The Principles and Practice of Change

The Principles and Practice of Change

This Reader, along with the companion volume *Discovering Leadership* edited by Jon Billsberry, form part of the Open University course *Making it Happen! Leadership, Influence and Change* (B204), a 60 point level two undergraduate course. The course is a compulsory element of the Foundation Degree in Leadership and Management and the BA (Hons) Leadership and Management, and an optional course in the BA (Hons) Business Studies.

Details of this and other Open University courses can be obtained from the Student Registration and Enquiry Service, The Open University, PO Box 197, Milton Keynes MK7 6BJ, United Kingdom: tel. +44 (0)845 300 6090, e-mail general-enquiries@open.ac.uk

Alternatively, you may visit the Open University website at http://www.open.ac.uk where you can learn more about the wide range of courses and packs offered at all levels by The Open University.

The Principles and Practice of Change

Edited By

Deborah Price

palgrave
macmillan

OU
Business
School

First published 2009 by
PALGRAVE MACMILLAN

Palgrave Macmillan in the UK is an imprint of Macmillan Publishers Limited,
registered in England, company number 785998, of Houndmills, Basingstoke,
Hampshire RG21 6XS.

Palgrave Macmillan in the US is a division of St Martin's Press LLC,
175 Fifth Avenue, New York, NY 10010.

Palgrave Macmillan is the global academic imprint of the above companies
and has companies and representatives throughout the world.

Palgrave® and Macmillan® are registered trademarks in the United States,
the United Kingdom, Europe and other countries.

ISBN-13: 978-0-230-57585-1
ISBN-10: 0-230-57585-4

This book is printed on paper suitable for recycling and made from fully
managed and sustained forest sources. Logging, pulping and manufacturing
processes are expected to conform to the environmental regulations of the
country of origin.

A catalogue record for this book is available from the British Library.

A catalog record for this book is available from the Library of Congress.

10 9 8 7 6 5 4 3 2 1
18 17 16 15 14 13 12 11 10 09

Printed and bound in Great Britain by
CPI Antony Rowe, Chippenham, Wiltshire

Contents

Figures, Tables and Exhibits

Figures

Tables

Exhibits

Acknowledgements

The author and publishers are grateful to the following for permission to reproduce copyright material: Taylor & Francis for extracts from R. Todnem (2005) 'Organisational Change Management: A Critical Review', *Journal of Change Management*, vol. 5, no. 4, pp. 369–80; R. K. Smollen (2006) 'Minds, Hearts and Deeds: Cognitive, Affective and Behavioural Responses to Change', *Journal of Change Management*, vol. 6, no. 2, pp. 143–58; R. Gill (2003) 'Change Management or Change Leadership', *Journal of Change Management*, vol. 3, no. 4, pp. 307–18. Harvard Business School Publishing for extracts from M. Beer and N. Nohria (2000) 'Cracking the Code of Change', *Harvard Business Review*, May–June, pp. 133–41; J. P. Kotter (1995) 'Leading Change: Why Transformation Efforts Fail', *Harvard Business Review*, March–April, pp. 56–67; J. P. Kotter and L. A. Schlesinger (1979) 'Choosing Strategies for Change', *Harvard Business Review*, March–April, pp. 106–14. Elizabeth Moss Kanter for the use of her article, 'Managing the Human Side of Change'. Academy of Management for extracts from D. A. Nadler and M. L. Tushman (1989) 'Organizational Frame Bending: Principles for Managing Reorientation', *The Academy of Management Review*, vol. 10, no. 3, pp. 194–204. Sage for extracts from D. Dunphy and D. Stace (1993) 'The Strategic Management of Corporate Change', *Human Relations*, vol. 46, no. 8, pp. 905–20, copyright © *Human Relations*. Inderscience for extracts from J. S. Oakland and S. J. Tanner (2006) 'Quality Management in the 21st Century: Implementing Successful Change', *International Journal of Productivity and Quality Management*, vol. 1, nos 1–2, pp. 69–87, copyright © Inderscience. Wiley-Blackwell for extracts from M. Doyle (2002) 'Selecting Managers for Transformational Change', *Human Resource Management Journal*, vol. 12, no. 1, pp. 3–16. Informs for extracts from D. Meyerson and M. Scully (1995) 'Tempered Radicalism and the Politics of Ambivalence and Change', *Organization Science*, vol. 6, no. 6, pp. 585–600. Every effort has been made to contact all the copyright-holders, but if any have been inadvertently omitted the publishers will be pleased to make the necessary arrangements at the earliest opportunity.

Introduction

Deborah Price

This book has been produced as part of the Open University course B204; Leadership, Influence and Change: Making a difference. The course follows a practise-based pedagogy which encourages students to explore the relationship between the theories and concepts they acquire and how these relate to what they do when dealing with or managing change.

The course is structure such that Part I is written in a very tutorial style. The aim here is to familiarise students with the key themes and influences which underpin the notion of change. The part starts by considering the drivers for change. Using examples from the media, we draw the student's attention to the ways in which the environmental context creates the demands which drive change within organisations. From here we develop the connection between the environment and the types of change needed before going on to look at how each of the different types of change presents. Lastly the part looks at the linear models which suggest ways in which practitioners might apply those changes.

In Part II the theme of types of change is continued. We start with Beer and Nohria's notion of Theory E and Theory O change, which illustrates the ways in which change within organisations needs to be cognisant of both the economic and human implications of change. We then use Nadler and Tushman's paper on 'Organizational Frame Bending' to look at how radical strategic change within organisations requires the pulling together of work, people, formal and informal structures and formal and informal processes. Lastly we use Dunphy and Stace's 1993 article to emphasise the situational approach to change, one which moves away from the polarisation between economic and human considerations to one which allows for a more fluid approach incorporating both.

Having framed the relationship between the environment, the types of demands this places on organisations, and the types of change that these demands imply, in Part III we consider the ways in which practitioners are encouraged to manage this change. The part begins with Kotter's 1995 paper on 'Leading Change'. The paper is used to illustrate the ways in which the literature often advocates single and generically applicable frameworks for managing change, regardless of the impetus for that change. We then use the Oakland and Tanner paper to present an empirical approach which resulted in the construction of a more dynamic approach to managing change. By positioning change as two interlocked loops Oakland and Tanner create a more iterative framework for managing change. Lastly we include an article from the Victorian Quality Council, in which they present some clear and pragmatic guidelines for managing the processes of change.

Until now we have present a fairly linear understanding of change. We have noted how change is driven by context and how that context presupposes a range of ways in which those managing the change are advised to act. In Part IV we consider how the human factor that may frustrate that smooth transition from what we are to what we want to be. We start with Kotter and Schlesinger's 1979 paper, Choosing Strategies for Change. In here the authors consider why people resist change and proffer a range of mechanisms for dealing with such resistance. In consolidating this perspective we then use Moss-Kanter paper on Managing the Human side of Change. Lastly we encourage students to think a little more deeply about the rationale behind resistance to change. By presenting Roy Kark Smollen's paper on the Cognitive, Affective and Behavioural ways in which people react to change, we hope to encourage students to think about the limitations of perceiving all resistance as being rational and logical.

In Part V we look at where responsibility for the success of change rests. Here we consider the role of leadership. In doing so we do not seek to debate the distinctions between management and leadership, rather we seek to consider the characteristics suggested as being appropriate for producing successful change. The part starts with Mike Doyle's article on selecting managers for transformational change. Here, he suggests that the effectiveness of the traditional approach of having a unitary change leader is compromised by the increasingly complex nature of change. Moreover, where people are selected as change leaders, there is little evidence to suggest that they are selected on grounds other than their ability to do their own job well. We then present Roger Gill's paper which questions whether change should be managed or lead, this draws on the need for an integrative model of change leadership. Lastly we look at a non-traditional approach to leading change, that of Debra Meyerson's Tempered Radicals. Here we encourage students to think of the ways in which the leadership of successful change is not always driven by those with rank or status. Rather that people at any level of the organisation can bring about change if they care enough about the organisation and are committed enough to drive that change.

Part VI of the book is a short directory of Tools and Techniques of change. As part of the course that this book is produced to support, students will be walking through a process of change and are encouraged to try and test a range of tools and techniques to see how useful (or otherwise) they are and how they impact their decisions. The tools and techniques included can be used for a range of purposes, and we suggest rather than prescribe where these might be used.

This book would not have been possible but for the help of many people. Those whose names I miss, please forgive me, your contribution was non-the-less valued. Sincere thanks to Caroline Ramsey, the Course Team Chair of B204: Making It Happen! Leadership, Influence and Change, for her support, encouragements and wisdom. The production of this book has been a team effort and I would like to thank the two course managers, Emir Forken and Jo Woods. Their expertise smoothed what would have otherwise been a very bumpy path. Thanks also to Gill Gowans at The Open University (Copublishing) and Penny Holzmann (Editor) for their constructive comments and guidance. And to Palgrave's Commissioning Editor, Ursula Gavin, for her help in seeing this project through to fruition.

Part I

Introduction

The first part of this book aims to set the context regarding the issue of Organisational Change. In setting this context, there are a number of objectives that we have set out to achieve:

We aim to briefly introduce what we understand by the term 'organisational change' and then go on to consider the factors that impel us to change; drivers for change.

We then build on these drivers for change to consider the nature of the relationship between the context within which the organisation finds itself, and the demands that this context places on the organisation.

We then consider how the demands placed on the organisation imply the appropriateness of particular types of change, which, according to the literature enable the organisation to adapt in a manner which is both timely and appropriate.

Last we look at the some of the linear models of change that the literature offers us as guidelines for successful change management.

Having briefly contextualised just some of the fundamental issues relating to change, we then present the Paul Strebel (1995) article entitled 'Choosing the Right Change Path'. In this article Strebel builds on the relationship between the environment and the organisation that we considered earlier, as well as introducing you to ideas like resistance to change which we will build on later. Strebel strives to make clearer the types of relationships that can exist between strong and weak forces for change and strong and weak forces of resistance. Recognising this relationship, he contests, helps you to then select the most appropriate path for change. He concludes by noting that a key factor in the successful management of change is the pulling together of a plan for change which is advised by an understanding of the relationship between the strengths of the forces for change, whether or not the change is proactive or reactive and the strengths of the forces of resistance. Only by doing this, Strebel argues, can organisations take advantage of the environmental conditions and gain competitive advantage.

The last part of this section builds on the issues of environmental influences, types of change and scale of change, to present a paper entitled 'Organisational Change Management: A Critical Review'. In this paper Todnem By presents a review framed by how change is characterised in the literature he considers:

Change characterised by the rate of occurrence
Change characterised by how it comes about
Change characterised by scale

The usefulness of the Todnem By paper is three fold. First it illustrates the importance of thinking critically about the literature we read. By looking at the arguments in support of and arguments which contradict particular viewpoints, he encourages us to think about the strengths and the limitations of the theories and concepts we study. Second in doing this, he presents a range of accessible literatures which we would encourage students to read to add greater breadth and depth to their learning. Third, Todnem By emphasises the usefulness of the theories, he encourages us to question how the application of a particular theory or concept can really help us to make a difference.

The Context of Change

1

Deborah Price

Introduction

In 1947, Kurt Lewin noted that 'Group life is never without change' (1947, p. 13), rather that there are 'merely differences in the amount and type of change that exist' (ibid.). The idea that we are all constantly engaged in change to a greater or lesser degree provokes the question 'why?' Why is change so all-pervasive? What are the factors that impel us to change? In this first part we will consider the drivers for change; those forces which have the potential to make us alter the ways in which we do things.

Although framed within the context of organisational change, the drivers for change that we will look at also have a considerable impact on both social and personal change.

Drivers for Change

Organisations exist for a purpose. That purpose may be to contribute to the health and welfare of society, to improve the well-being of disadvantaged groups or to maximise the financial returns to the organisation's shareholders. Regardless of their motives, organisations necessarily function within a multi-faceted external environment, an environment which influences what they should and should not and can and cannot do (Figure 1.1 – The Context of Organisations).

The environment within which organisations exist can be viewed at three levels; at a macro level, the Far Environment comprises the wider world within which the organisation operates. It is important to note that the organisation has little power to control or influence the Far Environment, and as such, changes in the external environment tend to dictate the need for change to the organisation. At a meso level, the Near Environment is one with which the organisation has a much more reciprocal relationship. Organisations

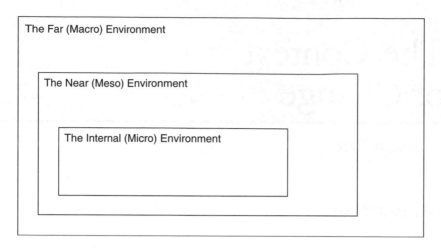

Figure 1.1   The context of organisations

exchange information and communicate with their Near Environment and are thus much more able to negotiate any necessary change. Last, the micro or Internal Environment. This comprises the internal workings of the organisation. It is predominantly controlled by the management of the organisation albeit factors from the Far Environment have a direct impact on what managers are able to do.

The Far Environment

The Far Environment is often characterised by the acronym PESTLE[1], and we will look briefly at each of these factors.

P – Political Drivers for Change

The political environment consists of the governmental ideologies, practices and systems which form the basis for the environment(s)[2] in which the organisation operates. As governments themselves adapt to a rapidly changing world (e.g. wars, political unrest, environmental disasters and changing ecological conditions), so their policies and systems change. It is incumbent on organisations to make the necessary changes to ensure that what they do, and how they do it, doesn't conflict with the political requirements.

Illustrative Case Study

Imagine that you are the manager of the local maternity hospital. Consider what changes you might need to think about in following circumstances?

A dramatic increase in the number of babies being delivered to foreign-born mothers has prompted calls for more money to be ploughed into NHS maternity services. According to a report by the BBC, yearly spending on maternity care has soared by more than £200 million since 1998.

Figures show that one out of four babies is now born to a mother born overseas, with the number of babies rising by 64,000 since the mid 1990s. This is compared to the figures for British mothers which, conversely, has fallen by 44,000 per year.

Liberal Democrat health spokesman Norman Lamb described the situation as 'deeply worrying'. 'It is essential that every expectant mother has access to reliable and safe maternity facilities,' he said.

'The government is happy to reap the economic benefits of migrant workers but not willing to provide capacity to cope with the extra pressure which they bring to the NHS. They cannot have it both ways,' he added.

Meanwhile, Professor Philip Steer, editor of the British Journal of Obstetrics and Gynaecology, said: 'The Department of Health has been taken by surprise'.

'The demographic change, the sheer numbers, has in some areas increased very substantially without there being any forward planning really to allow for that.'

(*Source*: http://www.kiddicare.com/webapp/wcs/stores/servlet/newsarticle0_53304_10751_-1_10001 downloaded on 28.06.08)

E – Economic Drivers for Change

The economic drivers for change likewise have both national and international dimensions. The economy within which organizations function has an impact on their workforce, on their suppliers, on their customers and on the value of the money that they have. To compound the impact, national economies exist within a global economic climate. Taxation, interest rates and exchange rates all affect the organisation's ability to achieve its objectives.

Illustrative Case Study

Consider the impact that the changing economic climate has on those trying to run viable estate agency businesses.

'Estate agents feeling the pinch': Mira Bar Hillel, *Evening Standard* 14 April 2008.

A third of Britain's estate agents could be forced to close this year as the number of house sales plunge.

Predictions made by the biggest network of independent estate agencies, Movewithus, estimate that around 4,000 of the country's 12,000 property businesses will shut by December.

⟶

Illustrative Case Study Continued

→

The move will be direct result of the credit crunch, which experts predict will cause an estimated 45,000 repossessions, 20,000 job losses in the City of London and a rise in mortgage repayments for around three million households.

Robin King, director of Movewithus, said the current climate meant fewer people wanted to buy property, with first time buyers and families being squeezed out of the market altogether.

He added that estate agent closures would be 'massive', after sales within his network dropped by between 30 and 50%.

(*Source*: http://www.thisismoney.co.uk/news/article.html?in_article_id=440367&in_page_id=2downloaded on 28.06.08)

S – Socio-Cultural Drivers for Change

The socio-cultural drivers for change reflect the standards set by society at large. They determine what is right and proper, and in so doing reflect the ways in which people are expected to behave. As societal standards are locally derived, this means that each society creates social conventions appropriate to itself. Organizations operating internationally therefore need to be aware of the cultural differences which exist between the different societies in which they work. Socio-cultural values may initially represent those values held informally by the community, however, where values are very strongly held, these may find their way into codified law, that is, politicians respond to societal pressure to make conformance to the values a legal requirement rather than allow people to decide whether or not they will conform.

Illustrative Case Study

Below is an excerpt from an article about Anita Roddick, the founder of The Body Shop. The article indicates not only the way in which Roddick was instrumental in changing socio-cultural values but also the way in which this change in values then became codified in law.

Michael McCarthy in The Independent *argues that Roddick deserves a place in the pantheon of revolutionary thinkers who changed the world.*

He says that Roddick's originality did not lie just in the achievements she is famous for, in the fields of animal rights, human rights, fair trade and environmental protection. It was in the idea, entirely novel 40 years ago when she started out, of business as a force for social change.

She opened the first Body Shop in Brighton in 1976, and began selling ethical cosmetics that were not tested on animals. It was something many people felt strongly about – and they sold like hotcakes. In the end, the rest of the cosmetics industry had to follow, but not without Roddick's tireless campaigning, eventually leading the UK government to ban the animal testing of cosmetics.

→

Illustrative Case Study Continued

$\longrightarrow$

Roddick believed business could change the world. Her goal was to show that capitalism itself, having despoiled the world for two centuries, could in the right hands repair it. She made this happen most of all in the area of fair trade, a concept previously considered inimical to global business practice.

As a result of making the Body Shop a pioneer in raising standards for suppliers, she helped to demonstrate that trade was indeed better than aid for the poor people of developing countries. It created sustainable communities, rather than dependency.

(*Source*: http://www.worldbusinesslive.com/article/738022/anita-roddick-business-revolutionary/ downloaded on 28.06.08)

T – Technological Drivers for Change

Technological drivers for change relate not only to new developments in and new uses of technology, but also to new means of production. Technology is now a substantial part of most people's lives, affecting the ways in which they communicate and socialise as well as the ways in which they work. Advances in technology offer organisations the potential to do things faster, more cheaply and better, but this use of technology often comes with some costs. People need to be trained to use new systems, processes and procedures and the organisation has to consider how soon an even newer, better and smarter technology will come along. The rapid rate of technological advancement means that organisations need to be aware of how new advances can force change upon them.

Illustrative Case Study

Consider how people may respond to the following example of technologically driven change.

New Zealand students able to use txt language in exams

From Wikinews, **Thursday, November 9, 2006**

The New Zealand Qualifications Authority (NZQA) has announced that a shorter version of English known as txt language will be acceptable in the external end of year exams. Txt language is where words are shortened for easier mobile phone usage, for example, txt is for text, lol is for laugh out loud, brb is for be right back, etc.

Txt language has been approved if the marker can see that the paper 'clearly shows the required understanding', however the NZQA still advises not to use it. Bali Haque, deputy chief executive of NZQA, said: 'Students should aim to make their answers as clear as possible. Markers involved in assessing NCEA (National Certificate of Educational Achievement) exams are trained professionals, experienced in interpreting the variety of writing styles and language uses encountered during the marking process,' Mr Haque is confident that marker will understand txt language.

(*Source*: http://en.wikinews.org/wiki/New_Zealand_students_able_to_use_txt_language_in_exams)

L – Legal Drivers for Change

The legal drivers for change relate to the regulatory systems which control what an organisation is allowed and is not allowed to do. Legal systems determine acceptable and unacceptable behaviours, they also determine the sanctions that people will be subject to if they break the rules. Organisations have little choice but to change what they do in order that they comply with the law, even if making those changes has costs to the organisation.

Illustrative Case Study

Smoking ban 'costs pub takings'

The landlord of a Kent pub is to send a petition to the government to try to get the smoking ban revised, claiming it has cost him 25% of his takings.

John Davis, who runs the Plough Inn, in New Romney, said he knew other pubs who had lost up to 35% in income.

He said he would have preferred to have one of the rooms in his pub changed instead of 'throwing everyone outside'.

The Department of Health said there was significant evidence the legislation had had a positive effect on pubs.

'There is considerable evidence from other countries that have introduced smokefree laws that the impact on business can be positive,' a spokesperson said.

'We will continue to monitor the impact of the smokefree legislation, with a full review due to be completed within three years'.

'We have seen no significant evidence to date that implies that smokefree legislation... will create any long-term economic problems for pubs or the hospitality trade in general.'

(*Source*: http://news.bbc.co.uk/1/hi/england/kent/7147786.stm downloaded on 28.06.08)

E – Environmental Drivers for Change

As the global community strive for more sustainable ways of working and of living, so organisations need to be more aware of the impact of their actions and inactions. Some 'ethical' business practices are mandated by law, others are not. However, even where no legislation exists, companies need to guard against unethical practices, not simply on moral grounds but because the consequences of such behaviour may cause customers to switch to another company, generate bad publicity or deter people from investing in the company. As people increasingly demand sustainable ways of working, so organisations need to adapt to the most ethical and environmentally friendly ways of working.

Illustrative Case Study

Imagine you are the purchasing manager of a large supermarket chain who does not sell Fairtrade coffee. Having read the article below think about what changes you might need to make to meet this increasing demand?

From 1 June 2008, the Fairtrade minimum price for Arabica coffee will increase to ensure that farmers continue to receive a price which covers the cost of sustainable production.

This price adjustment will benefit more than 250 producer organisations across the developing world – around one million farmers and their families.

'I represent more than one million family farmers who need Fairtrade pricing to put food on the table and keep their kids in school,' said Raul de Aguila, a Peruvian coffee grower and Cafédirect board member. 'No other label or certification system ensures a fair income for a hard day's work. This increase will have a direct and positive impact on the lives of Fairtrade Certified coffee farmers around the world.'

The price increase is the result of extensive field research into the real costs of sustainable production to ensure that Fairtrade continues to address the needs of coffee-producing communities. The research was followed by a multi-stakeholder review process involving producers, consumers and industry representatives from more than twenty countries around the world. Penny Newman, CEO of Cafédirect, says, *'It's our mission to create secure, sustainable livelihoods for growers, and this decision is a step in the right direction. Working closely with our grower partners, Cafédirect champions the need to continually assess the Fairtrade pricing structure to ensure its relevant to their needs.'*

Fairtrade is the only certification model that guarantees prices to farmers that meet strict social and environmental sustainability criteria, and the FAIRTRADE Mark has become one of the most recognized consumer labels in the UK . Research by DEFRA this year showed that more than eighty percent of the UK public say they have heard of Fairtrade, and more than half of those people said they made an effort to buy it.

According to Ian Bretman, Deputy Director of the Fairtrade Foundation in the UK and FLO Board member, *'The conscious consumer demands high-quality products that make a difference in the world. The research is clear: consumers are willing to pay more for Fairtrade products because they help lift farmers out of poverty. This moderate price increase in Fairtrade coffee will not undercut the dramatic growth of consumer demand for Fairtrade products; on the contrary, it gives concerned consumers additional evidence that Fairtrade truly delivers on its promise of farmer empowerment.'*

(*Source*: Adapted from: http://www.fairtrade.org.uk/press_office/press_releases_and_statements/archive_2007/dec_2007/small_scale_coffee_farmers_to_benefit_from_international_increase_in_fairtrade_price.aspx downloaded on 28.06.08)

The Near Environment

The Near environment comprises a mixture of stakeholder groups. Stakeholders are people who have a vested interest in the activities of the organisation, for example,

Suppliers
Customers

Competitors
Collaborators
Partners
Potential stakeholders

Depending on the nature of their relationship with the organisation, stakeholders will be more or less able to drive change. In considering their relationship with the organisation, three categories of stakeholders are considered.

Dependent Stakeholders

These are groups whose are reliant on their relationship with the organisation. This may be because the organisation stocks a rare product, because they offer particular therapies or treatments or because their role is important to the welfare of others (e.g. police, fire service or the armed forces).

Co-Dependent Stakeholders

These are groups who have a reciprocal relationship with the organisation. It is in the interest of both parties that the organisation is as successful as possible in what it does. For example, customers might depend on a product but the organisation depends on their buying this. Collaborators work together to optimise service delivery in the most efficient and effective ways possible. And shareholders invest in a company in order that they can get a return on that investment.

Independent Stakeholders

These are groups who are not reliant on what the organisation does on a daily basis, but may wish to react to stop the organisation from behaving in a particular way. For example, local residents or environmental groups may object to organisational plans to convert fields into a car park. Even though they are not directly a part of the organisation, they may still be powerful enough to prevent you from taking a particular course of action or to get the authorities to mandate that you take a particular course of action.

The Internal Environment

The Internal Environment comprises the relationship between staff, managers, the organisation's structure and culture and the processes and the systems.

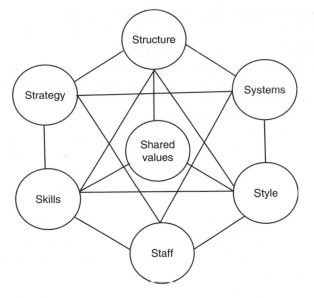

Figure 1.2 McKinsey seven S model

Drivers for change emanating from the Internal Environment are often those related to people wanting to improve the things that they do, develop new and better ways of working or solve problems with current practice. The Internal Environment is the point at which organisational change takes place; however, it is important to recognise the interconnectedness of each of the elements of this environment. This is usefully illustrated by the McKinsey Seven S Model. (See Figure 1.2)

The McKinsey Seven S Model draws attention to the idea that a change in any one part of the Internal Environment will have a greater or lesser effect on another part of the Internal Environment. As such those planning and leading change need to be aware of the consequences of their plans.

Types of Change

The impact that the external environment has in driving change within an organisation is not limited to the different environmental sectors. It is also affected by the rate of change taking place. David (2001) calls this environmental stability. The speed and magnitude of change taking place in the external environment places particular demands on organisations both in terms of their ability to respond to the changes and in terms of the type of change needed to meet those demands.

Many authors have considered the relationship between the degree of stability or turbulence in the external environment, and the structure of the organisation. Burns and Stalker (1961) noted that where the external environment was characterised by stability and predictability, then a centralised and bureaucratic structure was perfectly acceptable. There are unlikely to be any rapid changes in the environment which would require the organisation to respond quickly. Contrarily, where the external environment was deemed uncertain or unpredictable, then organisations with flatter organisational structures were deemed more appropriate. Their lack of centralised decision-making and tall structure meant that they were able to adapt quickly to the changing circumstances.

Lawrence and Lorsch (1967) argued that where environmental uncertainty existed, then there was a need to divide large organisations into smaller and more responsive sub-units. These sub-units could then adapt quickly to sudden and dramatic environmental changes. Alternatively, where the external environment was relatively stable, then it was appropriate to retain a single large organisational structure.

The second relationship that emerges between the external environment and an organisation is the relationship between the degree of dynamism in the external environment and the type of change that this demands. Senior and Fleming (2006) summarise this relationship in a tabular form (Table 1.1 – Environmental Conditions and Types of Change).

Table 1.1 Environmental conditions and types of change

Environmental forces	Types of change		
Ansoff and McDonnell (1990)	Dunphy and Stace (1993)[a]	Grundy (1993)	Burnes (2004)
Predictable	Fine-tuning	Smooth incremental	Incremental
Forecastable by extrapolation	Incremental adjustment		
Predictable threats and opportunities	Modular transformation	Bumpy incremental	
Partially predictable opportunities	Corporate transformation		Punctuated equilibrium
Unpredictable surprises		Discontinuous	Continuous transformation

Note: [a] We will not be discussing the Dunphy and Stace (1993) paper here as you will be reading this in full later on in your studies.

Source: Adapted from Senior and Fleming, 2006, p. 284.

Smooth Incremental Change (Grundy, 1993)

According to the Table 1.1, smooth incremental change (Figure 1.3) is suited to stable external environments. It is change that evolves slowly and follows a clear path for change through which those directing the change involve all of those people affected by the change. People are supported, coached and trained so that they can contribute to the process of change and feel comfortable with the outcome.

Because the changes are relatively minor, people are able to cope with them. People remain within what Arnold et al. call the 'range of stability' (1998, p. 423); that is, those involved in the change are comfortable in that they are able to deal psychologically, emotionally and physically with the demands made on them by the process of change. The tempo of change remains the same. People begin one change with a clear sense of what the objectives for change are, they work logically through the implementation process until the objectives are achieved and, once that change is completed the next change process begins.

Bumpy Incremental Change

Bumpy Incremental change (Figure 1.4 – Bumpy Incremental Change) is appropriate where there is some degree of predictability in the external environmental

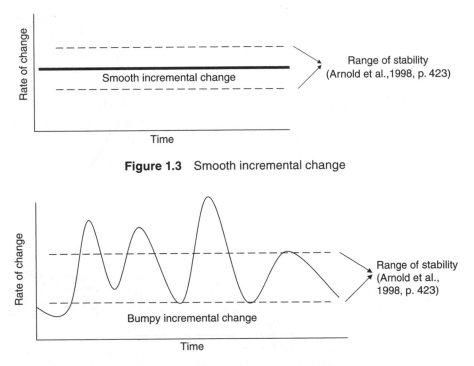

Figure 1.3 Smooth incremental change

Figure 1.4 Bumpy incremental change

conditions – but not sufficient predictability to be absolutely sure about the frequency, duration or the magnitude of the changes which might happen. As such, change within the organisation is periodic and is of sufficient magnitude to disrupt the status quo.

Bumpy incremental change involves a degree of discomfort for people. It takes them out of their 'range of stability' (ibid.). It does this because in order to achieve the goals of change the old ways in which worked are challenged and there is insufficient time to adopt the same supportive coaching and mentoring approach that is often used in smooth incremental change.

Discontinuous Change (Grundy, 1993)

Discontinuous change (Figure 1.5 – Discontinuous Change) is a dramatic and radical change in the ways in which things are done. Such dramatic change is necessitated by either a crisis or by an opportunity. A crisis may have arisen in the external environment, a sudden shift in conditions which has affected not only your own organisation, but all other organisations that work in the same context as you. Alternatively, the crisis may have arisen because of the actions of your competitors, as such it is only your organisation which is affected. Last, the crisis may have arisen as a result of bad management on the part of your company. In any of these situations, the key issue is that the crisis is of sufficient magnitude that it poses a serious threat to the viability of the organisation.

Contrarily, it may be that the organisation is not facing a crisis, rather it has spotted potential in the market. Rather than discontinuous change being purely reactive, that is, people responding to a crisis, here people are aware of an opportunity, one which needs to be taken advantage of immediately. Again the issue is speed, it is necessary to act quickly to make sure that your organisation takes advantage of that opportunity before anybody else does.

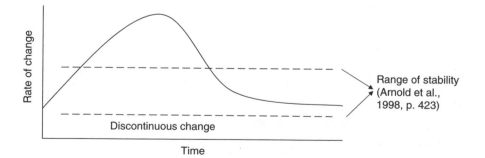

Figure 1.5 Discontinuous change

Discontinuous change challenges the status quo by disrupting the usual ways of doing things. It takes people out of their 'range of stability' (ibid.). The need for speed implies that people are 'instructed' as to what they need to do, rather than being consulted. By doing this, those managing a process of discontinuous change aim to bring about short-term compliance. Time is vital and the organisation needs to act quickly; managers can work on gaining people's longer term commitment to the change once the crisis is over.

Burnes (2004) contributes two additional types of change.[3]

Punctuated Equilibrium

Punctuated equilibrium (Figure 1.6 – Punctuated Equilibrium) is a type of change characterised by sudden bursts of activity. It is based on the understanding that whilst incremental change forms a good base for ensuring that the organisation conforms to the demands placed on it by the external environment, those demands are not always evolutionary. There are times when the external environment itself is shaken by radical change, and when that happens, organisations too need to change radically. As such people can remain with their 'range of stability' (Arnold et al., 1998, p. 423) during the periods of incremental change, but are then taken out of this range at the moments of dramatic, radical change.

Continuous Transformation

The last type of change that Burnes (2004) mentions is that of continuous transformation (Figure 1.7 – Continuous Transformation). In noting that the environmental context of the twenty-first century is characterised by dramatic change, then the slow plodding notion of simply trying to keep pace with changes in the external environment (by incremental change or punctuated equilibrium models) is not sufficient. Rather organisations need to proactively reinvent themselves if they are going to survive.

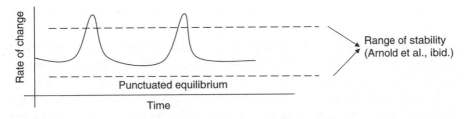

Figure 1.6 Punctuated equilibrium

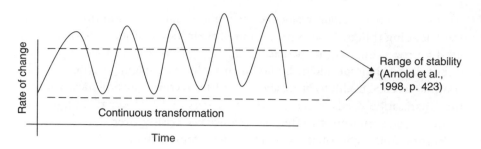

Figure 1.7   Continuous transformation

The nature of this change is dramatic. It challenges old ways of thinking as well as old ways of working. Such change takes people outside of their range of stability.

Conclusion

So far we have recognised that organisations in the twenty-first century act and interact with a range of different environments ranging from the Far Environment, through the Near Environment and into the Internal Environment. Each one of these environments is multi-faceted and each facet of each environment may place different and indeed competing demands on the organisation. We will now go on the consider how the organisation deals with those demands, that is what models of change can we use to guide the transition between where we are now and where we ultimately want to be?

Linear Models of Change

Linear models of change are frameworks which provide logical and sequential prescriptions for the processes of change. Such models map out the processes of change from the first recognition of the need (or desirability) for change through to the practicalities of implementation. They advocate a series of managerially driven activities, each of which feeds in to the next stage in the process.

This logical approach to change is premised on the rational model of decision-making. A model which advocates that problems within an organisation can be clearly defined, potential solutions generated and evaluated and a clear and unambiguous strategy for resolution devised. The five stage model (Figure 1.8 – The Rational Decision-Making Model) starts with the clear definition of the problem. The more specific the definition is, the more

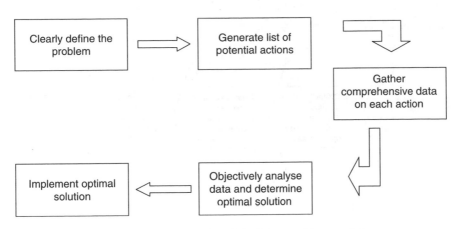

Figure 1.8   The rational decision-making model

focussed and therefore appropriate the solution will be. Next, having defined the problem, a list of potential courses of action is generated. Then, for each item on the list, a comprehensive set of data is gathered to advise the evaluation process. Next is the evaluation process. Based purely on the objective data gathered, a decision is made as to the ideal solution. Last, that solution is implemented.

The rational decision-making model has been criticised for its simplicity; it fails to account for the complexity of organisations. Perhaps the most famous critique came from Herbert Simon, who advocated that rather than follow a totally rational model of decision-making, managers satisfice. That is they make the best decision possible whilst acknowledging the limitations of decision that they have made. Underpinning the notion of satisficing is the idea that 'most human decision-making, whether individual or organisational, is concerned with the discovery and selection of *satisfactory* alternatives; only in exceptional cases is it concerned with the discovery of optimal alternatives' (Simon, cited in Pugh and Hickson, 1996, p. 134. Italics added).

Basing linear models of change on the rational model of decision-making therefore has implications for the outcome of change. One has to question whether in managing a change process we are seeking an optimal outcome or one which is simply satisfactory. Despite the linear models of change being open to similar criticisms as the rational model of decision-making, linear models are useful. They provide a consistent structure through which people can plan and execute change. They reduce the risk that some key part of the change process might be missed, and they are easily understood. Daft (2006) describes a four stage linear model of change. (Figure 1.9 – Four Stage Model of Change.)

Figure 1.9 Four stage model of change

Source: Adapted from Daft, 2006, p. 394.

Impetus for Change

The impetus for change is the force which drives for change. What Daft notes, is that this force can come from two sources, internal drivers for change and external drivers for change. Consideration of both is important. The drivers for change determine not only the need for change but the speed with which that change needs to be brought about.

Whilst we tend to consider internal and external drivers for change as distinct entities, it is worth noting that they are often inexorably linked.

To Illustrate

When changes in the economic environment result in interest rate rises, the costs for an organisation also rise. In order to deal with those increased costs, the organisation may decide to change working practices in order to improve efficiency. The impetus to change is driven by a need to adapt to changes in the external market. However, changes in the rate of interest rate also increase the cost of living for people working in the company. As a result, they may demand higher wage increases.

When considering the drivers for change, it is also worth noting that the external and internal factors which create the need for change seldom arrive as single events or issues. The increase in interest rates alluded to earlier is one single event which may occur at the same time as new legislation is brought in, or new governmental targets are launched or a new humanitarian aid crisis arises. Drivers for change often present a complex picture from which people in organisations have to pick their priorities.

Stage 1 – Define the Need for Change

Daft (ibid.) advocates that regardless of the drivers for change, people within organisations are not prepared to change unless they perceive that there is a crisis. That is, that change is the least damaging option for them. However, few organisations lurch from one crisis to another, and it would be generally thought unwise for organisations to simply wait for the next crisis to come along before introducing change. Rather than focus on a crisis, change needs to be managed as an ongoing process in which the need for change is communicated through identifying a performance gap. A performance gap is the difference between what we are doing and what we should be doing. Addressing the performance gap can be a means to resolving a problem (reactive) which already exists, or can be the opportunity (proactive) to develop, elaborate or improve what we are currently doing. Either way the performance gap is used as a means of demonstrating to people the difference between where the organisation is now and where the organisation needs or would like to be.

By recognising the performance gap, people are able to define what changes need to take place, whether these are changes in practice, changes in structure or change in culture.

Stage 2 – Initiate Change

This is the stage at which the plans for change are devised. It is the stage in which people search for solutions which meet the needs for change surfaced previously. Daft notes two approaches here. In the first those directing the change adapt solutions that either they have used previously or that they have seen used elsewhere. Alternatively they create new and innovative solutions themselves. The approach taken will to a large extent be governed by the need for change and the type of change needed. Where the change required is familiar, or similar to previous changes, then the solutions may be adapted from previous ways of managing change. However, where the drivers for change are complex and ambiguous, then the ways of managing that change may need to be new and innovative.

Stage 3 – Implement Change

Daft advocates that implementing change is a process of overcoming resistance. That people will naturally resist change, and therefore need to be effectively persuaded of the benefits of change. Failure to persuade people to participate in the change means that their resistance may undermine the organisation's ability to achieve its desired goals. A range of strategies are suggested from communicating with people and advising them of the benefits of change at one end through to the use of power to instruct people to participate in the change.

Daft's linear model of change offers a very generic framework within which one can think about change within organisations. Senior and Fleming (2006) present a much more detailed breakdown of the processes involved in planned change.

The Senior and Fleming model (Figure 1.10) divides the process of managing change into three distinct stages: Description, Options and Implementation.

Stage 1 – Descriptive Phase

In the descriptive phase, the intention is to narrow the focus on the specific requirements of the change. By describing the problem and then seeking

Phases	Stages	Actions appropriate for each stage
Description	1. Situation Summary	Recognise the need for change either to solve a problem or take advantage of an opportunity; Test out others' views on the need for change; Using appropriate diagnostic techniques, confirm the presence of hard complexity and a difficulty rather than a mess.
	2. Identify objectives and constraints	Set up objectives for systems of interest; Identify constraints on the achievement of the objectives.
	3. Identify performance measures	Decide how the achievement of the objectives can be measured.
Options	4. Generate options	Develop ideas for change into clear options for achievement of the objectives; Consider a range of possibilities.
	5. Edit options and detail selected options	Describe the most promising options in some detail; Decide, for each option, what is involved and how it will work.
	6. Evaluate options against measures	Evaluate the performance of the chosen options against the performance criteria identified in stage 3.
Implementation	7. Develop implementation strategies	Select preferred option(s) and plan how to implement.
	8. Carry out the planned changes	Involve all concerned; Allocate responsibilities; Monitor progress.

Figure 1.10   Senior and Fleming model

Source: Senior and Fleming, 2006, p. 313.

the view of others, people are able to surface a range of perspectives on the issue which can then be tested using diagnostic techniques. By creating a very specific focus, we are much more able to produce clear objectives and set a clear pathway towards achieving those objectives. The use of diagnostic tools is a way of checking the assumptions we make in the descriptions of change. Such tools and techniques provide a structured set of dimensions, metrics or lenses through which we can view the situation.

The application of such tools and techniques refines the focus further, allowing for specific intentions to be translated in to practical objectives.

In producing the specific objectives, those planning the change need to be aware of the ways in which the circumstances of change influence what they can and cannot do.

Objectives then are devised in line with the demands (Stewart, 1982) made on people, that is, what is the change specifically meant to achieve? The constraints impose limitations on how the group or individual could go about achieving their objectives. As such constraints may include limited time, limited resources, not have the necessary technical skills or being unable to get all the people involved to agree. These demands and constraints then frame the choices those planning the change are able to make.

Once the objectives have been decided, the description stage advocates that clear performance measures be devised. It is important at this stage that those planning the change have a clear idea of what it is they are going to measure and how they are going to measure it.

Stage 2 – The Options Stage

The options stage is the stage in which the plans for change as devised. Based on the analyses and the objectives devised in the description stage, people now draw together some ideas about what needs to be done to bring about the desired changes.

The evaluation of options is the point at which those managing the change identify the actions most likely to achieve the objectives of the change.

Once the options have been evaluated, the processes of change are refined and implemented.

Stage 3 – The Implementation Stage

The option(s) chosen will in many ways indicate the actions that need to be taken; however, this stage is about formalising those actions into clear implementation plans. The plans need to say what is going to be done, how, when and by whom. Time limits need to include the scheduling of the review processes as well as the actual implementation plan. The plan notes how those managing the change will communicate that change, how they will support and guide people through the change and how they will enable people to acquire the new skills, new knowledge or new ways of working necessary for the change to be successful.

Conclusion

Linear models of change provide those managing change with a clear process through which they plan and monitor change. The models incorporate time sequenced activities which guide those implementing change through from the investigation of the need for change to the outcomes. However, this simplicity can be problematic.

Summary

In this chapter, we have tried to take you quickly through some of the key issues related to organisational change. As we move forward through the course we will be exploring the practicality of some of the things you have learned. We will be asking you to think about the ways in which this learning influences your practice, and getting you to explore the consequences of trying to apply some of these theories and concepts. By encouraging you to engage with a range of academic papers and articles we want you to consolidate your learning; to engage critically with the literature and by use of reasoning and reflection help you to make a difference.

Notes

1. Political, Economic, Socio-Cultural, Technological, Legal, Environmental.
2. As more and more organisations operate globally, so they need to adapt to working in a range of different political contexts.
3. His notion of incremental change maps on to Grundy's notion of smooth incremental change.

Bibliography

Ansoff, I. I. and McDonnell (1990) *Implanting Strategic Management*, Englewood Cliffs, NJ, Prentice-Hall.

Arnold, J., Cooper, C. L. and Robertson, I. T. (1998) *Work Psychology – Understanding Human Behaviour in the Workplace*, London, Prentice Hall.

Buchanan, D. and Huczynski, A. (2004) *Organizational Behaviour: An Introductory Text* (5th edn), Essex, Pearson Education.

Burnes, B. (2004) *Managing Change*, Essex, UK, Pearson Education.

Burns, T. and Stalker, G. M. (1961) *The Management of Innovation*, London, Tavistock.

Carnell, C. (2007) *Managing Change in Organizations* (5th edn), Essex, Pearson Education.

Daft, R. (2006) *The New Era of Management*, Ohio, Thomson.

David, F. (2001) *Strategic Management- Concepts and Cases*, New Jersey, Prentice Hall.

Dunphy, D. and Stace, D. (1993) 'The strategic management of corporate change', *Human Relations*, vol. 46, no. 8, pp. 905–20.

Grundy, T. (1993) *Implementing Strategic Change*, London, Kogan Page.

Johnson, G. and Scholes, K. (1999) *Exploring Corporate Strategy* (5th edn), Essex, Pearson Education.

Lawrence, P. R. and Lorsch, J. W. (1967) *Organization and Environment*, Boston, MA, Harvard Business School.

Lewin, K. (1947) 'Frontiers in group dynamics: Concept, method and reality in social science; social equilibria and social change', *Human Relations*, vol. 1, no. 5, pp. 5–41.

Mullins, L. J. (2005) *Management and Organizational Behaviour* (7th edn), Essex, Pearson Education.

Senior, B. and Fleming, J. (2006) *Organizational Change* (3rd edn), Essex, Pearson Education.

Stewart, R. (1982) 'A model for understanding managerial jobs and behaviour', *Academy of Management Review*, vol. 7, no. 1, pp. 7–13.

Choosing the Right Change Path

Paul Strebel

Change management is suffering from competing approaches. On the one hand, chief executives put their companies through radical restructuring, with little account taken of the time and process needed to change skills and behavior. Then they are surprised to find that they have to repeat the exercise a few years later, because once the restructuring is over, change stops. On the other hand, executives influenced by theories of organizational behavior encourage deep cultural change in their companies from the bottom up and are surprised to find that financial performance, rather than improving, is suffering from the impact of external change drivers.

Barring a fortuitous combination of events, these competing approaches to managing change are doomed to failure. Programs based primarily on the change drivers, ignoring the forces of resistance, are as prone to failure as those dealing primarily with the forces of resistance, ignoring the change drivers. What is needed is the choice of a change path based on a diagnosis of both the forces of change and resistance.

The importance of the the forces of change and resistance was pointed out already in the 1940s by the psychologist, Kurt Lewin, who showed how the force field, or the tension between environmental change and psychological resistance, can be used to explain human behavior.[1] The same idea of a force field is frequently evoked in the context of change management and has resurfaced recently in the academic literature on organizational change.[2] But little, if anything, has been done to relate the force field to the choice of generic change paths.

By distinguishing between strong and weak forces of change, strong and weak forces of resistance, and the balance beween them, eight different change paths can be identified. The choice of the most appropriate path can be made by using a series of questions about the forces of change and resistance to diagnose a particular change situation. A simple graphical tool called a change arena can be used to diagram the change paths. The change arena can be employed to depict corporate change campaigns, incorporating a sequence of change paths, that explicitly take account of the variations in the interplay between the forces of change and resistance.[3]

Mapping out the Change Arena

When dealing with complex, multiphase change, the first step is to identify the forces for change and resistance acting on the company, as well as the generic change processes that might be used to deal with the forces. Change forces come in three basic forms:

- established trends in the socio-political, economic, technological, competitive, and organizational environments;
- turning points that reflect the limits to the established trends (limits to the existing resources, capacity, investment, growth) and the stimuli promoting new trends (innovation, life cycle shifts, new players);
- internal change drivers in the form of organizational shifts, new managers, and change agents.

The strength of a change force is reflected in the rate of change it is causing in the environment. From the company perspective, the strength of a change force is determined by its current or future impact on the company's performance (most frequently measured by market share, sales, or profits). A strong change force creates a substantial decline in the performance of a company that is not adapted to it, and improvement in the performance of a company that is adapted. Typically, the stronger the change force on an unadapted company, the larger the gap between what is needed for adapting to the force of change and where the company is today – that is, the greater the change requirements in terms of tangible and intangible resources, functional competencies and organizational capabilities.

The forces of resistance reflect the response of the company's internal and external stakeholders to the change requirements. Resistance comes in four basic forms:

- rigid structures and systems reflecting organizations, business technology, and stakeholder resources that are not consistent with the forces of change;
- closed mindsets reflecting business beliefs and strategies that are oblivious to the forces of change;
- entrenched cultures reflecting values, behaviors, and skills that are not adapted to the forces of change;
- counterproductive change momentum driven by historical or other change drivers that are not relevant to the most urgent forces of change.

There is a natural hierarchy in terms of the difficulty and time required to break down the various forms of resistance: Internal structures and systems (excluding technology) typically can be altered most rapidly and readily; more time is required to convert closed business mindsets to the need for change; cultural change involving behaviors and skills is much more difficult and time consuming; counterproductive change typically constitutes the strongest form of resistance because it encompasses the other forms. (To get rid of the resistance, the supporting structure and systems have to be altered, mindsets have to be changed, and new behaviors and skills have to be learned.) Most change processes involve several, if not all the forms of resistance. The overall strength of the resistance can be summarized in terms of the time and resources needed to realign the company, or business unit, and its status quo agents, with the force of change.

Four generic change processes can be distinguished for dealing with the forces of change and resistance. Although these can be found in various forms in the literature on change management,[4] in the present context they can be described most simply in terms of the four domains of the change arena shown in Exhibit 2.1, each domain corresponding to a different combination of strong/weak forces of change and resistance.

In the top left-hand corner, weak change forces hardly affect an industry or company with strong resistance. Since the resistance threshold has not been reached, the status quo prevails and no change occurs. Status quo agents set the

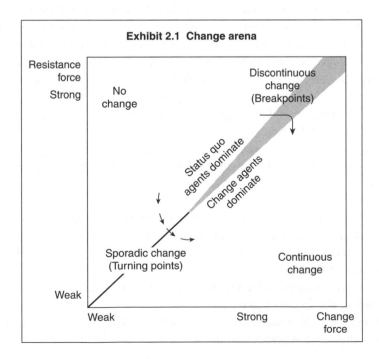

Exhibit 2.1 Change arena

tone by emphasizing continuity based on old behavior.[5] This is typical of closed, inward-looking systems such as regulated markets and bureaucratic government organizations subject only to weak forces of change. Provided the force does not increase, the system may continue with this posture indefinitely.

In the opposite, bottom right-hand corner of the arena, the forces of change are strong and the resistance is weak. The forces of change far exceed the resistance threshold, so the system adapts continuously to the change forces. This represents a flexible industry or company that responds to strong forces in the environment, one in which there is little resistance to change. All the participants perceive the forces for change. There are few status quo agents; almost everyone is a change agent. Whenever adapta ion is required, the full house of change agents ensures that the system responds accordingly.[6] Small new companies and independent business units facing strong forces, especially those in high-tech and financial service industries, often come close to continuous adaptation. The closest are firms in high-volume, competitive markets for commodities and financial instruments, in which there are no obstacles to change.

Bisecting the change arena is a diagonal which marks the boundary between the dominance of the status quo agents and the forces of resistance on the one side, and the dominance of the change agents and forces of change on the other side. Along the diagonal the forces of change and resistance are finely balanced. A slight alteration in the balance can shift the dominant influence in the system between the status quo and change agents.

In the bottom left-hand corner of the arena where the forces of change are weak and the resistance is weak, the boundary between old and new behavior is easily crossed. Neither the status quo nor the change agents are strongly entrenched; both are present with approximately equal influence on either side. The impact of the forces of change and resistance fluctuates because chance events can easily alter the balance between them. The alternating dominance of the forces of change and resistance results in sporadic change: change when the resistance threshold is breached from time to time.[7] If the change force continues to grow with low resistance, it causes the gradual conversion of status quo agents into change agents and results in a *turning point*. Many intermediate-volume markets and medium-sized companies are flexible enough to adapt to weak change forces in a sporadic way. The absence of large stakes, or weak resistance to change, makes it relatively easy for their participants to act as change agents. Moreover, frequent adaptation prevents them from becoming overly committed to the status quo.

In the top right-hand corner, where strong forces put pressure on systems with strong resistance, the change can be sharply discontinuous, forming a *breakpoint*. The transition between status quo and change agent behavior is characterized by a sudden sharp jump which is represented by the shaded part of the boundary line in the change arena. To the left of the boundary below the resistance threshold no change occurs, despite the fact that the change forces are strong; the status quo agents dominate largely. These are the markets and organizations where structure and stakes in the status quo initially neutralize the forces for change. Moderate pressure for change creates too few change agents to have a significant impact on the existing system. Strong pressure for change, of crisis proportions, is needed to undermine the status quo. Close to the boundary, chance events can make the difference in breaching the resistance threshold. Once the change forces exceed the resistance threshold, on the right hand side of the boundary, the resistance breaks down. Domination by the change agents occurs all of a sudden when the balance of power tips in their favor. A massive shift takes place from status quo to change agent behavior, thereby triggering a breakpoint.[8]

Breakpoints in rigid systems are the stuff that revolutions, market crashes, and radical corporate reorganizations are made of. The abandonment of the Bretton Woods agreement and the oil price shocks of the 1970s, for example, introduced an era of sharply fluctuating exchange and interest rates, which completely changed competitive conditions in many industries from one moment to the next. The breakpoints in the financial markets in the late 1980s and the collapse of the command economies in the early 1990s have reinforced the trend toward more frequent radical shifts in the competitive environment and in organizations. As long as strong forces continue to confront strong resistance, breakpoints will be frequent.

However, the change arena suggests that all four change types are relevant. The continuing and varying tension between the forces of resistance and change, between the status quo and a new order, determines the type of change that occurs. Even if one change type is in the limelight because of overall economic conditions, the position of individual industries, companies, and business units differs and evolves over time. The location of a business in the change arena during a particular period shapes the kind of change that the business is likely to experience.

When managers intervene they typically alter the configuration of the forces for change and resistance. The company moves around in the change arena tracing out a change path. Viable change paths are those which successfully adapt the company to its environment. To identify a viable change path, a series of questions about the relative strength of the forces of change change and resistance must be answered. These questions are summarized in Table 2.1 in the form of an outline of the change path diagnostic.

The first question that must be answered is: How strong are the forces of change and what is their impact on the company's performance? It is important to distinguish between situations in which the forces of change are already having a strong negative impact on the performance of the company (these are situations calling for *reactive change*) and situations in which the company is doing well and the forces of change have yet to affect performance (those calling for *proactive change*).

Table 2.1   Change path diagnostic

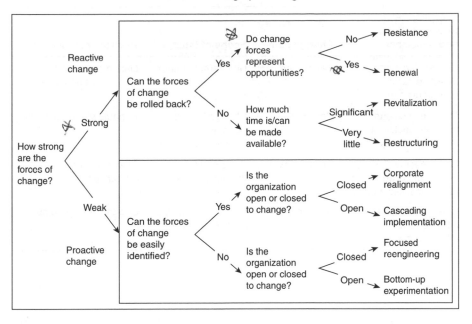

Identifying Reactive Change Paths

In the case of reactive change, the manager and company have to respond to well developed forces of change and resistance. The company is close to the edge of a breakpoint (see Exhibit 2.1). To identify a viable change path under these conditions, the relevant question to be answered is: What is the balance between the forces of change and resistance? Or, more explicitly, can the forces of change be rolled back? The answer depends on the nature of the forces of change and the resources and time at the disposal of the company. The characteristics of the corresponding reactive change paths are summarized in Table 2.2.

Change Forces Can Be Rolled Back – If the change force can be rolled back, then the less radical change associated with renewal or resistance will be appropriate (See Table 2.2). The key issue is whether the change force represents a business opportunity or threat? If the change force is a business threat, then the company is best off on a path of resistance using its resources and existing momentum to either avoid or role back the change force. By contrast, the company obviously should adapt to a change force that represents a business opportunity. Since the change force can be neutralized, adaptation typically is limited to parts of the organization on a path of renewal. Adaptation often

Table 2.2 Reactive change paths

Interplay between forces of change and resistance	Change path	Scope of change	Pace of change process
Change force can be rolled back; represents a threat	Resistance	No internal change	Depends on ability to contain change force
Change force can be rolled back; but is an opportunity	Renewal	Change limited to parts of the organization	Periodic stepwise change
Change force cannot be rolled back; time is available	Revitalization	Ongoing change throughout the organization	Slow continuous adaptation
Change force cannot be rolled back; very little time available	Restructuring	Intense change on a few dimensions	Sudden change jump

removes the need for further change, until the pressure builds up again. If so, this results in sporadic, stepwise change.

■ *A resistance path* is appropriate when strong resistance that is closed to change confronts a change force that is a threat but can be contained. The resistance path presumes the firm can avoid a potential organizational breakpoint by working on its environment to create more stable conditions where the change force is weaker. What little change occurs internally is directed toward reducing the pressure exerted by the change force. The resistance path often involves interacting with government and public agencies, trade and industry associations, and other external groups that can channel and reduce the forces of change in the business environment.

A resistance path often involves the pursuit of a niche formula, designed to avoid need for sharp change by finding a corner of the market protected from the change force. This formula is generally more useful for smaller players. Rolex, Audemars-Piguet, and the other up-market Swiss watch companies carved out a high-quality niche that shielded them from the massive breakpoint created by Seiko, Citizen, and other East Asian competitors. As one of their managers put it, 'We have never heard of the Japanese.'

Niche formulas are common in the German-speaking world. Specialized, high-quality products represent the strategy of thousands of medium-sized and small German companies, the so-called 'Mittelstand'. They have created highly profitable, well-protected niches in the world market. From their niches, the

Mittelstand contribute a great deal to Germany's record exports, despite the discontinuities faced by the more exposed major players.

- *A renewal path* is appropriate when the change force represents an opportunity that can be exploited with stepwise change. The scope of the change is typically limited to parts of the company and the pace is sporadic. Both internal and external organization with various stakeholders may be involved. Through adaptation, renewal takes the pressure off and weakens the change force.

In the 1980s, Procter & Gamble (the detergent giant) and Frito-Lay (the potato chip maker owned by Pepsi) invaded the $2.2 million cookie market that Nabisco had dominated for almost a century. With a heavy barrage of advertising, Frito-Lay was said to have captured 20 percent of the Kansas City market in a few weeks. Procter & Gamble spent $20 million on advertising and promotion for a comfortable 25 percent share in six months. Nabisco's initial reaction was to add more chocolate chips to its 'Chips Ahoy' hard cookies. Stock analysts on Wall Street were not convinced by this lame response and their commentary increased the pressure for change. (See arrow 1 in Exhibit 2.2.)

Management then decided to shake up its complacent mindset and shake off Nabisco's reputation as 'a sleepy sales company that did little to push its products'. It initiated a renewal of the product range with the company's

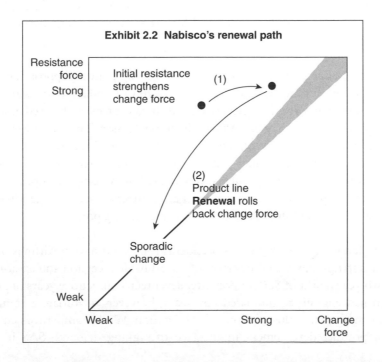

Exhibit 2.2 Nabisco's renewal path

biggest cookie development project in years. Sixteen months after Frito-Lay's first attack, a new Nabisco line with fifteen varieties, called Almost Home, appeared on supermarket shelves. Presented as 'the moistest, chewiest, most perfectly baked cookies the world has ever tasted...well, almost', the new line was supported by a $25 million advertising counterattack. When the dust finally settled, Frito-Lay's market share had fallen back to 8 percent, Procter & Gamble's to 20 percent. Nabisco with its established warehousing, distribution, and sales strengths had renewed its product line and captured 35 percent of the soft cookie segment (arrow 2 in Exhibit 2.2).

The renewal path was appropriate for Nabisco, because the change force could be rolled back by exploiting the strengths of the company to attack the competition and enter the market for chewy cookies. The adaptation to the change force was limited to a change in mindset with only part of the organization being involved, in this case, the product development and marketing departments. Once this had been done, the competition dealt with, and the demand for chewy cookies satisfied, the force for change was much weaker.

Change Forces Cannot Be Rolled Back – If the change force cannot be rolled back, only the more radical change associated with restructuring and revitalization will be able to adapt the company to the change force. The key issue is how much time is, or can be made available before the change force overwhelms the resistance?[9] When enough time is available, entrenched cultural resistance and momentum can be reduced gradually to initiate a corporate turning point followed by a pervasive revitalization. When the time available is short, restructuring will be needed to break the resistance. The two paths are contrasted below.

■ *A revitalization path,* involving a reactive turning point, is appropriate when resistance based on culture and momentum must be adapted to a strong and growing change force. The strong external change forces can be used indirectly to drive the internal organizational change processes. The pace of change is typically slow, but continuous and all-encompassing. Under these conditions, lowering the resistance usually stimulates the change forces by converting status quo agents into change agents. Revitalization can only be implemented if the firm can protect itself from the negative effects of the change force long enough to accomplish the necessary cultural turning point.

When Jan Carlson took over as president, the Scandinavian Airlines System (SAS) was struggling with the impact of a worldwide recession and an accumulated two-year deficit of $30 million after seventeen consecutive years of profits. Carlson had enough accumulated resources, however, to initiate a change in strategic momentum plus a cultural revitalization. While competitors cut back on new product development in the face of sagging demand, SAS invested

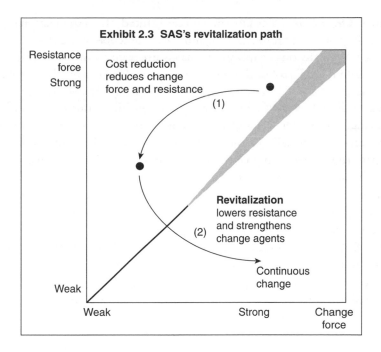

Exhibit 2.3 SAS's revitalization path

heavily in its Businessman's Airline Program. Among strategic initiatives were a cost reduction drive, a punctuality drive, a new corporate identity, and new marketing projects. These moves opened the company up and by improving performance reduced the external pressure, thereby, providing the time for more fundamental change (arrow 1 in Exhibit 2.3).

The centerpiece of the change process, however, was a cultural revolution. Responsibility for action was delegated downward to the front line, putting employees in charge. Management was asked to serve as consultants rather than as leaders of the organization. To implement the cultural revolution, Carlson and his team personally visited the front line all over the company and established a training program for 20,000 managers and employees on the new concept of service. According to Carlson, 'Giving a person freedom to take responsibility for his ideas, decisions, and actions is to release hidden resources.'

By encouraging the change agents both inside and outside SAS to move into action, Carlson stimulated a gradual process of fundamental change (arrow 2 in Exhibit 2.3). This turning point approach was facilitated by the time that could be made available and avoided the organizational trauma associated with breakpoint restructuring.

■ *A restructuring path,* involving a reactive breakpoint, is appropriate when a strong and growing change force confronts strong resistance that is closed to change. On this path, because time is very limited, the organization is given a sharp shock to adapt it to the environment. The scope of the change is highly focused, typically on organizational hardware such as structure and systems. This facilitates control of the transition and avoids possible disintegration.

Organizational restructuring – via acquisition, divestment, reorganization, downsizing, and so on – is a common way of trying to respond to an external breakpoint, especially in the Anglo-Saxon world. In continental Europe and Japan, the restructuring often takes place within a larger industrial group, where the parent company and related banks play a major role. For companies with strong forces of resistance, the shock created by a radical change imposed from the top down is often the only way of unfreezing existing structures before the forces of change overwhelm the company.

When Bob Horton took over as chairman of BP in early 1990, he initiated Project 1990, which was designed to transform the bureaucratic, civil service culture of the company. Its purpose was to make BP capable of discovering and unleashing corporate entrepreneurs to find new opportunities for the company's dwindling oil reserves. The number of businesses, layers of management, committees, head office staff, and so on were cut. This initial streamlining lowered the resistance to change somewhat and by reducing costs also lowered the change pressure. (See arrow 1 in Exhibit 2.4.)

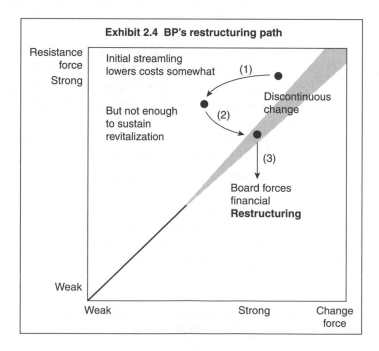

Exhibit 2.4 BP's restructuring path

Workshops, communication and training programs were used to promote a new culture based on values of 'openness, care, teamwork, empowerment and trust. People will be expected to take decisions themselves, rather than through committees,' said Horton.[10] But costs had not been reduced enough to sustain this revitalization effort (arrow 2 in Exhibit 2.4).

BP was facing a more immediate problem in the form of the worldwide economic downturn, which severely constrained the company's ability to maintain the tempo of exploration, debt repayments and dividends. The conflict between the longer run internal objectives of Project 1990, to create a more entrepreneurial culture, and the external market forces of contraction seriously compromised the whole change effort. BP announced its first historic loss in the first quarter of 1992. And on June 25th, Bob Horton resigned in 'what appeared to be a coup by his fellow directors'. In the presence of strong financial pressure, with an organization still closed to radical change and with time running out, the Board had little choice. It put BP through a forced process of restructuring based on radical cost reduction, as well a new financial policy of lower dividends and reduced investment in exploration (arrow 3 in Exhibit 2.4).

Putting Together a Change Campaign

A complete radical change campaign, as the BP example illustrates, may require several moves in the change arena. The initial position of the company and the constellation of forces may be such that, in the time available, all the change requirements cannot be achieved with a single change path. There may be a set of change forces of differing urgency. To deal with a set of change forces, a change campaign is needed in the form of a sequence of change paths.

A reactive change campaign can be used to come from behind and leapfrog the competition. Under these conditions, there is often a company-specific change force with a strong financial impact, together with a competitive change force with somewhat longer run impact. Being the greatest threat to survival, the strongest change force must be dealt with in the first phase of the change campaign, while the weaker change force(s) is/are dealt with in the subsequent phase(s). Once the necessary resources and competence have been acquired to deal with the strongest change force, competence can be added to deal with the other forces.

A classic example of how such a reactive change campaign evolves is provided by the Harley Davidson story. 'At the start of the 1980s, few people gave Harley-Davidson much chance to survive. The last U.S. motorcycle maker was being battered by the Japanese. Its share of the super heavyweight motorcycle market had fallen from 75 percent in 1973 to 25 percent.' As Peter Reid pointed out in his book on Harley Davidson, more than half the machines coming off

Harley's assembly line had missing parts; the dealers had to fix them up before they could be sold.

The first phase of the change campaign was triggered by the appointment of Vaugh Beals as CEO in 1975. He intervened immediately to protect Harley's operations from the immediate financial and competitive change forces in order to keep the company in business. He appealed to the banks for financial support to restructure the balance sheet; a quality control program was set up with the chief engineer to repair the bikes before selling them to the dealers; the design skills of William G. Davidson, grandson of one of the founders, were deployed in the form of styling innovations to stem the erosion of market share.

During the second phase, Beals and his team intervened to revitalize the production operations with new skills and behaviors. After a visit to Honda's plant in Marysville, Ohio, and a successful pilot program, they decided to introduce just-in-time inventory control and quality improvement. Some of the workers laughed at the idea of replacing Harley's computerized control system, overhead conveyors, and high-rise parts storage with just-in-time push carts. To deal with the resistance, Harley executives spent months meeting with employees from all departments. The employees were involved in planning the system and working out the details. 'No changes were implemented until the people involved understood and accepted them. It took two months before the consensus decision was made to go ahead. That was a Friday – and we started making the changes on Monday.' The employees responded with initiative. The company followed up by teaching workers the use of statistical tools needed for quality control, training plant managers to become team leaders, and helping suppliers to use similar methods.

Having laid the quality and cost foundation for its comeback, Harley turned to the third phase of the campaign: adding perceived value through renewal of marketing. First, it won five years of declining import tariff protection against the big Japanese bikes. Then to shape the mindset of its customers a series of TV commercials announced Super Ride, a demonstration program inviting bikers to try out a new Harley at any of the 600 or more dealers. As a result, potential buyers were increasingly convinced that Harley had solved its quality control problems. Super Ride became so successful that Harley takes a fleet of demo bikes to all motorcycle rallies. Money was also spent boosting dealers and forming the Harley Owners Group (HOG). The club sponsors bikers' events virtually every weekend from April to November all over the country and includes managers and their wives: 'HOG is one way we differentiate ourselves from our Japanese competitors.' Indeed, Honda tried and failed to create its own version of HOG.

In 1983, Harley moved from the red to the black in terms of profitability. Its market share started climbing again. By 1989, Harley had recaptured almost 50 percent of the super-heavyweight bike market, with profits of $26.9 million on sales of $810.1 million.

The overall change process can be summarized graphically by mapping out the intervention paths in the change arena as shown in Exhibit 2.5 for Harley-Davidson.

- *Path 1:* Resistance path to stay in the game by shielding operations from the most urgent change forces with financial restructuring and W. Davidson's designs
- *Path 2:* Revitalizing to catch up with the Japanese by changing the culture and moving production toward continuous improvement
- *Path 3:* Renewal to outperform the Japanese by incremental addition of value through marketing (Super Ride and HOG programs)

The key to the success of Harley's change campaign was the way in which the change paths were sequenced to deal with the stronger change forces first, thereby clearing the way for dealing with the weaker ones. Furthermore, each change path was consistent with the strength of the corresponding forces of change and resistance.

The timing of the transition between the paths is crucial. If the process moves too soon from one path to the next, the basis for supporting the next path may not be sufficient. On the other hand, if the process is too slow, the company may miss the window of opportunity that often opens up after an industry breakpoint.

Exhibit 2.5 Harley-Davidson leapfrog: Sequence of change paths

Creating Proactive Breakpoints and Turning Points

In the case of proactive change, the change forces have yet to affect performance. Typically, there is enough time for whatever change path might be envisaged. However, the change requirements are often difficult to specify, because, as an industry leader, the company has no other example to follow. In addition, when a company is ahead of the competition, and when there is no performance crisis, it is much more difficult to mobilize the organization for change than when it has to react to the moves of others. In situations that call for proactive change, people may agree intellectually that something more is needed to stay ahead, but when things are going well, it is not easy to get an emotional commitment to change from comfortable status quo agents.

The main diagnostic question to be answered when selecting a proactive change path is whether the forces of change can be easily identified? When the change forces are easy to identify, action is called for to capitalize on the new environment as soon as possible before the competitors do so. By contrast, when the environmental change forces are difficult to identify, a more exploratory response is needed to give the organization the opportunity to discover the direction of the new change forces. The corresponding proactive change paths are described below and summarized in Table 2.3.

Table 2.3   Creating proactive change

Forces of change and resistance	Change path	Nature of path	Motivation to change
Change force easy to identify; organization closed to change	Corporate Realignment	Organizational contrast with another approach	Challenge to resolve organizational tension
Change force easy to identify; organization open to change	Cascading implementation	Progressive adaptation to change forces	Participative commitment
Change force difficult to identify; organization closed to change	Focused Re-engineering	Benchmarking. Explicit focused comparisons	Threat implicit in performance of benchmark
Change force difficult to identify; organization open to change	Bottom-up experimenting	Learning by example from successful internal change	Competition to match example

Change Forces Can Be Identified – The key to mobilizing for emerging change forces that can be identified is to bring the external change forces into the organization, to create a tension between where the organization is and where it should be going. Typically, status quo agents can only be converted into change agents if they feel the change force directly in the form of a threat to their position, or an opportunity to improve it. Successful proactive change managers have found numerous ways of converting the identifiable external change forces into internal change drivers. The question is whether the organization is open or closed to change?

Corporate Realignment – If the organization is closed to change, then it has to be jolted into recognizing the forces of change: for example, by challenging the company internally with another organization that is closer to the force of change – that is, by initiating a breakpoint in the form of an organizational realignment.

A common approach to an organizational realignment is through an acquisition or merger. Helmut Maucher of Nestlé anticipated the global consolidation of the food industry and tried to revitalize the company by streamlining procedures and shifting power from the head office on Lake Geneva into the field. Although these actions improved performance somewhat, they also increasd the resistance to globalization by strengthening the power of the geographic zones and the accompanying national cultures (arrow 1 in Exhibit 2.6).

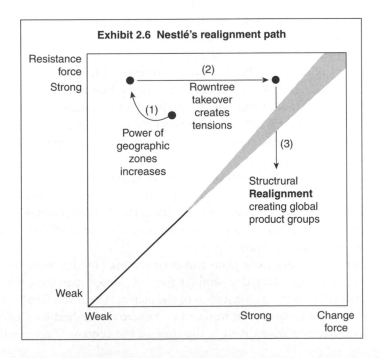

Exhibit 2.6 Nestlé's realignment path

Little else changed, until Nestlé was exposed internally, through the acquisition of Rowntree, to a different way of doing things that reflected the globally oriented forces of change. The acquired Rowntree became Nestlé's first center for a global product line, in this case, confectionery. The tension between this new global product line and the zonal structure created dissatisfaction with the existing situation, thereby, providing the motivation for fundamental change (arrow 2 in Exhibit 2.6). In response to this tension, Nestlé put itself through a structural breakpoint – in the form of two new global, strategic product groups, one of which included confectionery – as part of a corporate realignment from a local to a global orientation (arrow 3 in Exhibit 2.6).

In the absence of the Rowntree acquisition (or some other motivating event), it would have been very difficult to generate the organizational energy to support fundamental change. The size and inertia in the Nestlé organization precluded the use of a more gradual turning point. On the other hand, relative to top-down reactive restructuring, Nestlé's proactive realignment provided much more time for the organization to take ownership of the need for change.

Cascading Implementation – If the organization is open to change, then it can be asked to begin implementing. The key managers can be encouraged to become change agents to exploit the change force in their busness units, both in a stepwise organizational turning point and in a cascading implementation from the top down through the organization.

When Seiko's planning department issued their report on market saturation and the increasing weakness in watch prices, Ichiro Hattori, the CEO, felt that the company should do something. The question was how to get a company with very healthy profits to respond to such a weak change force. Hattori first made the threat more real by highlighting Matsushita's plans for a TV watch in addition to the pressure on prices. He then began at the top by asking his fellow directors on the board what Daini Seikosha's response should be to the competitive situation. They opted for diversification into electronic equipment.

When he was satisfied with their answers he moved to the second stage, a companywide conference for approximately 50 senior managers. Each was asked to 'propose a three-year strategic plan at the divisional and departmental levels relating to the corporate survival scenario for 1990 incorporating diversification into electronic equipment'.

In early 1982, once these plans had been accepted by the board, the third stage began with a three-day seminar for 250 junior managers who were asked to develop the implementation of the plan at their level. Finally, a Total Quality Control program was initiated to 'ensure the highest level of corporatewide implementation'. And at the time of the centenary celebrations in

1982, the corporate identity and name was changed to the Seiko Instruments and Electronics Co. Ltd.

It took longer than expected to get corporate-wide consensus and to develop the necessary new manufacturing and engineering expertise. Moreover, the diversification cost was more than anticipated and the customers wanted a wider product range. Yet Seiko easily achieved its diversification target in 1986, four years ahead of schedule. By then Seiko had developed a new line of sophisticated graphics devices that accounted for 50 percent of sales. The collaborative cascade approach had allowed Hattori to create a proactive turning point from above. (See the four arrows in Exhibit 2.7; these are not numbered, because they are all part of the same cascading process.)

Change Forces Difficult to Identify – Getting people to feel the external change force inside the company is most difficult when the change forces themselves are difficult to identify. The challenge is to create a mobilizing sense of discomfort with the way things are as opposed to the way they should be. How this can best be achieved depends on whether the organization is closed or open to change.

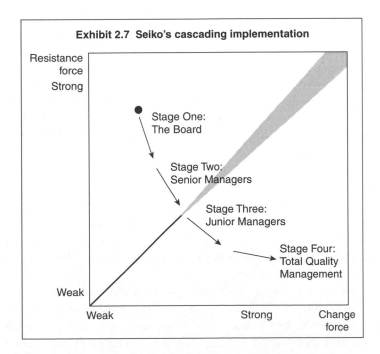

Exhibit 2.7 Seiko's cascading implementation

Focused Re-engineering – If the organization is closed to change, some way must be found of getting it to identify the forces of change – for example, through explicit comparison (benchmarking) with other players (customers, suppliers, competitors, or leaders in other industries with similar processes). The first key to success is a breakpoint in mindset. Then, based on the benchmarking or other analysis, processes and systems can be redesigned from scratch. This serves to improve efficiency and effectiveness by eliminating the waste of resources and time and focusing on the needs of the customer. Relative to corporate realignment, such re-engineering of the affected sytems and processes leads to a more focused breakpoint.

Bottom-Up Experimenting – If the organization is open to change, it can be stimulated to identify the forces of change by encouraging experimentation to find an example of successful internal change that embodies the change force. Once an example of successful change has been produced, it can be used as a cultural change driver to create an organizational turning point from the bottom up in the rest of the organization.

Such change often emerges in unexpected ways, at unexpected places. For example, in a move to cut costs, the manager of the Energy Chemicals Division of a major oil company temporarily stopped all field trips by the research and technology staff from the central laboratory. As anticipated, this decision produced strong reactions from both the sales force and the technology unit: the sales force complained that they could not do their work without a technologist on site; technology complained that they no longer had field trips to test their new products. Unintentionally, however, this dissatisfaction provided the opening for more fundamental change (arrow 1 in Exhibit 2.8).

Since the technologists could not come on site, the sales force started trying to do the bottle and field tests itself. In Safniyah, one of the largest Saudi fields, the salesman spent time in the field lab, blending and trying new chemical combinations, calling the central lab by telephone for advice. Through this process he developed an innovative new blend. The client received a detailed report on the results of the new product trials within two days and the company quickly won a six month contract. Samples of the new blend and copies of the test report were sent to the central lab for review. The central lab responded by sending new samples to the sales force for field trials. Gradually an exchange of ideas and methods developed, with the central lab concentrating on perfecting and developing fundamentally new chemicals, while in the field the sales force blended these to satisfy the specific needs of new customers.

As sales began to improve with new products and product adaptations visible in the lab and the field, the manager of the division and his team began to realize that the key to success was not only cost cutting, but also new products and customized service. Product development was then further

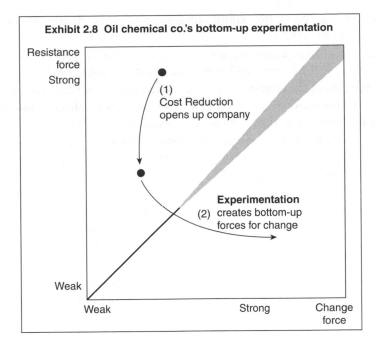

Exhibit 2.8 Oil chemical co.'s bottom-up experimentation

encouraged in the central lab, while field labs were set up in all markets where they didn't already exist. The Energy Chemicals Division developed a reputation for providing good products in a short time with excellent after-sales service. Competitors were caught off guard, the division's market share expanded and its success began to be noticed in other parts of the corporation.

In effect, a proactive turning point had occurred from the bottom up. Management had inadvertently created the organizational space needed for experimentation in the field. It quickly recognized what was going on and encouraged the new process (arrow 2 in Exhibit 2.8).

Conclusion

Assessing the strength of the forces of change and resistance provides a framework for choosing between eight different change paths. Of the eight paths, seven (all but the resistance path) have to do with reducing the forces of resistance inside the organization to respond to the impact of the forces of change. The way in which this can best be done depends on the strength of the change forces. The main distinction is between reactive change paths (for dealing with strong change forces that have already affected performance) and proactive change paths (for taking advantage of weak change forces whose impact has yet to be felt).

When the change forces are strong, the key issue is whether, and when, the resistance will be overcome? Resistance that is capable of dominating the change force gives the company the choice of adapting with limited renewal, or resisting. By contrast, change forces that cannot be neutralized, must be fully adapted to – either with slow deep revitalization when there is enough time and resources available, or with sharp, rapid restructuring when time is short.

When the change forces are weak and have yet to affect performance, the key question for initiating proactive change is whether the forces can be readily identified? If so, the most appropriate change path is determined by how open or closed the organization is to change. A radical realignment is typically needed in closed organizatons to exploit the emerging opportunity in time; cascading implementation, or some other turning point approach, can be used in open organizations. By contrast, if the change forces themselves themselves are difficult to identify, the challenge is to create a mobilizing sense of discomfort with thing as they are. In closed organizations, a way must be found of creating a breakpoint in the managerial mindset (by benchmarking, for example). Open organizations, on the other hand, can be stimulated to identify the forces of change with bottom-up experimentation.

To adapt to more than one change force, a change campaign is required in the form of a sequence of change paths, to deal with the stronger change forces first, thereby clearing the way for exploiting the weaker ones. Each of the change paths in the campaign should reflect the configuration of the forces acting on the part of the business to be changed. The transition between the paths must allow enough time to provide a sufficient basis for the next phase of the campaign, while being quick enough to capitalize on competitive opportunities. And the change campaign must be ongoing; as soon as companies stop dealing with change forces, they run into trouble, as illustrated by the recent experience of both SAS and Harley Davidson.

As they become more proficient at managing change, especially proactive change, leading companies become the force of change in the industry. Ideally, they develop the capability of managing internal turning points and breakpoints, both reactively and proactively, in order exploit environmental change and outpace the competition.

_____ **_Notes_** _____

1. Lewin, Kurt (1947) 'Frontiers in group dynamics, concept method and reality in social science; social equilibria and social change', _Human Relations,_ vol. 1, pp. 2–38.
2. See, for example, Ginsberg, A. and Bucholz, A. (1990) 'Converting to for-profit status: Corporate responsiveness to radical change,' _Academy of Management Journal,_ vol. 33,

no. 3, pp. 445–77, for a discussion of what they call inductive and inertial forces. (See Myer, A., Brooks, G. and Goes, J. (1990) 'Environmental jolts and industry revolutions: Organizational responses to discontinuous change', *Strategic Management Journal,* vol. 11, pp. 93–110, for a review of the literature on different patterns of change.)

3. This article is based on my recently published book, Strebel, P. (1992) *Breakpoints: How Managers Exploit Radical Business Change*, Boston, MA, Harvard Business School Press, which contains the sources of the quotes and examples of change management other than the BP story.

4. For a summary of the literature or the change processes see Strebel, P. and Välikangas, L. 'Organizational change processes in a force field,' *International Review of Strategic Management* (forthcoming).

5. This is essentially the steady state behavior described for example by Cyert, R. M. and March, J. G. (1963) *A Behavioral Theory of the Form*, Englewood Cliffs, NJ, Prentice Hall.

6. This is similar to the evolutionary adaptation described for example by Lawrence, P. R. and Lorsch, J. W. (1967) *Organization and the Environment*, Boston, MA, Harvard Business School.

7. Sporadic Change is essentially the logical incrementalism described by Quinn, J. B. (1978) 'Strategic change: Logical incrementalism', *Sloan Management Review,* vol. 20, pp. 7–12.

8. Discontinuous Change has been described, for example, by Meyer, A. D. (1982) 'Adapting to environmental jolts', *Administrative Science Quarterly,* vol. 27, pp. 515–37.

9. For a discussion on the urgency of change, see Fry, J. N. and Killing, J. P. (1989) *Strategic Analysis and Action* (2nd edn), Englewood Cliffs, NJ, Prentice Hall, Ch. 12.

10. Most of the BP story and all the quotes are taken from Hargreaves, I. (1992) 'When thoroughness is not enough', *Financial Times,* 26 June, p. 19; Lascelles, D. (1992) 'Horton is ousted as Chairman of British Petroleum,' *Financial Times,* 26 June, p. 1. See also Simon, D. (1991) 'Managing cultural change at BP', *Target-Management Development Review,* vol. 4, no. 3, pp. 16–19.

Organisational Change Management: A Critical Review

3

Rune Todnem By

Introduction

Change management has been defined as 'the process of continually renewing an organization's direction, structure, and capabilities to serve the ever-changing needs of external and internal customers' (Moran and Brightman, 2001, p. 111). According to Burnes (2004) change is an ever-present feature of organisational life, both at an operational and strategic level. Therefore, there should be no doubt regarding the importance to any organisation of its ability to identify where it needs to be in the future, and how to manage the changes required getting there. Consequently, organisational change cannot be separated from organisational strategy, or vice versa (Burnes, 2004; Rieley and Clarkson, 2001). Due to the importance of organisational change, its management is becoming a highly required managerial skill (Senior, 2002). Graetz (2000, p. 550) goes as far as suggesting 'Against a backdrop of increasing globalisation, deregulation, the rapid pace of technological innovation, a growing knowledge workforce, and shifting social and demographic trends, few would dispute that the primary task for management today is the leadership of organisational change.'

Since the need for change often is unpredictable, it tends to be reactive, discontinuous, ad hoc and often triggered by a situation of organisational crisis (Burnes, 2004; De Wit and Meyer, 2005; Luecke, 2003; Nelson, 2003). Although the successful management of change is accepted as a necessity in order to survive and succeed in today's highly competitive and continuously evolving environment (Luecke, 2003; Okumus and Hemmington, 1998), Balogun and Hope Hailey (2004) report a failure rate of around 70 per cent of all change programmes initiated. It may be suggested that this poor success rate indicates a fundamental lack of a valid framework of how to implement and manage

Todnem, R. (2005) 'Organisational change management: A critical review', *Journal of Change Management*, vol. 5, no. 4, pp. 369–80.

organisational change as what is currently available to academics and practitioners is a wide range of contradictory and confusing theories and approaches (Burnes, 2004). Guimaraes and Armstrong (1998) argue that mostly personal and superficial analyses have been published in the area of change management, and according to Doyle (2002) there is even evidence to suggest that with only a few exceptions existing practice and theory are mostly supported by unchallenged assumptions about the nature of contemporary organisational change management. Edmonstone (1995, p. 16) supports this observation when stating 'many of the change processes over the last 25 years have been subject to fundamental flaws, preventing the successful management of change'.

Even though it is difficult to identify any consensus regarding a framework for organisational change management, there seems to be an agreement on two important issues. Firstly, it is agreed that the pace of change has never been greater then in the current business environment (Balogun and Hope Hailey, 2004; Burnes, 2004; Carnall, 2003; Kotter, 1996; Luecke, 2003; Moran and Brightman, 2001; Okumus and Hemmington, 1998; Paton and McCalman, 2000; Senior, 2002). Secondly, there is a consensus that change, being triggered by internal or external factors, comes in all shapes, forms and sizes (Balogun and Hope Hailey, 2004; Burnes, 2004; Carnall, 2003; Kotter, 1996; Luecke, 2003), and, therefore, affects all organisations in all industries.

While there is an ever-growing generic literature emphasising the importance of change and suggesting ways to approach it, very little empirical evidence has been provided in support of the different theories and approaches suggested (Guimaraes and Armstrong, 1998). The purpose of this article is, therefore, to provide a critical review of theories and approaches currently available in a bid to encourage further research into the nature of organisational change with the aim of constructing a new and pragmatic framework for the management of it. In order to do so the article has adopted Senior's (2002) three categories of change as a structure with which to link other main theories and approaches. These three categories have been identified as change characterised by the rate of occurrence, by how it comes about, and by scale. Although total quality management (TQM), business process re-engineering (BPR) and other change initiatives embrace several of these characteristics (Balogun and Hope Hailey, 2004; Pettinger, 2004) this article will concentrate on the main characteristics of change and not on individual change initiatives. Finally, the article identifies some areas for further research.

Change Characterised by the Rate of Occurrence

The early approaches and theories to organisational change management suggested that organisations could not be effective or improve performance if they were constantly changing (Rieley and Clarkson, 2001). It was argued that people need routines to be effective and able to improve performance (Luecke, 2003). However, it is now argued that it is of vital importance to organisations that people are able to undergo continuous change (Burnes, 2004; Rieley and Clarkson, 2001). While Luecke (2003) suggests that a state of continuous change can become a routine in its own right, Leifer (1989) perceives change as a normal and natural response to internal and environmental conditions.

Table 3.1 identifies the main types of change categorised by the rate of occurrence to be discontinuous and incremental change. However, different authors employ different terminology when describing the same approach. While Burnes (2004) differentiates between incremental and continuous change, other authors do not. Furthermore, to make it even more confusing, Grundy (1993) and Senior (2002) distinguish between smooth and bumpy incremental change.

Grundy (1993, p. 26) defines discontinuous change as 'change which is marked by rapid shifts in either strategy, structure or culture, or in all three'. This sort of rapid change can be triggered by major internal problems or by considerable external shock (Senior, 2002). According to Luecke (2003) discontinuous change is onetime events that take place through large, widely separated initiatives, which are followed up by long periods of consolidation and stillness and describes it as 'single, abrupt shift from the past' (Luecke, 2003, p. 102).

Advocates of discontinues change argue this approach to be cost-effective as it does not promote a never-ending process of costly change initiatives, and that it creates less turmoil caused by continuous change (Guimaraes and Armstrong, 1998). Nelson (2003, p. 18) states that 'Change cannot be relied upon to occur at a steady state, rather there are periods of incremental change sandwiched between more violent periods of change which have contributed to the illusion of stability once assumed to be the case.'

Although the discontinuous approach to change is still employed in recent change initiatives (Duncan *et al.*, 2001) there seems to be a consensus among contemporary authors that the benefits from discontinuous change do not

Table 3.1 Change characterised by the rate of occurrence 1

Type of change	Balogun and Hope Hailey (2004)	Burnes (2004)	Grundy (1993)	Luecke (2003)	Senior (2002)
Discontinuous		✓	✓	✓	
Incremental		✓			
Smooth incremental			✓		✓
Bumpy incremental			✓		✓
Continuous	✓	✓			✓
Continuous incremental				✓	
Punctuated equilibrium	✓	✓			

last (Bond, 1999; Grundy, 1993; Holloway, 2002; Love *et al.*, 1998; Taylor and Hirst, 2001). According to Luecke (2003) this approach allows defensive behaviour, complacency, inward focus, and routines, which again creates situations where major reform is frequently required.

What is suggested as a better approach to change is a situation where organisations and their people continually monitor, sense and respond to the external and internal environment in small steps as an ongoing process (Luecke, 2003). Therefore, in sharp contrast to discontinuous change, Burnes (2004) identifies continuous change as the ability to change continuously in a fundamental manner to keep up with the fast-moving pace of change. ✏

Burnes (2004) refers to incremental change as when individual parts of an organisation deal increasingly and separately with one problem and one objective at a time. Advocates of this view argue that change is best implemented through successive, limited, and negotiated shifts (Burnes, 2004). Grundy (1993) suggests dividing incremental change into smooth and bumpy incremental change. By smooth incremental change Grundy (1993) identifies change that evolves slowly in a systematic and predictable way at a constant rate. This type of change is suggested to be exceptional and rare in the current environment and in the future (Senior, 2002). Bumpy incremental change, however, is characterised by periods of relative peacefulness punctuated by acceleration in the pace of change (Grundy, 1993; Holloway, 2002). Burnes' (2004) and Balogun and Hope Hailey's (2004) term for this type of change is punctuated equilibrium.

The difference between Burnes' (2004) understanding of continuous and incremental change is that the former describes departmental, operational, ongoing changes, while the latter is concerned with organisation-wide strategies and the ability to constantly adapt these to the demands of both the external and internal environment. In an attempt to simplify the categories, Luecke (2003) suggests combining continuous and incremental change. However, it can be suggested that this combination makes it difficult to differentiate between departmental and organisation-wide approaches to change management. Therefore, for the purpose of this article Table 3.2 suggests a combination of the above-mentioned change characteristics.

Table 3.2   Change characterised by the rate of occurrence 2
Type of change
Discontinuous change
Incremental change
Bumpy incremental change
Continuous change
Bumpy continuous change

Smooth incremental change has been deleted from the list as it is seen as an outdated approach to change (Grundy, 1993). Furthermore, Burnes' (2004) and Balogun and Hope Hailey's (2004) punctuated equilibrium model has been merged with Grundy's (1993) bumpy incremental change model as they both are describing the same approach. Furthermore, Table 3.2 distinguishes between incremental change and continuous change to enable the differentiation between operational, on-going changes, and strategies implemented throughout the whole organisation to enable it to constantly adapt to the demands of both the external and internal environment. Bumpy continuous change is suggested as an additional category with the assumption that just as there will be periods of relative serenity punctuated by acceleration in the pace of change when it comes to operational changes (Grundy, 1993; Senior, 2002), the same can arguably be the case for organisation-wide strategies.

Change Characterised by How It Comes about

When characterised by how change comes about, there are several different approaches, as identified in Table 3.3. However, the literature is dominated by planned and emergent change (Bamford and Forrester, 2003). Even though there is not one widely accepted, clear and practical approach to organisational change management that explains what changes organisations need to make and how to implement them (Burnes, 2004) the planned approach to organisational change attempts to explain the process that bring about change (Burnes, 1996; Eldrod II and Tippett, 2002). Furthermore, the planned approach emphasises the importance of understanding the different states which an organisation will have to go through in order to move from an unsatisfactory state to an identified desired state (Eldrod II and Tippett, 2002).

The planned approach to change was initiated in 1946 by Lewin (Bamford and Forrester, 2003), who was a theorist, researcher and practitioner in interpersonal, group, intergroup, and community relationships (Eldrod II and

Table 3.3 Change characterised by how it comes about

Type of change	Burnes (1996)	Dunphy and Stace (1993)	Senior (2002)
Planned	✓		✓
Emergent	✓		✓
Contingency		✓	
Choice	✓		

Tippett, 2002). Lewin (1946 in Burnes, 2004) proposed that before change and new behaviour can be adopted successfully, the previous behaviour has to be discarded. According to Lewin (1952 in Eldrod II and Tippett, 2002) a successful change project must, therefore, involve the three steps of unfreezing the present level, moving to the new level and refreezing this new level. This model of change recognises the need to discard old behaviour, structures, processes and culture before successfully adopting new approaches (Bamford and Forrester, 2003).

Even though this three-step model was adopted as a general framework for understanding the process of organisational change, it is rather broad (Eldrod II and Tippett, 2002). Several authors have, therefore, developed Lewin's work in an attempt to make it more practical (Bamford and Forrester, 2003). By reviewing more than 30 models of planned change, Bullock and Batten (1985) developed a four-phase model of planned change that splits the process into exploration, planning, action and integration. According to Burnes (2004) this is a highly applicable model for most change situations. The model looks at the processes of change, which describe the methods employed to move an organisation from one state to another, and the phases of change, which describe the stages an organisation must go through to achieve successful change implementation (Bullock and Batten, 1985).

Although the planned approach to change is long established and held to be highly effective (Bamford and Forrester, 2003; Burnes, 2004), it has come under increasing criticism since the early 1980s (Kanter *et al.*, 1992; Burnes, 1996). Firstly, it is suggested that the approach's emphasis is on small-scale and incremental change, and it is, therefore, not applicable to situations that require rapid and transformational change (Burnes, 1996, 2004; Senior, 2002).

Secondly, the planned approach is based on the assumptions that organisations operate under constant conditions, and that they can move in a pre-planned manner from one stable state to another (Bamford and Forrester, 2003). These assumptions are, however, questioned by several authors (Burnes, 1996, 2004; Wilson, 1992) who argue that the current fast-changing environment increasingly weakens this theory. Moreover, it is suggested that organisational change is more an open-ended and continuous process than a set of pre-identified set of discrete and self-contained events (Burnes, 1996, 2004). By attempting to lay down timetables, objectives and methods in advance it is suggested that the process of change becomes too dependent on senior managers, who in many instances do not have a full understanding of the consequences of their actions (Wilson, 1992).

Thirdly, the approach of planned change ignores situations where more directive approaches are required. This can be a situation of crisis, which requires major and rapid change, and does not allow scope for widespread consultation or involvement (Burnes, 1996, 2004; Kanter *et al.*, 1992). Finally, the critics argue that the planned approach to change presumes that all stakeholders in a change project are willing and interested in implementing it, and that a common agreement can be reached (Bamford and Forrester, 2003). This presumption clearly ignores organisational politics and conflict, and assumes these can be easily identified and resolved (Burnes, 1996, 2004).

In response to this criticism of the planned approach to organisational change, the emergent approach has gained ground. Rather than seeing change to be top-down driven, the emergent approach tends to see change driven from the bottom up (Bamford and Forrester, 2003; Burnes, 1996, 2004). The approach suggests change to be so rapid that it is impossible for senior managers effectively to identify, plan and implement the necessary organisational responses (Kanter *et al.*, 1992). Therefore, the responsibility for organisational change has to become increasingly devolved (Wilson, 1992).

The emergent approach to change emphasises that change should not be perceived as a series of linear events within a given period of time, but as a continuous, open-ended process of adaptation to changing circumstances and conditions (Burnes, 1996, 2004; Dawson, 1994). The emergent approach stresses the unpredictable nature of change, and views it as a process that develops through the relationship of a multitude of variables within an organisation. Apart from only being a method of changing organisational practices and structures, change is also perceived as a process of learning (Altman and Iles, 1998; Davidson and De Marco, 1999; Dunphy and Stace, 1993).

According to the advocates of the emergent approach to change it is the uncertainty of both the external and internal environment that makes this approach more pertinent than the planned approach (Bamford and Forrester, 2003). To cope with the complexity and uncertainty of the environment it is suggested that organisations need to become open learning systems where strategy development and change emerges from the way a company as a whole acquires, interprets and processes information about the environment (Dunphy and Stace, 1993). The approach stresses a promotion of 'extensive and in-depth understanding of strategy, structure, systems, people, style and culture, and how these can function either as sources of inertia that can block change, or alternatively, as levers to encourage an effective change process' (Burnes, 1996, p. 14). Furthermore, Burnes (1996, p. 13) argues, 'successful change is less dependent on detailed plans and projections than on reaching an understanding of the complexity of the issues concerned and identifying the range of available options. It can, therefore, be suggested that the emergent approach to change is more concerned with change readiness and facilitating for change than to provide specific pre-planned steps for each change project and initiative.

Although Pettigrew and Whipp (1993) argue there are no universal rules when it comes to leading and managing change, several advocates of the emergent approach have suggested sequences of actions that organisations should comply with. However, many of these suggestions tend to be rather abstract in nature and difficult to apply (Burnes, 2004). There are some authors who offer more practical guidance to organisations and managers. Three of these authors are Kanter (1983, 1989), Kanter *et al.* (1992), Kotter (1996) and Luecke (2003). Table 3.4 combines Kanter's (Kanter *et al.*, 1992) Ten Commandments for Executing Change, Kotter's (1996) Eight-Stage Process for Successful Organisational Transformation, and Luecke's (2003) suggested Seven Steps in order to identify similarities and differences between these models.

As the emergent approach to change is relatively new compared to the planned approach, it is argued that it still lacks coherence and a diversity of techniques (Bamford and Forrester, 2003; Wilson, 1992). Another criticism of the emergent approach is that it consists of a rather disparate group of models and approaches that tend to be more united in their scepticism to the planned approach to change than to an agreed alternative (Bamford and Forrester, 2003; Dawson, 1994). However, according to Burnes (1996) the general applicability and validity of the emergent approach to organisational change depends on whether or not one believes that all organisations operate in dynamic and unpredictable environments to which they constantly have to adapt. If so, Burnes (1996, p. 14) argues 'the emergent model is suitable for all organizations, all situations and at all times'.

Dunphy and Stace (1993) do not agree with this view and argue 'managers and consultants need a model of change that is essentially a "situational" or "contingency model", one that indicates how to vary change strategies to achieve "optimum fit" with the changing environment' (Dunphy and Stace, 1993, p. 905). They advocate an approach that reflects not only that organisations are operating in ever-changing environments, but also that there is a range of approaches to change. Furthermore, it is argued that the planned and emergent approaches to change should not be seen as the entire spectrum of change events. An approach of contingency to change that supports a 'one best way for each' organisation approach rather than a 'one best way for all' approach is therefore suggested. The contingency approach to change is founded on the theory that the structure and the performance of an organisation are dependent on the situational variables that it faces (Dunphy and Stace, 1993). No two organisations are alike, and will not necessarily face the same variables. Therefore, their operations and structures may be different (Dunphy and Stace, 1993). However, contingency theory in general has been criticised for the difficulty of relating structure to performance and that the theory assumes that organisations and managers do not have any significant influence and choice over situational variables and structure (Burnes, 1996).

Burnes (1996, p. 16) suggests that an organisation does not necessarily have to adapt to the external environment, and advocates an approach of choice by suggesting 'there is certainly evidence that organizations wishing to maintain or promote a particular managerial style can choose to influence situational variables to achieve this. The point is that rather than having little choice,

Table 3.4 A comparison of three models of emergent change

Kanter et al.'s Ten Commandments for Executing Change (1992)	Kotter's Eight-Stage Process for Successful Organisational Transformation (1996)	Luecke's Seven Steps (2003)
1) Analyse the organisation and its need for change		1) Mobilise energy and commitment through joint identification of business problems and their solutions
2) Create a vision and a common direction	3) Developing a vision and strategy	2) Develop a shared vision of how to organise and manage for competitiveness
3) Separate from the past		
4) Create a sense of urgency	1) Establishing a sense of urgency	
5) Support a strong leader role		3) Identify the leadership
6) Line up political sponsorship	2) Creating a guiding coalition	
7) Craft an implementation plan		
8) Develop enabling structures	5) Empowering broad-based action	
9) Communicate, involve people and be honest	4) Communicating the change vision	
10) Reinforce and institutionalise change	8) Anchoring new approaches in the culture	6) Institutionalise success through formal policies, systems, and structures
	6) Generating short-term wins	
	7) Consolidating gains and producing more change	
		4) Focus on results, not on activities
		5) Start change at the periphery, then let it spread to other units without pushing it from the top
		7) Monitor and adjust strategies in response to problems in the change process

rather than being forced to change their internal practices to fit in with external variables, organizations can exercise some choice over these issues.'

Change Characterised by Scale

When it comes to change characterised by scale there is less confusion as there seems to be some wider agreement. According to Dunphy and Stace (1993), change identified by scale can be divided into four different characteristics: fine-tuning, incremental adjustment, modular transformation, and corporate transformation. Fine-tuning, also known as convergent change (Nelson, 2003), describes organisational change as an ongoing process to match the organisation's strategy, processes, people and structure (Senior, 2002). It is usually manifested at a departmental or divisional level of the organisation. The purpose of fine-tuning is, according to Dunphy and Stace (1993), to develop personnel suited to the present strategy, linking mechanisms and create specialist units to increase volume and attention to cost and quality, and refine policies, methods and procedures. Furthermore, the fine-tuning should foster both individual and group commitment to the excellence of departments and the organisation's mission, clarify established roles, and promote confidence in accepted beliefs, norms, and myths (Dunphy and Stace, 1993). According to Senior (2002) incremental adjustment involves distinct modifications to management processes and organisational strategies, but does not include radical change.

Modular transformation is change identified by major shifts of one or several departments or divisions. In contrast to incremental adjustment this change can be radical. However, it focuses on a part of an organisation rather than on the organisation as a whole (Senior, 2002). If the change is corporate-wide and characterised by radical alterations in the business strategy it is described as corporate transformation (Dunphy and Stace, 1993). According to Dunphy and Stace (1993) examples of this type of change can be reorganisation, revision of interaction patterns, reformed organisational mission and core values, and altered power and status.

Recommendations for Further Research

Drawing on the reported poor success rate of change programmes in general, the lack of empirical research on change management within organisations, and an arguably fundamental lack of a valid framework for organisational change management, it is recommended that further research into the nature of change management is conducted. The first step in this process should be to carry out exploratory studies in order to increase the knowledge of organisational change management. Such studies should enable an identification of critical success factors for the management of change. Furthermore, in order to construct a valid framework for change management it is arguably necessary to enable measurement of the success rate of change initiatives. Methods of measurements should, therefore, be designed.

Conclusion

It is evident from this article that change is an ever-present element that affects all organisations. There is a clear consensus that the pace of change has never been greater than in the current continuously evolving business environment. Therefore, the successful management of change is a highly required skill. However, the management of organisational change currently tends to be reactive, discontinuous and ad hoc with a reported failure rate of around 70 per cent of all change programmes initiated (Balogun and Hope Hailey, 2004). This may indicate a basic lack of a valid framework of how to successfully implement and manage organisational change since what is currently available is a wide range of contradictory and confusing theories and approaches, which are mostly lacking empirical evidence and often based on unchallenged hypotheses regarding the nature of contemporary organisational change management.

By providing a critical review of current change management theories and approaches, applying Senior's (2002) three categories of change as the focal structure, this article has made an attempt to highlight the need for a new and pragmatic framework for change management. In order to construct such a framework it is recommended that further exploratory studies of the nature of change and how it is being managed should be conducted. Such studies would arguably identify critical success factors for the management of change. The article also suggests that methods of measuring the success of organisational change management should be designed in order to evaluate the value of any new frameworks suggested.

_____ *References* _____

Altman, Y. and Iles, P. (1998) 'Learning, leadership, teams: corporate learning and organisational change', *Journal of Management Development,* vol. 17, no. 1, pp. 44–55.

Balogun, J. and Hope Hailey, V. (2004) *Exploring Strategic Change* (2nd edn), London, Prentice Hall.

Bamford, D. R. and Forrester, P. L. (2003) 'Managing planned and emergent change within an operations management environment', *International Journal of Operations & Production Management,* vol. 23, no. 5, pp. 546–64.

Bond, T. C. (1999) 'The role of performance measurement in continuous improvement', *International Journal of Operations & Production Management,* vol. 19, no. 12, pp. 1318–34.

Bullock, R. J. and Batten, D. (1985) 'It's just a phase we're going through: a review and synthesis of OD phase analysis', *Group and Organization Studies,* 10 (December), pp. 383–412.

Burnes, B. (1996) 'No such thing as…a "one best way" to manage organizational change', *Management Decision,* vol. 34, no. 10, pp. 11–18.

Burnes, B. (2004) *Managing Change: A Strategic Approach to Organisational Dynamics* (4th edn), Harlow, Prentice Hall.

Carnall, C. A. (2003) *Managing Change in Organizations* (4th edn), Harlow: Prentice Hall.

Davidson, M. C. G. and De Marco, L. (1999) 'Corporate change: education as a catalyst', *International Journal of Contemporary Hospitality Management,* vol. 11, no. 1, pp. 16–23.

Dawson, P. (1994) *Organizational Change: A Processual Approach*, London, Paul Chapman.

De Wit, B. and Meyer, R. (2005) *Strategy Synthesis: Resolving Strategy Paradoxes to Create Competitive Advantage* (2nd edn), London, Thomson Learning.

Doyle, M. (2002) 'From change novice to change expert: Issues of learning, development and support', *Personnel Review,* vol. 31, no. 4, pp. 465–81.

Duncan, M., Mouly, S. and Nilakant, V. (2001) 'Discontinuous change in the New Zealand police service: a case study', *Journal of Managerial Psychology,* vol. 16, no. 1, pp. 6–19.

Dunphy, D. and Stace, D. (1993) 'The strategic management of corporate change', *Human Relations,* vol. 46, no. 8, pp. 905–18.

Edmonstone, J. (1995) 'Managing change: an emerging consensus', *Health Manpower Management,* vol. 21, no. 1, pp. 16–19.

Eldrod II, P. D. and Tippett, D. D. (2002) 'The "death valley" of change', *Journal of Organizational Change Management,* vol. 15, no. 3, pp. 273–91.

Graetz, F. (2000) 'Strategic change leadership', *Management Decision,* vol. 38, no. 8, pp. 550–62.

Grundy, T. (1993) *Managing Strategic Change*, London, Kogan Page.

Guimaraes, T. and Armstrong, C. (1998) 'Empirically testing the impact of change management effectiveness on company performance', *European Journal of Innovation Management,* vol. 1, no. 2, pp. 74–84.

Holloway, S. (2002) *Airlines: Managing to Make Money*, Aldershot, Ashgate.

Kanter, R. M. (1983) *The Change Masters: Corporate Entrepreneurs at Work*, London, International Thomson Business Press.

Kanter, R. M. (1989) *When Giants Learn to Dance: Mastering the Challenges of Strategy, Management, and Careers in the 1990s*, London, Routledge.

Kanter, R. M., Stein, B. A. and Jick, T. D. (1992) *The Challenge of Organizational Change*, New York, The Free Press.

Kotter, J. P. (1996) *Leading Change*, Boston, MA, Harvard Business School Press.

Leifer, R. (1989) 'Understanding organizational transformation using a dissipative structural model', *Human Relations,* vol. 42, no. 10, pp. 899–916.

Love, P. E. D., Gunasekaran, A. and Li, H. (1998) 'Improving the competitiveness of manufacturing companies by continuous incremental change', *The TQM Magazine,* vol. 10, no. 3, pp. 177–85.

Luecke, R. (2003) *Managing Change and Transition*, Boston, MA, Harvard Business School Press.

Moran, J. W. and Brightman, B. K. (2001) 'Leading organizational change', *Career Development International,* vol. 6, no. 2, pp. 111–18.

Nelson, L. (2003) 'A case study in organizational change: implications for theory', *The Learning Organization,* vol. 10, no. 1, pp. 18–30.

Okumus, F. and Hemmington, N. (1998) 'Barriers and resistance to change in hotel firms: an investigation at unit level', *International Journal of Contemporary Hospitality Management,* vol. 10, no. 7, pp. 283–88.

Paton, R. A. and McCalman, J. (2000) *Change Management: A Guide to Effective Implementation* (2nd edn), London, SAGE Publications.

Pettigrew, A. M. and Whipp, R. (1993) *Managing Change for Competitive Success*, Cambridge, Blackwell.

Pettinger, R. (2004) *Contemporary Strategic Management*, Basingstoke, Palgrave MacMillan.
Rieley, J. B. and Clarkson, I. (2001) 'The impact of change on performance', *Journal of Change Management,* vol. 2, no. 2, pp. 160–72.
Senior, B. (2002) *Organisational Change* (2nd edn), London, Prentice Hall.
Taylor, P. and Hirst, J. (2001) 'Facilitating effective change and continuous improvement: The Mortgage Express way', *Journal of Change Management,* vol. 2, no. 1, pp. 67–71.
Wilson, D. C. (1992) *A Strategy of Change*, London, Routledge.

Part II
Types of Change

Introduction

In Part I we considered the environmental contexts within which organisations find themselves, and we introduced the idea of different types of change. In Part II we will be building more substantially on this issue of types of change. The part starts with the Harvard Business Review article by Beer and Nohria entitled 'Cracking the Code of Change'.

In their article, Beer and Nohria elaborate on this connection between the environmental context and the type of change needed, noting how the connection also implies the need for particular approaches to change. By this they mean that once the goals for change have been clarified, it is important to consider the extent to which the process of change should be process or person driven. Theory E, they argue, would advocate a process focus; a systems driven strategy motivated by the need to achieve clear economic gains. Contrarily, Theory O would be a more person driven approach in which organisational capabilities are built by investing in people, developing the culture and creating motivation and commitment.

The second article in this part is Nadler and Tushman's 1989 paper entitled 'Organizational Frame Bending: Principles for Managing Reorientation'. In this paper, the authors characterise the type of change needed by organisations as being strategic, organisation wide and profound. As such, change is motivated by the need to reorient the organisation to the environment in which it finds itself. The success of this re-orientation, they argue, is dependent on a clear understanding of what large scale change implies. Throughout the paper they present a series of matrices which frame different change contexts and allow those directing the change to map their own context against a range of different dimensions. By considering the type of change needed, the relative intensity of the change and the complexity of the organisation, Nadler and Tushman offer a range of principles to help guide the planning and the implementation of change.

The third paper in this part is Dunphy and Stace's 1993 article entitled 'The Strategic Management of Corporate Change'. Arguing that the complex nature of environmental conditions mitigates against the creation of a unitary model for change, Dunphy and Stace use data from their empirical work to help them to create a more contingent model of change. Their research showed in particular that there was a need to balance Organizational Development approaches, people oriented strategies akin to Beer and Nohria's Theory O, with the need for radical transformational change, change which was disruptive and directive. As such they refute the idea that process driven change and people driven change are oppositional, arguing instead that there should be a fluid relationship in which managers and change leaders can move between the two depending on the circumstances.

Cracking the Code of Change

Michael Beer and Nitin Nohria

Until now, change in business has been an either-or proposition: either quickly create economic value for shareholders or patiently develop an open, trusting corporate culture long term. But new research indicates that combining these 'hard' and 'soft' approaches can radically transform the way businesses change.

The new economy has ushered in great business opportunities – and great turmoil. Not since the Industrial Revolution have the stakes of dealing with change been so high. Most traditional organizations have accepted, in theory at least, that they must either change or die. And even Internet companies such as eBay, Amazon.com, and America Online recognize that they need to manage the changes associated with rapid entrepreneurial growth. Despite some individual successes, however, change remains difficult to pull off, and few companies manage the process as well as they would like. Most of their initiatives – installing new technology, downsizing, restructuring, or trying to change corporate culture – have had low success rates. The brutal fact is that about 70% of all change initiatives fail.

In our experience, the reason for most of those failures is that in their rush to change their organizations, managers end up immersing themselves in an alphabet soup of initiatives. They lose focus and become mesmerized by all the advice available in print and on-line about why companies should change, what they should try to accomplish, and how they should do it. This proliferation of recommendations often leads to muddle when change is attempted. The result is that most change efforts exert a heavy toll, both human and economic. To improve the odds of success, and to reduce the human carnage, it is imperative that executives understand the nature and process of corporate change much better. But even that is not enough. Leaders need to crack the code of change.

For more than 40 years now, we've been studying the nature of corporate change. And although every business's change initiative is unique, our research suggests there are two archetypes, or theories, of change. These archetypes are

Beer, M. and Nohria, N. (2000) 'Cracking the Code of Change', *Harvard Business Review*, May–June, pp. 133–41.

based on very different and often unconscious assumptions by senior executives – and the consultants and academics who advise them – about why and how changes should be made. Theory E is change based on economic value. Theory O is change based on organizational capability. Both are valid models, each theory of change achieves some of management's goals, either explicitly or implicitly. But each theory also has its costs – often unexpected ones.

Theory E change strategies are the ones that make all the headlines. In this 'hard' approach to change, shareholder value is the only legitimate measure of corporate success. Change usually involves heavy use of economic incentives, drastic layoffs, downsizing, and restructuring. E change strategies are more common than O change strategies among companies in the United States, where financial markets push corporate boards for rapid turnarounds. For instance, when William A. Anders was brought in as CEO of General Dynamics in 1991, his goal was to maximize economic value – however painful the remedies might be. Over the next three years, Anders reduced the workforce by 71,000 people – 44,000 through the divestiture of seven businesses and 27,000 through layoffs and attrition. Anders employed common E strategies.

Managers who subscribe to Theory O believe that if they were to focus exclusively on the price of their stock, they might harm their organizations. In this 'soft' approach to change, the goal is to develop corporate culture and human capability through individual and organizational learning – the process of changing, obtaining feedback, reflecting, and making further changes. U.S. companies that adopt O strategies, as Hewlett-Packard did when its performance flagged in the 1980s, typically have strong, long-held, commitment-based psychological contracts with their employees.

Managers at these companies are likely to see the risks in breaking those contracts. Because they place a high value on employee commitment, Asian and European businesses are also more likely to adopt an O strategy to change.

Few companies subscribe to just one theory. Most companies we have studied have used a mix of both. But all too often, managers try to apply theories E and O in tandem without resolving the inherent tensions between them. This impulse to combine the strategies is directionally correct, but theories E and O are so different that it's hard to manage them simultaneously – employees distrust leaders who alternate between nurturing and cutthroat corporate behavior. Our research suggests, however, that there is a way to resolve the tension so that businesses can satisfy their shareholders while building viable institutions. Companies that effectively combine hard and soft approaches to change can reap big payoffs in profitability and productivity. Those companies are more likely to achieve a sustainable competitive advantage. They can also reduce the anxiety that grips whole societies in the face of corporate restructuring.

In this article, we will explore how one company successfully resolved the tensions between E and O strategies. But before we do that, we need to look at just how different the two theories are.

A Tale of Two Theories

To understand how sharply theories E and O differ, we can compare them along several key dimensions of corporate change: goals, leadership, focus, process, reward system, and use of consultants. (For a side-by-side comparison, see the exhibit 'Comparing Theories of Change'.) We'll look at two companies in similar businesses that adopted almost pure forms of each archetype. Scott Paper successfully used Theory E to enhance shareholder value, while Champion International used Theory O to achieve a complete cultural transformation that increased its productivity and employee commitment. But as we will soon observe, both paper producers also discovered the limitations of sticking with only one theory of change. Let's compare the two companies' initiatives.

Goals. When Al Dunlap assumed leadership of Scott Paper in May 1994, he immediately fired 11,000 employees and sold off several businesses. His determination to restructure the beleaguered company was almost monomaniacal. As he said in one of his speeches: 'Shareholders are the number one constituency. Show me an annual report that lists six or seven constituencies, and I'll show you a mismanaged company.' From a shareholder's perspective, the results of Dunlap's actions were stunning. In just 20 months, he managed to triple shareholder returns as Scott Paper's market value rose from about $3 billion in 1994 to about $9 billion by the end of 1995. The financial community applauded his efforts and hailed Scott Paper's approach to change as a model for improving shareholder returns.

Champion's reform effort couldn't have been more different. CEO Andrew Sigler acknowledged that enhanced economic value was an appropriate target for management, but he believed that goal would be best achieved by transforming the behaviors of management, unions, and workers alike. In 1981, Sigler and other managers launched a long-term effort to restructure corporate culture around a new vision called the Champion Way, a set of values and principles designed to build up the competencies of the workforce. By improving the organization's capabilities in areas such as teamwork and communication, Sigler believed he could best increase employee productivity and thereby improve the bottom line.

Leadership. Leaders who subscribe to Theory E manage change the old-fashioned way: from the top down. They set goals with little involvement from their management teams and certainly without input from lower levels or unions. Dunlap was clearly the commander in chief at Scott Paper. The executives who survived his purges, for example, had to agree with his philosophy that shareholder value was now the company's primary objective. Nothing made clear Dunlap's leadership style better than the nickname he gloried in: 'Chainsaw Al'.

By contrast, participation (a Theory O trait) was the hallmark of change at Champion. Every effort was made to get all its employees emotionally committed to improving the company's performance. Teams drafted value statements, and even the industry's unions were brought into the dialogue. Employees were encouraged to identify and solve problems themselves. Change at Champion sprouted from the bottom up.

Focus. In E-type change, leaders typically focus immediately on streamlining the 'hardware' of the organization – the structures and systems. These are the elements that can most easily be changed from the top down, yielding swift financial results. For instance, Dunlap quickly decided to outsource many of Scott Paper's corporate functions – benefits and payroll administration, almost all of its management information systems, some of its technology research, medical services, telemarketing, and security functions. An executive manager of a global merger explained the E rationale: 'I have a [profit] goal of $176 million this year, and there's no time to involve others or develop organizational capability.'

By contrast, Theory O's initial focus is on building up the 'software' of an organization – the culture, behavior, and attitudes of employees. Throughout a decade of reforms, no employees were laid off at Champion. Rather, managers and employees were encouraged to collectively reexamine their work practices and behaviors with a goal of increasing productivity and quality. Managers were replaced if they did not conform to the new philosophy, but the overall firing freeze helped to create a culture of trust and commitment. Structural change followed once the culture changed. Indeed, by the mid-1990s, Champion had completely reorganized all its corporate functions. Once a hierarchical, functionally organized company, Champion adopted a matrix structure that empowered employee teams to focus more on customers.

Process. Theory E is predicated on the view that no battle can be won without a clear, comprehensive, common plan of action that encourages internal coordination and inspires confidence among customers, suppliers, and investors. The plan lets leaders quickly motivate and mobilize their businesses, it compels them to take tough, decisive actions they presumably haven't taken in the past. The changes at Scott Paper unfolded like a military battle plan. Managers were instructed to achieve specific targets by specific dates. If they didn't adhere to Dunlap's tightly choreographed marching orders, they risked being fired.

Meanwhile, the changes at Champion were more evolutionary and emergent than planned and programmatic. When the company's decade-long reform began in 1981, there was no master blueprint. The idea was that innovative work processes, values, and culture changes in one plant would be adapted and used by other plants on their way through the corporate system. No single person, not even Sigler, was seen as the driver of change. Instead, local leaders took responsibility. Top management simply encouraged experimentation from the ground up, spread new ideas to other workers, and transferred managers of innovative units to lagging ones.

Reward System. The rewards for managers in E-type change programs are primarily financial. Employee compensation, for example, is linked with financial incentives, mainly stock options. Dunlap's own compensation package – which ultimately netted him more than $100 million – was tightly linked to shareholders interests. Proponents of this system argue that financial incentives guarantee that employees' interests match stockholders' interests. Financial rewards also help top executives feel compensated for a difficult job – one in which they are often reviled by their onetime colleagues and the larger community.

The O-style compensation systems at Champion reinforced the goals of culture change, but they didn't drive those goals. A skills-based pay system and a corporatewide gains-sharing plan were installed to draw union workers and management into a community of purpose. Financial incentives were used only as a supplement to those systems and not to push particular reforms. While Champion did offer a companywide bonus to achieve business goals in two separate years, this came late in the change process and played a minor role in actually fulfilling those goals.

Use of Consultants. Theory E change strategies often rely heavily on external consultants. A SWAT team of Ivy League–educated MBAs, armed with an arsenal of state-of-the-art ideas, is brought in to find new ways to look at the business and manage it. The consultants can help CEOs get a fix on urgent issues and priorities. They also offer much-needed political and psychological support for CEOs who are under fire from financial markets. At Scott Paper, Dunlap engaged consultants to identify many of the painful cost-savings initiatives that he subsequently implemented.

Theory O change programs rely far less on consultants. The handful of consultants who were introduced at Champion helped managers and workers make their own business analyses and craft their own solutions. And while the consultants had their own ideas, they did not recommend any corporate program, dictate any solutions, or whip anyone into line. They simply led a process of discovery and learning that was intended to change the corporate culture in a way that could not be foreseen at the outset.

Comparing Theories of Change

Our research has shown that all corporate transformations can be compared along the six dimensions shown here. Table 4.1 outlines the differences between the E and O archetypes and illustrates what an integrated approach might look like.

Table 4.1 Comparing theories of change

Dimensions of change	Theory E	Theory O	Theories E and O combined
Goals	maximize shareholder value	develop organizational capabilities	explicitly embrace the paradox between economic value and organizational capability
Leadership	manage change from the top down	encourage participation from the bottom up	set direction from the top and engage the people below
Focus	emphasize structure and systems	build up corporate culture: employees behavior and attitudes	focus simultaneously on the hard (structures and systems) and the soft (corporate culture)
Process	plan and establish programs	experiment and evolve	plan for spontaneity
Reward System	motivate through financial incentives	motivate through commitment – use pay as fair exchange	use incentives to reinforce change but not to drive it
Use of Consultants	consultants analyze problems and shape solutions	consultants support management in shaping their own solutions	consultants are expert resources who empower employees

In their purest forms, both change theories clearly have their limitations. CEOs who must make difficult E-style choices understandably distance themselves from their employees to ease their own pain and guilt. Once removed from their people, these CEOs begin to see their employees as part of the problem. As time goes on, these leaders become less and less inclined to adopt O-style change strategies. They fail to invest in building the company's human resources, which inevitably hollows out the company and saps its capacity for sustained performance. At Scott Paper, for example, Dunlap trebled shareholder returns but failed to build the capabilities needed for sustained competitive advantage – commitment, coordination, communication, and creativity. In 1995, Dunlap sold Scott Paper to its longtime competitor Kimberly-Clark.

CEOs who embrace Theory O find that their loyalty and commitment to their employees can prevent them from making tough decisions. The temptation is to postpone the bitter medicine in the hopes that rising productivity will improve the business situation. But productivity gains aren't enough when fundamental structural change is required. That reality is underscored by today's global financial system, which makes corporate performance instantly transparent to large institutional shareholders whose fund managers are under enormous pressure to show good results. Consider Champion. By 1997, it had become one of the leaders in its industry based on most performance measures. Still, newly instated CEO Richard Olsen was forced to admit a tough reality: Champion shareholders had not seen a significant increase in the economic value of the company in more than a decade. Indeed, when Champion was sold recently to Finland-based UPM-Kymmene, it was acquired for a mere 1.5 times its original share value.

Managing the Contradictions

Clearly, if the objective is to build a company that can adapt, survive, and prosper over the years, Theory E strategies must somehow be combined with Theory O strategies. But unless they're carefully handled, melding E and O is likely to bring the worst of both theories and the benefits of neither. Indeed, the corporate changes we've studied that arbitrarily and haphazardly mixed E and O techniques proved destabilizing to the organizations in which they were imposed. Managers in those companies would certainly have been better off to pick either pure E or pure O strategies – with all their costs. At least one set of stakeholders would have benefited.

The obvious way to combine E and O is to sequence them. Some companies, notably General Electric, have done this quite successfully. At GE, CEO Jack Welch began his sequenced change by imposing an E-type restructuring. He demanded that all GE businesses be first or second in their industries. Any unit that failed that test would be fixed, sold off, or closed. Welch followed that up with a massive downsizing of the GE bureaucracy. Between 1981 and 1985, total employment at the corporation dropped from 412,000 to 299,000. Sixty percent of the corporate staff, mostly in planning and finance, was laid off. In this phase, GE people began to call Welch 'Neutron Jack', after the fabled bomb that was designed to destroy people but leave buildings intact. Once he had wrung out the redundancies, however, Welch adopted an O strategy. In 1985, he started a series of organizational initiatives to change GE culture. He declared that the company had to become 'boundaryless', and unit leaders across the corporation had to submit to being challenged by their subordinates in open forum. Feedback and open communication eventually eroded the hierarchy. Soon Welch applied the new order to GE's global businesses.

Unfortunately for companies like Champion, sequenced change is far easier if you begin, as Welch did, with Theory E. Indeed, it is highly unlikely that E would successfully follow O because of the sense of betrayal that would involve. It is hard to imagine how a draconian program of layoffs and downsizing can leave intact the psychological contract and culture a company has so patiently built up over the years. But whatever the order, one sure problem with sequencing is that it can take a very long time; at GE it has taken almost two decades. A sequenced change may also require two CEOs, carefully chosen for their contrasting styles and philosophies, which may create its own set of problems. Most turnaround managers don't survive restructuring – partly because of their own inflexibility and partly because they can't live down the distrust that their ruthlessness has earned them. In most cases, even the best-intentioned effort to rebuild trust and commitment rarely overcomes a bloody past. Welch is the exception that proves the rule.

So what should you do? How can you achieve rapid improvements in economic value while simultaneously developing an open, trusting corporate culture? Paradoxical as those goals may appear, our research shows that it is possible to apply theories E and O together. It requires great will, skill – and wisdom. But precisely because it is more difficult than mere sequencing, the simultaneous use of O and E strategies is more likely to be a source of sustainable competitive advantage.

One company that exemplifies the reconciliation of the hard and soft approaches is ASDA, the UK grocery chain that CEO Archie Norman took over in December 1991, when the retailer was nearly bankrupt. Norman laid off employees, flattened the organization, and sold off losing businesses – acts that usually spawn distrust among employees and distance executives from their people. Yet during Norman's eight-year tenure as CEO, ASDA also became famous for its atmosphere of trust and openness. It has been described by executives at Wal-Mart – itself famous for its corporate culture – as being 'more like Wal-Mart than we are'. Let's look at how ASDA resolved the conflicts of E and O along the six main dimensions of change.

Explicitly confront the tension between E and O goals. With his opening speech to ASDA's executive team – none of whom he had met – Norman indicated clearly that he intended to apply both E and O strategies in his change effort. It is doubtful that any of his listeners fully understood him at the time, but it was important that he had no conflicts about recognizing the paradox between the two strategies for change. He said as much in his maiden speech: 'Our number one objective is to secure value for our shareholders and secure the trading future of the business. I am not coming in with any magical solutions. I intend to spend the next few weeks listening and forming ideas for our precise direction. ... We need a culture built around common ideas and goals that include listening, learning, and speed of response, from the stores upwards. [But] there will be management reorganization. My objective is to establish a clear focus on the stores, shorten lines of communication, and build one team.' If there is a contradiction between building a high-involvement organization and restructuring to enhance shareholder value, Norman embraced it.

Set direction from the top and engage people below.   From day one, Norman set strategy without expecting any participation from below. He said ASDA would adopt an everyday-low-pricing strategy, and Norman unilaterally determined that change would begin by having two experimental store formats up and running within six months. He decided to shift power from the headquarters to the stores, declaring: 'I want everyone to be close to the stores. We must love the stores to death; that is our business.' But even from the start, there was an O quality to Norman's leadership style. As he put it in his first speech: 'First, I am forthright, and I like to argue. Second, I want to discuss issues as colleagues. I am looking for your advice and your disagreement.' Norman encouraged dialogue with employees and customers through colleague and customer circles. He set up a 'Tell Archie' program so that people could voice their concerns and ideas.

Making way for opposite leadership styles was also an essential ingredient to Norman's – and ASDA's – success. This was most clear in Norman's willingness to hire Allan Leighton shortly after he took over. Leighton eventually became deputy chief executive. Norman and Leighton shared the same E and O values, but they had completely different personalities and styles. Norman, cool and reserved, impressed people with the power of his mind – his intelligence and business acumen. Leighton, who is warmer and more people oriented, worked on employees' emotions with the power of his personality. As one employee told us, 'People respect Archie, but they love Allan.' Norman was the first to credit Leighton with having helped to create emotional commitment to the new ASDA. While it might be possible for a single individual to embrace opposite leadership styles, accepting an equal partner with a very different personality makes it easier to capitalize on those styles. Leighton certainly helped Norman reach out to the organization. Together they held quarterly meetings with store managers to hear their ideas, and they supplemented those meetings with impromptu talks.

Focus simultaneously on the hard and soft sides of the organization. Norman's immediate actions followed both the E goal of increasing economic value and the O goal of transforming culture. On the E side, Norman focused on structure. He removed layers of hierarchy at the top of the organization, fired the financial officer who had been part of ASDA's disastrous policies, and decreed a wage freeze for everyone – management and workers alike. But from the start, the O strategy was an equal part of Norman's plan. He bought time for all this change by warning the markets that financial recovery would take three years. Norman later said that he spent 75% of his early months at ASDA as the company's human resource director, making the organization less hierarchical, more egalitarian, and more transparent. Both Norman and Leighton were keenly aware that they had to win hearts and minds. As Norman put it to workers: 'We need to make ASDA a great place for everyone to work.'

Plan for spontaneity. Training programs, total-quality programs, and top-driven culture change programs played little part in ASDA's transformation. From the start, the ASDA change effort was set up to encourage experimentation and evolution. To promote learning, for example, ASDA set up an experimental store that was later expanded to three stores. It was declared a risk-free zone, meaning there would be no penalties for failure. A cross-functional task force 'renewed', or redesigned, ASDA's entire retail proposition, its organization, and its managerial structure. Store managers were encouraged to experiment with store layout, employee roles, ranges of products offered, and so on. The experiments produced significant innovations in all aspects of store operations. ASDA's managers learned, for example, that they couldn't renew a store unless that store's management team was ready for new ideas. This led to an innovation called the Driving Test, which assessed whether store managers' skills in leading the change process were aligned with the intended changes. The test perfectly illustrates how E and O can come together: it bubbled up O-style from the bottom of the company, yet it bound managers in an E-type contract. Managers who failed the test were replaced.

Let incentives reinforce change, not drive it. Any synthesis of E and O must recognize that compensation is a double-edged sword. Money can focus and motivate managers, but it can also hamper teamwork, commitment, and learning. The way to resolve this dilemma is to apply Theory E incentives in an O way. Employees' high involvement is encouraged to develop their commitment to change, and variable pay is used to reward that commitment. ASDA's senior executives were compensated with stock options that were tied to the company's value. These helped attract key executives to ASDA. Unlike most E-strategy companies, however, ASDA had a stock-ownership plan for all employees. In addition, store-level employees got variable pay based on both corporate performance and their stores' records. In the end, compensation represented a fair exchange of value between the company and its individual employees. But Norman believed that compensation had not played a major role in motivating change at the company.

Use consultants as expert resources who empower employees. Consultants can provide specialized knowledge and technical skills that the company doesn't have, particularly in the early stages of organizational change. Management's task is figuring out how to use those resources without abdicating leadership of the change effort. ASDA followed the middle ground between Theory E and Theory O. It made limited use of four consulting firms in the early stages of its transformation. The consulting firms always worked alongside management and supported its leadership of change. However, their engagement was intentionally cut short by Norman to prevent ASDA and its managers from becoming dependent on the consultants. For example, an expert in store organization was hired to support the task force assigned to renew ASDA's first few experimental stores, but later stores were renewed without his involvement.

By embracing the paradox inherent in simultaneously employing E and O change theories, Norman and Leighton transformed ASDA to the advantage of its shareholders and employees. The organization went through personnel changes, unit sell-offs, and hierarchical upheaval. Yet these potentially destructive actions did not prevent ASDA's employees from committing to change and the new corporate culture because Norman and Leighton had won employees' trust by constantly listening, debating, and being willing to learn. Candid about their intentions from the outset, they balanced the tension between the two change theories.

By 1999, the company had multiplied shareholder value eightfold. The organizational capabilities built by Norman and Leighton also gave ASDA the sustainable competitive advantage that Dunlap had been unable to build at Scott Paper and that Sigler had been unable to build at Champion. While Dunlap was forced to sell a demoralized and ineffective organization to Kimberly-Clark, and while a languishing Champion was sold to UPM-Kymmene, Norman and Leighton in June 1999 found a friendly and culturally compatible suitor in Wal-Marr, which was willing to pay a substantial premium for the organizational capabilities that ASDA had so painstakingly developed.

In the end, the integration of theories E and O created major change – and major payoffs – for ASDA. Such payoffs are possible for other organizations that want to develop a sustained advantage in today's economy. But that advantage can come only from a constant willingness and ability to develop organizations for the long term combined with a constant monitoring of shareholder value – E dancing with O, in an unending minuet.

Organizational Frame Bending: Principles for Managing Reorientation

David A. Nadler and Michael L. Tushman

One of the hallmarks of American business in the past decade has been the attempts by large organizations to manage large-scale planned change. In some cases – AT&T, Chrysler, and Apple, for example – the efforts have been dramatic and have captured public attention. Other cases, such as Corning Glass, Xerox, Citicorp, and GTE, have received less attention, but the changes have been no less profound.

The concept of planned organizational change is not new; but this most recent generation of changes is somewhat different from what has gone before. First, they typically are initiated by the leaders of organizations rather than consultants or human resource specialists (although they have played significant roles in some cases). Second, they are closely linked to strategic business issues, not just questions of organizational process or style. Third, most of the changes can be traced directly to external factors, such as new sources of competition, new technology, deregulation or legal initiatives, maturation of product sets, changes in ownership, or shifts in fundamental market structure. Fourth, these changes affect the entire organization (whether it be a corporation or a business unit) rather than individual SBUs (strategic business units) or departments. Fifth, they are profound for the organization and its members because they usually influence organizational values regarding employees, customers, competition, or products. As a result of the past decade's changes, there are now more large visible examples than ever before of successful planned organizational change.

Nadler, D.A. and Tushman, M.L. (1989) 'Organizational frame bending: Principles for managing reorientation', *The Academy of Management Review*, vol. 10, no. 3, pp. 194–204.

Our work has brought us into contact with a number of examples of these changes.[1] In general, they have been changes that encompass the whole organization, have occurred over a number of years, and have involved fundamental shifts in the way the organization thinks about its business, itself, and how it is managed. Our experience has included changes that both internal and external observers rate as successes, some that have been described as failures, and some that are still going on.

Our purpose in this article is to share some insights, generalizations, and hunches about large-scale organizational changes, working from our perspective of close observations. We begin by reviewing some basic concepts of organization and change that have shaped the way we think about and observe these events. Next, we briefly describe an approach to differentiating among various types of organization change. Finally, we devote the rest of the article to our concept of 'frame bending' – a particular kind of large-scale change found in complex organizations.

Basic Concepts of Organization and Change

Thinking about Organizations

We view organizations as complex systems that, in the context of an environment, an available set of resources, and a history, produce output. To illustrate, we have developed a model that consists of two major elements (see Exhibit 5.1). The first is strategy, the pattern of decisions that emerges over time about how resources will be deployed in response to environmental opportunities

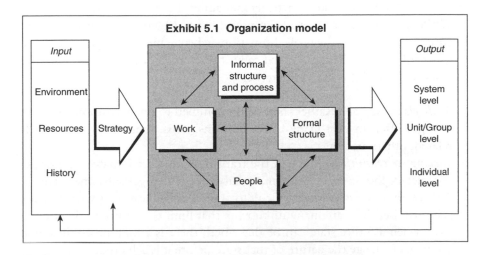

Exhibit 5.1 Organization model

and threats. The second is organization, the mechanism that is developed to turn strategy into output. Organization includes four core components: work, people, formal structures and processes, and informal structures and processes. The fundamental dynamic is congruence among these elements. Effectiveness is greatest when a firm's strategy is consistent with environmental conditions and there is internal consistency, or fit, among the four organizational components. Our model emphasizes that there is no one best way to organize. Rather, the most effective way of organizing is determined by the nature of the strategy as well as the work, the individuals who are members of the organization, and the informal processes and structures (including culture) that have grown up over time.[2]

While our model implies that congruence of organizational components is a desirable state, it is, in fact, a double-edged sword. In the short term, congruence seems to be related to effectiveness and performance. A system with high congruence, however, can be resistant to change. It develops ways of insulating itself from outside influences and may be unable to respond to new situations.[3]

Organizational Change

From time to time, organizations are faced with the need to modify themselves. The change may involve one or more elements of the organizational system, or it may involve a realignment of the whole system, affecting all of the key elements – strategy, work, people, and formal and informal processes and structures. A central problem is how to maintain congruence in the system while implementing change, or how to help the organization move to a whole new configuration and a whole new definition of congruence. Critical issues in managing such changes include (1) managing the political dynamics associated with the change, (2) motivating constructive behavior in the face of the anxiety created by the change, and (3) actively managing the transition state.[4]

While these approaches have been useful for managers and implementors of organizational change, they have limitations when applied to large-scale, complex organizational changes. Specifically, these larger-scale changes entail at least some of the following characteristics:

- ■ *Multiple transitions.* Rather than being confined to one transition, complex changes often involve many different transitions. Some may be explicitly related; others are not.
- ■ *Incomplete transitions.* Many of the transitions that are initiated do not get completed. Events overtake them, or subsequent changes subsume them.
- ■ *Uncertain future states.* It is difficult to predict or define exactly what a future state will be; there are many unknowns that limit the ability to describe it. Even when a future state can be described, there is a high probability that events will change the nature of that state before it is achieved.

■ *Transitions over long periods of time*. Many large-scale organization changes take long periods of time to implement – in some cases, as much as three to seven years. The dynamics of managing change over this period of time are different from those of managing a quick change with a discrete beginning and end.

All these factors lead to the conclusion that the basic concepts of transition management must be extended to deal with the additional issues posed by large-scale changes.[5]

Types of Organizational Change

As a first step toward understanding large-scale organizational change, we have developed a way of thinking about the different types of change that organizations face. Change can be considered in two dimensions. The first is the scope of the change – that is, subsystems of the organization versus the entire system. Changes that focus on individual components, with the goal of maintaining or regaining congruence, are *incremental* changes. For example, adapting reward systems to changing labor market conditions is an incremental, systems-enhancing change. Changes that address the whole organization, including strategy, are *strategic* changes. These changes frequently involve breaking out of a current pattern of congruence and helping an organization develop a completely new configuration. Incremental changes are made within the context, or frame, of the current set of organizational strategies and components. They do not address fundamental changes in the definition of the business, shifts of power, alterations in culture, and similar issues. Strategic changes change that frame, either reshaping it, bending it or, in extreme cases, breaking it. For example, when John Sculley took the reins from Steven Jobs at Apple Computer, or when Lee Iacocca took over at Chrysler, systemwide changes followed.

The second dimension of change concerns the positioning of the change in relation to key external events. Some changes are clearly in response to an event or series of events. These are called *relative* changes. Other changes are initiated, not in response to events but in anticipation of external events that may occur. These are called *anticipatory* changes. (The relationship between the dimensions can best be described using the illustrations shown in Exhibit 5.2). Four classes of change are the result:

■ *Tuning*. This is incremental change made in anticipation of future events. It seeks ways to increase efficiency but does not occur in response to any immediate problem.
■ *Adaptation*. This is incremental change that is made in response to external events. Actions of a competitor, changes in market needs, new technology, and so on, require a response from an organization, but not one that involves fundamental change throughout the organization.

■ *Reorientation.* This is strategic change, made with the luxury of time afforded by having anticipated the external events that may ultimately require change. These changes do involve fundamental redirection of the organization and are frequently put in terms that emphasize continuity with the past (particularly values of the past). Because the emphasis is on bringing about major change without a sharp break with the existing organization frame, we describe these as *frame-bending changes*. For example, the sweeping changes initiated by Paul O'Neil and Fred Federholf at ALCOA are frame-bending changes in that they are not driven by performance crisis (that is, they are proactive) and they build on ALCOA's past even though they involve widespread organization change.

■ *Re-creation.* This is strategic change necessitated by external events, usually ones that threaten the very existence of the organization. Such changes require a radical departure from the past and include shifts in senior leadership, values, strategy, culture, and so forth. Consequently, we call these *frame-breaking changes*. Examples of these reactive, systemwide changes abound, and include those at National Cash Register, U.S. Steel, AT&T, GM, ICI, and SAS.

Building on this classification scheme, these different types of change can be described in terms of their intensity (Exhibit 5.3). Intensity relates to the severity of the change and, in particular, the degree of shock, trauma, or discontinuity created throughout the organization. Strategic changes are obviously more intense than incremental changes, which can frequently be implemented without altering an organization's basic management processes. Reactive changes are more intense than anticipatory changes because of the necessity of packing substantial activity into a short period of time without the opportunity to prepare people to deal with the trauma. There is also less room for error and correction.

Relative intensity is further affected by organizational complexity. Organizations become more difficult to change as they increase in complexity – complexity

Exhibit 5.2 Types of organizational change

	Incremental	Strategic
Anticipatory	Tuning	Reorientation
Reactive	Adaptation	Re-creation

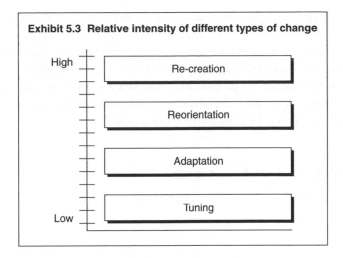

Exhibit 5.3 Relative intensity of different types of change

High

Re-creation

Reorientation

Adaptation

Tuning

Low

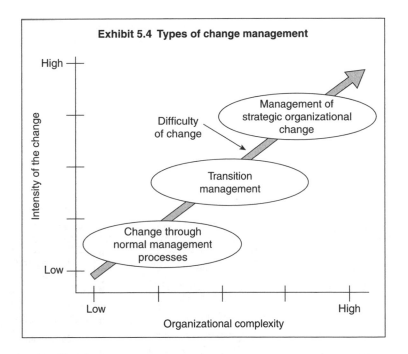

Exhibit 5.4 Types of change management

High

Intensity of the change

Difficulty of change

Management of strategic organizational change

Transition management

Change through normal management processes

Low

Low   High

Organizational complexity

determined by (1) size of the organization in terms of employees and (2) the diversity of the organization in terms of the number of different businesses, geographic dispersion, and so on. Smaller organizations with a few highly related businesses are easier places in which to implement changes than are larger, highly diverse organizations.

If we put these concepts together, we get a map of the difficulty of organizational change (see Exhibit 5.4). The least difficult changes are those that are low intensity and take place in fairly noncomplex settings. The most difficult changes are those that are high intensity (strategic) and take place in highly complex settings. Our focus is on strategic organizational change. Re-creations are the most risky and traumatic form of change, and our assumption is that managers would rather avoid the costs and risks associated with them. The challenge, then, is to effectively initiate and implement reorientations, or frame-bending change, in complex organizations.

Observations of Effective Organizational Frame Bending

In the last section, we identified the activities and elements that characterize effective organizational re-creation. The principles have been organized into four clusters for discussion purposes, and we will refer to them as *principles of effective frame bending*. First, there are those principles associated with initiating change. Next there is a set of principles having to do with how the reorientation is defined, or the *content of change*, and another set having to do with *leading change*. Finally, there are principles associated with *achieving change*, relating to the activities that are required to implement, sustain, and complete reorientations over long periods of time. The clusters and principles are displayed in Exhibit 5.5.

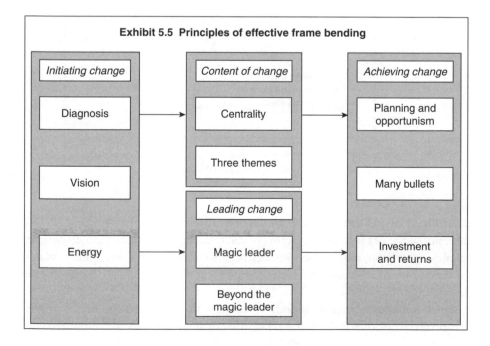

Exhibit 5.5 Principles of effective frame bending

Initiating change	Content of change	Achieving change
Diagnosis	Centrality	Planning and opportunism
	Three themes	
Vision		Many bullets
	Leading change	
Energy	Magic leader	Investment and returns
	Beyond the magic leader	

The Diagnosis Principle

Managing organizational reorientation involves managing the *what* as well as the *how*. The *what* concerns the content of the change: what strategies and elements of organization will have to be changed to enable the organization effectively to anticipate, respond to, and even shape the challenges to come. While much of the focus of this perspective is on the process of managing reorientations, the content is nevertheless critically important.

Identification of the appropriate strategic and organizational changes comes from diagnostic thinking – analyzing the organization in its environment, understanding its strengths and weaknesses, and analyzing the implication of anticipated changes. Diagnosis typically involves the collection, integration, and analysis of data about the organization and its environment. It involves assessment of the organization usually based on some underlying model of organizational effectiveness.

Effective reorientations are characterized by solid diagnostic thinking. In these cases, managers have spent time understanding the potential *environmental challenges and forces,* be they technological, regulatory, competitive, or otherwise. They have worked to identify the *critical success factors* associated with achieving effective anticipation or response. They have looked hard at the *organizational strengths and weaknesses,* thus gaining a systematic view on what has to change and why.

In contrast, the less effective reorientation suffers from a lack of diagnosis and the quick adoption of 'solutions in search of problems', which often comes about through *organizational mimicry.* In these cases, the senior management of one organization observes how 'model' organizations (the referents vary – they could be industry leaders, generally respected companies, and so on) are responding to or anticipating change and they then copy what the model is doing. What they fail to grasp is that the model organization typically has done diagnostic work and has identified a set of changes unique to its own conditions. Because the management of the model organization has participated in the diagnostic work, it has both the understanding and the commitment that results from the process. Thus, mimicking organizations not only adopt strategies that are not designed for the problems or challenges they face, but do so in a manner that leads to low commitment to change. Little wonder that they tend to fail.[6]

The Vision Principle

An effective reorientation involves movement from one state to another. The most effective reorientations include a fully developed description of the desired future state. Since the nature of the change is usually both very broad and profound, this description is more than a statement of objectives or goals; it is a *vision* of what the organization hopes to be once it achieves the reorientation. This vision may range from a set of principles or values all the way to detailed papers outlining specific strategic objectives, operating modes, organizational structures, and so on. In most cases, it addresses values as well as performance. Overall, most visions touch in some way on each of the following points:

- *Rational.* A description of why the vision is needed, or why the change is required.
- *Stakeholders.* A discussion of the organization's stakeholders and what it seeks to provide for them.
- *Values.* A description of the core values and/or beliefs that drive the organization of the change.
- *Performance objectives.* A definition of what will characterize effective performance of the organization (and in some cases individuals) once the change has been achieved.
- *Organizational structure or processes.* How the organization will be structured or will work to achieve the vision.
- *Operating style.* A discussion of some of the specific elements of how people in the organization (particularly managers) will operate and interact with each other. In some cases, this is an attempt to describe the required culture in operational terms.

Visions are developed for a number of different purposes. They are directional, signalling where the reorientation is headed. They are symbolic, providing a point for rallying and identification. They are educational, helping individuals to understand the events around them. Finally, they are energizing.

In this context, effective visions seem to be ones that are credible, responsive to the current (or anticipated) problems, and provide a balance of specificity and ambiguity. Effective visions also have a balance of new and old or sustaining ideas, values, or perspectives. In contrast to recreations (in which a break with the past is often necessary and appropriate), effective visions for reorientations often are crafted to have 'resonance' – to meld with themes from the organization's past.

Effective reorientations tend to have visions that are responsive to the issues raised in diagnosis and meet many of the criteria listed above. Less effective reorientations either have no vision or have visions that are flawed, are the result of mimicry, or have been developed in a way that does not facilitate the creation of understanding and/or commitment.[7]

A final note on vision. The question of whether or not to make a vision public has been faced in a number of reorientations. While the issue is important, no definitive answer has yet been identified. Clearly, the vision needs to be made public at some point. The directional, energizing, and educational goals of the vision cannot be met if it is kept secret. On the other hand, there are many cases of premature articulation of vision leading to negative consequences. In what some have called the 'rush to plexiglass', certain companies have developed vision statements and immediately distributed them throughout the company, using posters, documents, plaques, pins, plexiglass 'tombstones', and so on. When the vision is poorly thought out, when it is not clear how the vision will be achieved, or (perhaps most importantly) when the vision is very much at odds with current management behavior, employees tend to greet such statements with justified skepticism; the net result is a loss of management credibility. In some cases, this problem has been dealt with by clearly positioning the vision as aspirational and recognizing that this is not the way the organization functions today.

The Energy Principle

One of the great strengths of organizations is that they contain tremendous forces for stability. They are able to withstand threats and challenges to the established order. The flip side of this characteristic is that organizations (and particularly successful ones) can be inherently resistant to change, particularly change that undermines strongly held values and beliefs. Energy must be created to get change initiated and executed.

Organizational reorientation presents a particular dilemma. In a crisis situation (for example, the Tylenol poisoning case, the Union Carbide disaster at Bhopal, or deregulation at AT&T) the clear, present danger of organizational failure creates the energy needed to make change happen. Reorientation, by definition, is different because it involves changes in anticipation of the events that may make it necessary. The need for change may be apparent only to a small number of people. For the majority of people in the organization – and sometimes this includes much of senior management – the need for change is often not clear.[8]

Effective reorientations seem to be initiated by specific efforts to create energy. Most often this involves some effort – usually by leaders – to create a *sense of urgency*, and somehow to communicate and convey that sense of urgency throughout the organization. In some cases, a sense of urgency can be created by presenting information that shatters widespread assumptions about the current situation. But this tactic addresses the intellectual inertia. Urgency and energy are emotional issues, and experience indicates that people and organizations develop the energy to change when faced with real *pain*.

The larger and more intense the change, the more extreme the pain needed to mobilize individuals to consider doing things differently. There are a number of different ways in which pain can be created. Most of them involve employees participating in the process of data collection, discovery, and comparison of their organization against accepted benchmarks (frequently competitors). Some re-orientations have been started by getting senior managers to spend time with customers, use competitive products or services, or visit companies that are competitive analogs (the now familiar 'trip to Japan'). Since individuals have a unique capacity for denial, multiple intense exposures may be necessary to create the required depth of emotional reaction.

The problem is that pain can create energy that is counterproductive. The consequences of pain can be dysfunctional behavior as well as functionally directed action. Negative information can lead to certain defensive reactions, such as denial, flight, or withdrawal. To the extent that the organization is characterized by pathology, the creation of pain or urgency may stimulate mal-adaptive responses. Therefore, the challenge is to develop methods of creating pain that will create energy and catalyze action.

Successful reorientations involve the creation of a sense of urgency right at the limits of tolerance – just at the point where responses border on defensive. At the same time, efforts are made to track dysfunctional or pathological responses and find ways to redirect the energy in positive ways. In many less effective reorientations, sufficient energy has not been generated early or broadly enough. This is particularly true in very large organizations that have the capacity to absorb or buffer pain.

The next two principles assume that change has been initiated, and focus on the content of the change. These will be followed by two principles regarding the role of leadership in reorientation.

The Centrality Principle

For a change to engage the entire organization, it must be clearly and obviously linked to the core strategic issues of the firm. The positioning and labeling of the re-orientation are critical. Successful long-term changes are positioned as strategic imperatives that are compelling to members of the organization. Usually, the connection is so clear and has so much validity that the relationship of the change to company health and survival is obvious. For example, the emphasis on quality and customer service at Xerox and ALCOA were clearly linked to their enhanced competitiveness. Where changes are not seen as central to the survival, health, or growth of the organization, they tend to be transient, existing only so long as the perceived interest of senior management lasts. For a change to 'catch', employees have to see a clear connection with core organizational and individual imperatives.

To the degree the change is central, it raises another dilemma. If the organization has been successful and has built some degree of congruence over the years, employees may resist wholesale changes. In many successful long-term changes, managers worked to make sure that the core themes of the change (and the vision) had organizational resonance – that is, that they seemed related to and consistent with some of the historical core values of the organization.

But how can one find themes with strategic centrality in an organization of great diversity? It appears to be more difficult to find such themes across widely diverse businesses in large organizations. Success comes most often when generic themes, such as quality, competitiveness, or innovation, can be positioned across the businesses and then related with specificity to each particular operation's situation.[9]

The Three-Theme Principle

While a strategic change may involve a large number of specific activities, most managers of change find it necessary to identify themes to communicate and conceptualize the changes. Themes provide a language through which employees can understand and find patterns in what is happening around them. At the same time, however, they seem to be capable of integrating only a limited number of themes in the midst of all of the other transactions that make up daily life. Employees are bombarded with programs, messages, and directives. In many situations, individuals cope by figuring out which messages they can safely ignore. Usually, more are ignored than not. Successful long-term changes are characterized by a careful self-discipline that limits the number of major themes an organization gives its employees. As a general rule, managers of a change can only initiate and sustain approximately three key themes during any particular period of time.

The challenge in this area is to create enough themes to get people truly energized, while limiting the total number of themes. The toughest part is having to decide not to initiate a new program – which by itself has great merit – because of the risk of diluting the other themes.

Most successful reorientations are characterized by consistency of themes over time. It is consistency that appears to be most significant in getting people to believe that a theme is credible. The problem, then, is how to maintain consistency while simultaneously shaping themes to match changing conditions.[10]

The Magic Leader Principle

Another important component of a successful reorientation is an individual leader who serves as a focal point for the change, whose presence has some special 'feel' or 'magic'. Large-scale organizational change requires active and visible leadership to help articulate the change and to capture and mobilize the hearts and minds of the people in the organization. This kind of leadership relies on special effects created throughout the organization by the individual leader and, thus, this type of individual can be thought of as a *magic leader*. These leaders display the following characteristics:

- *Distinctive behaviors.* Magic leaders engage in three distinctive types of behavior that encourage employees to act in ways consistent with the desired change. The first is *envisioning* – creating an engaging and inspirational vision of a future state. Next is *energizing* – creating or stimulating energy through personal demonstration, rewards, and punishments, and setting high standards. Finally, there is *enabling* – helping to create the processes, resources, or structures that enable employees to do the things they have been motivated to do. The most successful large-scale change leaders exhibit elements of all three of these types of behavior.
- *Ability to create a sense of urgency.* The magic leader seems to be critical in creating a sense of urgency so essential to organizational changes. The leader is a key player in the creation and management of pain.
- *Guardianship of themes.* The leader is the guardian of the themes of the change. He or she is the one individual who can make sure the themes survive. Successful change managers exhibit great tenacity (or even stubbornness) in the articulation of themes over a period of years, in both good times and bad.
- *A mix of styles.* Magic leaders also display an interesting mix of management styles. On one hand, they appear to be directive and uncompromising in furthering their objectives for change. On the other hand, they seem to welcome participation and spend time getting people involved in shaping the change process. This combination of autocratic and democratic tendencies appears to be critical to their effectiveness.

The dilemma here is that while the individual magic leader is essential to successful reorientation, continued dependence on him or her can lead to disaster. The change can become too personalized; nothing happens unless that individual assumes personal sponsorship, and the next levels of management may become disenfranchised. Furthermore, when the leader makes mistakes (as he or she inevitably does) the magic may fade. The magic leader finds it difficult to live up to the fantasies that subordinates create. Thus the challenge is to fulfill the need for the leader at the very time when the organization needs to grow beyond the leader.[11]

The Leadership-is-Not-Enough Principle

While magic leadership is necessary, it cannot, by itself, sustain a large-scale change. Success depends on a broader base of support built with other individuals who act first as followers, second as helpers, and finally as co-owners of the change.

The expansion of the leadership of change beyond the magic leader requires efforts in two directions. The first complements the magic leader with leadership that focuses on the necessary elements of management control, or instrumental leadership.

The second broadens the base of leadership beyond one or two individuals. The most common way to achieve this is through the executive team of the organization. Successful changes are characterized by a large investment in the executive team, both as individuals and as a group. This team needs to share and own the vision, to become over time more visible as champions, and to come to grips collectively with the task of managing today's business while also managing the change to position tomorrow's business. In addition to the executive team, leadership can be expanded through the development and involvement of senior management and by efforts to develop leadership throughout the organization.[12]

The first seven principles have focused on how to initiate change, how to define the content of change, and the role of leadership. The final three principles have to do with the problem of sustaining change and achieving reorientation over time.

The Planning-and-Opportunism Principle

Profound organizational reorientation does not occur by accident. Rather, it is the result of intensive planning. On the other hand, it is naive to believe that reorientation in the face of uncertainty can occur by mechanistically executing a detailed operating plan. Successful reorientations involve a mix of planning and unplanned opportunistic action.

The argument for planning flows naturally out of many of the principles that have already been articulated. Diagnosis, the development of vision, the creation of energy, and the crafting of the content of the change all require in-depth thinking and planning. The system's nature and complexity of organizations also require that significant changes with multiple components be sequenced and linked together. A number of successful reorientations have involved six months to two years of planning prior to any public action.

At the same time, there is a valid argument for the inherent limitations of planning. By definition, reorientations involve planning in the face of uncertainty. The architect of change does not know for sure what will occur environmentally in the future. Typically, unforeseen events – both positive and negative – will occur and have a profound impact on the reorientation. Some of these events are themselves consequences of the reorientation efforts – products of its success or failure at different stages. Each event may present an opportunity; to ignore them because 'they are not in the plan' would be foolish.

As a consequence, effective reorientations seem to be guided by a process of iterative planning; that is, the plans are revised frequently as new events and opportunities present themselves. This reflects the fact that planned organizational change involves a good deal of learning and that this learning can and should shape the development of the vision and reorientation itself. Thus the planned sequence of activity is balanced with what might be called *bounded opportunism*. However, it does not make sense nor is it effective to respond to every problem, event, or opportunity. Some potential courses of action may simply be inconsistent with the intent of the change or may drain energy from the core effort. It is within certain boundaries, then, that the effective architect of reorientation is opportunistic and modifies plans over time.[13]

The Many-Bullets Principle

The nature of organizational stability and resistance to change was discussed earlier. It clearly has implications for initiating change, but it also has ramifications for achieving change.

Organizations are typically resistant to change. Changes in one component of a system that do not 'fit' are frequently isolated and stamped out, much as the human body fights a foreign organism. In these cases, the forces for congruence are forces that work for stability. Similarly, individual behavior in organizations is frequently overdetermined. If an individual's patterns of activity were examined, one would see that there are multiple forces shaping it – for example, the design of the work, the activities of supervisors, the immediate social system, the rewards, the organizational structure, the selection system that attracted and chose the individual, and the physical setting. Indeed, there are frequently more factors reinforcing a pattern of behavior than are necessary. As a result, changing those patterns will require more than a modification of a single element of the environment.

Effective reorientations recognize the intractability of organizational and individual behavior and thus make use of many 'bullets' – as many different devices to change behavior as possible, incorporating intentionally redundant activities. They thus involve planned changes in strategy, the definition of work, structure, informal process, and individual skills – along with attitudes and perceptions.

In effective reorientations, managers use all available points of leverage to bring about change. Underlying the Many-Bullets Principle is the assumption that the organization ultimately must come to grips with the need to adjust its infrastructure to be consistent with, and supportive of, the change. As all the other work is being done, there is the less glamorous but still critical work of building the structures to enable and reinforce the changes. This is tough, detailed, and sometimes tedious work, but it is crucial. Things that need to be addressed include:

- Standards and measure of performance
- Rewards and incentives
- Planning processes
- Budgeting and resource allocation methods
- Information systems

The problem here is one of timing. The work cannot get too far ahead of the change, yet it cannot lag too far behind. Successful managers make skillful use of these levers to support and in some cases drive the change over time.[14]

The Investment-and-Returns Principle

The final principle concerns the amount of effort and resources that are required to achieve a truly effective re-orientation as well as the long time span that is usually required to realize the results of those efforts. There are two subpoints to this principle – one concerning investments (the *no-free-lunch* hypothesis) and one concerning returns (the *check-is-in-the-mail* hypothesis).

The No-Free-Lunch Hypothesis. Large-scale, significant organizational change requires significant investment of time, effort, and dollars. While change may yield significant positive results, it is not without its costs.

Successful changes are characterized by a willingness on the part of the changers to invest significant resources. The most scarce resource appears to be senior management time. Organizations engaging in large-scale change find it necessary to get senior managers involved in a range of activities – senior team meetings, presentations, attendance at special events, education, and training – all of which are necessary to perform the functions of leadership in the change. This broadening of ownership also requires a significant investment of time, particularly of the senior team. Less successful changes often prove to be those in which the investments of time were delayed or avoided because senior managers felt so overloaded with change activity that they could not do their work. In successful reorientations, senior managers saw change as an integral part of their work.

The dilemma here is that while the senior team's investment of time is essential, it may also cut into time that the team needs to spend being leaders for the rest of the organization. This could lead to charges that the senior team is too insular, too absorbed in its own process. The challenge is to manage the balance of these two demands.

The Check-Is-in-the-Mail Hypothesis. Organizational reorientation takes time. In particular, as the complexity of the organization increases, so does the time required for change. Each level of the organization engaged in the change takes its own time to understand, accept, integrate, and subsequently own and lead change. In many changes, it becomes important to sell and resell the change throughout many levels of the organization. Each level has to go through its own process of comprehending the change and coming to terms with it.

Organizations go through predictable states as they deal with a change and a set of themes:

- *Awareness,* People within the organization first become aware of the need to change and the dimensions of the change. They work to come to grips with this need and to understand what the change is all about.
- *Experimentations.* Small-scale efforts are made to experiment with the changes in a bounded and manageable setting. Efforts are made to see whether the change will really work in 'our unique setting'.
- *Understanding.* The experimentation leads to increased understanding of the change, its consequences and implications. At this point, employees begin to realize the scope of the change and what it may involve.
- *Commitment.* The leadership faces up to the decisions to change and makes a significant and visible commitment to take action.
- *Education.* Employees spend time acquiring the skills and information needed to implement the change. This may involve training or other transfers of skills.
- *Application to leveraged issues.* The new approach, perspective, and skills are applied to key issues or specific situations where there is leverage. This is done consciously, and even a bit awkwardly.
- *Integration into ongoing behavior.* The new changed behavior starts to become a way of life. Employees naturally (and unconsciously) are working in new ways.

Obviously, a change rarely follows the steps exactly as described above. Moreover, different levels of the organization may go through the stages at their own pace. But at some time, each part of the organization must come to grips with each of these issues in some way.

As a result, experience indicates that large-scale reorientations generally take from three to seven years in complex organizations. The efforts may entail false starts, derailments, and the necessity to start over in some places. In addition, significant payoffs may not be seen for at least two years. Again, there is a dilemma. People need to be persuaded to invest personally in the change before there is any evidence that it will pay off, either for the organization or for them personally. Their motivation is essential to success, but proven success is essential to their motivation. The challenge is to demonstrate (through experiments, personal example, or through 'face validity') that the change will ultimately pay off.[15]

Conclusion

This article has focused on the factors that characterize the most successful attempts at frame bending – large-scale, long-term organizational reorientation. But it would be a mistake to conclude without commenting on the very important, critical, and central aspects of organizational life and how these affect change.

Two elements are tightly intertwined with the implementation of organizational change – *power politics* and *pathology*. All organizations are political systems, and changes occur within the context of both individual and group aspirations. Thus strategic changes become enmeshed in issues that are ideological ('What type of company should we be?') as well as issues that are personal ('What's going to be the impact on my career?'). These are not aberrations; they are a normal part of organizational life. However, they will be magnified by and indeed may 'play themselves out' through the change. It is difficult to provide general guidance for dealing with this, since the issues vary greatly. However, the successful change manager works at understanding these dynamics, predicting their impact on the change and vice versa, and shaping the situation to make constructive use of them.[16]

Not all organizational life is adaptive. Organizations, like people, have their dark sides – their destructive or maladaptive responses to situations. Organizations develop stylized responses to problems and situations. These responses may be elicited by the intensity of a strategic change. An organization that engages in collective despair may become more despairing. Again, it is the leader who must understand the organizational pathology and confront it.

We have attempted here to share some initial views on a particular subset of organizational change – reorientations. Our belief is that reorientations are a particularly significant kind of change. While reorientations require sustained senior management attention, they are more likely to succeed than re-creations.

More and more organizations face the need for such change as competitive pressures increase. This article is another step in trying to understand this need and to provide guidance to those who are called upon to lead these organizations.

Notes

1. This article is based on observations of approximately 25 organizations in which we have done work over the past five years, and specifically our very close work with the most senior levels of management in planning and implementing significant, multiyear strategic-level changes in six particular organizations.

2. See Nadler, D. A. and Tushman, M. L. (1977) 'A diagnostic model for organization behavior' in Lawler, E. E. and Porter, L. W. (eds) *Perspectives on Behavior in Organizations*, New York, McGraw-Hill; and D. A. Nadler and M. L. Tushman, 'A Model for Organizational Diagnosis', *Organizational Dynamics.* Autumn 1980.

3. See M. L. Tushman, W. Newman, and E. Romanelli, 'Convergence and Upheaval: Managing the Unsteady Pace of Organizational Evolution', *California Management Review,* Fall 1986, 29–44. Also see M. L. Tushman and E. Romanelli, 'Organizational Evolution: A Metamorphosis Model of Convergence and Re-orientation' in B. L. Staw and L. I. Commings (Eds.), *Research and Organizational Behavior,* Greenwich, CT: JAI Press, 1985, p. 17.

4. R. Beckhard and R. Harris, *Organizational Transitions,* Reading, MA: Addison-Wesley, 1977; K. Lewin, 'Frontiers in Group Dynamics', *Human Relations,* 1947, 1, 5–41; and D. A. Nadler, 'Managing Organizational Change: An Integrative Perspective', *Journal of Applied Behavioral Science,* 1981, 17, 191–211.

5. See Beckhard and Harris, Endnote 4; and W. G. Benois, K. D. Benne; R. Chin, *The Planning of Change,* New York: Holt, Rinehart & Winston, 1961; and W. G. Bennis and B. Nanus, *Leadership: The Strategies for Taking Charge.* New York: Harper and Row, 1985.

6. See P. A. Goodman and Associates, *Change in Organizations: New Perspectives on Theory, Research, and Practice,* San Francisco: Jossey-Bass, 1982; and E. E. Lawler, D. A. Nadler, and C. Cammann, *Organizational Assessment,* New York: John Wiley & Sons, 1980.

7. J. M. Burns, *Leadership,* New York: Harper & Row, 1978; and Goodman et al., Endnote 6.

8. See Bennis et al., Endnote 5; Lewin, Endnote 4; and J. M. Pennings & Associates, *Organizational Strategy and Change,* San Francisco: Jossey-Bass, 1985.

9. See M. Kets de Vries and D. Miller, 'Neurotic Style and Organizational Pathology', *Strategic Management Journal,* 1984, 5, 35–55; and N. M. Tichy and M. A. Devanna. *The Transformational Leader.* New York: John Wiley & Sons, 1986.

10. See D. A. Nadler and M. L. Tushman, *Strategic Organization Design,* Glenview, IL: Scott, Foresman. 1988; J. B. Quinn, *Strategies for Change: Logical Incrementalism,* Homewood, IL: Irwin, 1980; and J. B. Quinn and K. Cameron (Eds.). *Paradox and Transformation.* Cambridge, MA: Ballinger, 1988.

11. See D. A. Nadler and M. L. Tushman, *Beyond the Charismatic Leader: Leadership and Organizational Change,* New York: Delta Consulting Group, 1987; and Tichy and Devanna, Endnote 9.

12. D. A. Nadler and M. L. Tushman, *Managing Strategic Organizational Change,* New York: Delta Consulting Group. 1986; and Nadler and Tushman, Endnote 11.

13. See Quinn, Endnote 10; and Tushman et al., Endnote 3.

14. See Nadler and Tushman, Endnote 10; and Pennings et al., Endnote 8.

15. See Quinn, Endnote 10; Quinn and Cameron, Endnote 10; and Tichy and Devanna, Endnote 9.

16. See Kets de Vries and Miller, Endnote 9; and Tichy and Devanna, Endnote 9.

The Strategic Management of Corporate Change

Dexter Dunphy and Doug Stace

Introduction

Advocates of particular change ideologies mostly claim that their model is universally applicable. However, turbulent times demand different responses in varied circumstances. So managers and consultants need a model of change that is essentially a 'situational' or 'contingency model', that is, one that indicates how to vary change strategies to achieve 'optimum fit' with the changing environment. Dunphy and Stace (1988) have developed a model of this kind with two critical dimensions: the scale of change needed to bring the organization back into fit with its environment, and the style of leadership required to bring about that change. In developing their model, they criticized the prevailing emphasis among OD writers up to the mid-1980s on the need for incremental rather than for radical or framebreaking change (Quinn, 1980; Golembiewski, 1979; Shaskin, 1984). Dunphy and Stace argued, with others (Miller, 1982; Kimberley and Quinn, 1984; Miller and Friesen, 1984; Harris, 1985; Shein, 1985; Peters, 1988) that turbulent and unpredictable environments may make radical change a necessity.

Since that time, the traditional OD emphasis on the positive value of incremental change has increasingly given way to acceptance and sometimes advocacy of transformational change. For example, Bartunek and Louis (1988) noted that 'Organizational development and organizational transformation represent two different approaches to the understanding of organizational change' (p. 97) but argued that the two approaches are compatible and 'considered jointly, inform the larger understanding of change' (p. 97). They noted that the traditional OD approach involves improvements 'within already accepted frameworks' (p. 100), i.e., first order change. On

Dunphy, D. and Stace, D. (1993) 'The strategic management of corporate change', *Human Relations*, vol. 46, no. 8, pp. 905–20.

the other hand, transformational approaches involve 'discontinuous shifts in frameworks' (p. 100), such as rethinking the organization's mission, i.e., second-order change. They did not, however, argue for synthesizing the two approaches but for continuing to treat both approaches separately, maintaining a debate between them.

In a review covering the development of OD into the 1980s, Mirvis (1988) documented the development of the movement from its innovative, even radical origins in the 1960s to a point where 'the OD movement has become an established discipline' where its proponents 'are, in effect, part of the establishment (p. 35). However, Mirvis judged that in 1988 OD was showing signs of escaping from a period of stagnation and 'reinventing itself... Theorists are attempting again to define what change really is: distinctions are being made between development transitions and transformations' (p. 47).

By 1990, Mirvis (1990) was including OT in OD, noting that this was a response to massive environmental change which had led half of the top 800 U.S. companies into massive restructurings. Similarly in 1991 Porras and Silvers (1991) referred to OT as 'second-generation OD'. They noted, however that since the OD area 'is so underdeveloped, it is our hope that sented here suggest that scholars working within the ecological framework may benefit by shifting their attention from the question of whether change is hazardous to the questions of under what conditions change may be hazardous or helpful... firms in dramatically changing environments may be compelled to adjust their strategies and structure in order to survive' (p. 73).

This is change of the kind referred to by Kanter, Stein, and Jick (1992) as 'revolutionary change', i.e., change 'so great that it must be considered a fresh start rather than an extension of what preceded it' (p. 173). Clearly most OD practitioners clung strongly to their belief in incrementalism for most of the 1980s but, faced by demands for more radical interventions, by the 1990s were looking for ways to reconcile the two divergent approaches to corporate change.

Dunphy and Stace (1988) also reviewed the debate between participative approaches to change and directive/coercive approaches. OD theorists have argued for a universally applicable leadership style that creates widespread organizational involvement in defining goals and implementing change (Eldon, 1987; Golembiewski, 1979; Quinn, 1980; Shaskin, 1984; Schein, 1985; Beer and Walton, 1987) while pluralist power writers have argued that directive and coercive approaches are often necessary to resolve significant conflicts of interests (Salancik and Pfeffer, 1978; Mason and Mitroff, 1981; Muczuk and Reimann, 1987). Interestingly enough, even participative approaches may not be as participative as they seem for, on the basis of empirical work, Newmann (1989) estimated that approximately two-thirds of a workforce typically choose not to participate in change programs even when they are given the opportunity (Neumann, 1989).

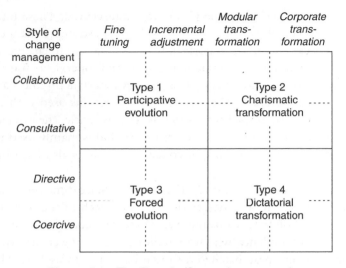

Figure 6.1 The Dunphy/Stace change matrix

Dunphy and Stace contend that different circumstances demand different styles of change leadership. In particular, transformative change may often demand directive/coercive leadership. Dunphy and Stace's contingency model (outlined in Figure 6.1) claims to be 'a more comprehensive approach to organizational change management strategies which finds a place for transformation as well as incrementalism and which accommodates the use of directive/coercive as well as collaborative means of achieving change' (Dunphy and Stace, 1988, p. 331). This article describes field research undertaken to test the Dunphy/Stace model's applicability and usefulness as an explanatory tool for understanding how and why organizations choose different change strategies.

Research Method

During 1988–89, a research study using the Dunphy/Stace model was conducted in the Australian service industry. The Australian service sector has been subjected to large-scale environmental change such as deregulation, increasing overseas competition, and technological innovation.

Thirteen Australian organizations were selected in banking, insurance, aviation, and international telecommunications. High, medium, and low performing organizations were included, independently ranked by three industry market analysts. The research involved structured interviews with over 450 executives, managers, and supervisors. At least eight members of each top executive team, including the CEO, were interviewed. These interviewees responded to forced-choice instruments on business strategy, change strategy, and HR practices. This article reports only results relevant to change strategies. A stratified random sample of middle managers and supervisors was also interviewed in each organization, using group interviews structured on a modified Delphi technique. Several of the forced-choice questions used with executives were also used with personnel at these levels. In this article, the extensive qualitative data gathered cannot be quoted at length and is mainly used to explain apparently discrepant results and, in condensed form, is also used in the case studies.

As a result of an initial pilot study, the Dunphy/Stace dimensions and model were modified to create four descriptive tvoes on each of the model's change leadership: Collaborative, Consultative, Directive, and Coercive. On each dimension, the respondents (who were senior executives) were asked to choose the description which best matched the organization as it was 3 years before the study (1985) and at the time of the study (1988). Modal scores were used, i.e., the description most frequently chosen was regarded as representative of the view of the executives in a particular organization.

Research Results

Research Results on the Scale of Change. Table 6.1 shows the results (as modal scores) on the scale of change. There are 26 observations, i.e., 13 organizations at two time periods. Two thirds of these cases experienced or were currently experiencing transformative change (our scale Types 3 and 4), reflecting the turbulence of these industries. (Of the 13 organizations, only four maintained the same scale of change over a period of 3–5 years). The table illustrates that

Table 6.1 Scale of change: Research results[a]

Type period	Type 1: fine tuning	Type 2: incremental adjustment	Type 3: modular transformation	Type 4: corporate transformation
3 years ago	4%	11%	8%	27%
Now (1988)	8%	11%	31%	—
Subtotals	12%	22%	39%	27%
Totals for alternate approaches	34% (incremental approaches)		66% (transformative approaches)	

Note: [a]*N* = 26, that is, 13 organizations in two time periods; figures given are based on modal responses of senior executives in each organization, and have been converted to percentages.

some organizations operated with the fairly minor changes of Fine Tuning or Incremental Adjustment but organizations changing in this way are a minority; Modular and Corporate Transformation have become the norm rather than the exception.

Research Results on the Style of Change Leadership

The second component of the change model is a continuum from collaborative, through consultative to directive and coercive leadership of corporate change. Our research enables us to describe the prevailing styles used to manage change in our 13 Australian service sector organizations at two time periods (see Table 6.2).

Table 6.2 shows how executives described the styles they used in managing corporate change processes. Clearly the predominant style is directive. These are measures, however, of the style of the executives, as rated by the executives themselves. We can ask two questions about this: 'Is their perception of their style shared by their subordinates?' and 'Is this leadership style also used for change management at lower levels?' As noted, we also interviewed a systematically selected sample of middle level managers and first line supervisors. In nine of the 13 organizations, there was exact correspondence between the scores of the executives and their subordinates; both the executives and their subordinate managers/supervisors agreed that their corporate leadership style was directive, or in one case coercive. In each of the other four cases the executive group saw their own style as consultative whereas a majority of the middle managers and supervisors saw it as directive. These four cases were all organizations where the field research showed that senior executives espoused consultative values, had embodied these values in a formal corporate value statement, and had

Table 6.2   Styles change leadership: Research results (at corporate level)[a]

Type period	Type 1: collaborative	Type 2: consultative	Type 3: directive	Type 4: coercive
3 years ago	—	11%	31%	8%
Now (1988)	—	19%	31%	—
Subtotals	—	30%	62%	8%
Totals for alternate approaches	34% (incremental approaches)		66% (transformative approaches)	

Note: [a]$N = 26$, that is, 13 organizations in two time periods; figures given are based on modal responses of senior executives in each organization, and have been converted to percentages.

also devoted considerable time and energy to a range of consultative activities. However, these activities were not necessarily perceived by supervisors, or if perceived evaluated as consultative. When asked, most supervisory respondents favored a directive corporate leadership style for their senior executives.

We also gathered data on the leadership style at business unit level. Ratings for this were obtained only from first line and middle managers. In nine organizations, middle managers/supervisors rated the change leadership style differently at the corporate and business unit levels. In eight cases, the shift was from ratings of 'directive' at corporate level to 'consultative' at business level. This strongly suggests that the traditional OD model is more widely applied at the business unit level than at the corporate level. The most probable explanation is that, as a general rule, major organizational change strategies are conceived at corporate level by senior executives who expect those below them to follow the strategies. At business unit level, however, there is consultation on the implementation of these strategies to ensure commitment and relevance. However, at neither level did we find any scores for collaboration, as defined in our Style Type 4.

Research Results for the Contingency Matrix. Using the Dunphy/Stace matrix shown in Figure 6.1, we are able to classify the overall strategies of the 13 organizations at two time periods (see Table 6.3). Table 6.3 shows clearly that the dominant strategy used in managing change has been 'Directive Transformation', that is, large-scale organizational transformation achieved by directive leadership. Fifty-two percent of our sample of 26 cases (13 organizations at two time periods) fall into the Dictatorial Transformation quadrant, although the majority are more accurately described as examples of directive transformation. Only 12% fall into the Charismatic Transformation quadrant, which has been widely advocated in the U.S. literature on Organizational Transformation, 20% fall into the Participative Evolution quadrant, the traditional OD approach. Sixteen

Table 6.3   Change strategies of sample organizations[a]

	Scale of change				
Style of change	Fine tuning	Incremental adjustment	Modular transformation	Corporate transformation	Total
Collaborative	—	—	—	—	0%
Consultative	8%	12%	12%	—	32%
Directive	4%	8%	26%	22%	60%
Coercive	—	4%	—	4%	8%
Total	12%	24%	38%	26%	100%

Note: [a]$N = 26$, that is, 13 organizations in two time periods; figures given are based on modal responses of senior executives in each organization, and have been converted to percentages.

percent fall into the Forced Evolution quadrant. The directive/coercive style of leadership (of corporate change) accounts for 68% of cases, the remaining 32% being consultative.

The Change Model and Corporate Performance

In the sample, there were two organizations which were relatively lower performers. We were interested therefore to compare their change strategies with medium to higher performing organizations. We found that the two lower performers were the only organizations using Fine Tuning change; one associated with the use of a Consultative Change Style, the other associated with the use of a Directive Change Style. How do the medium to high performers fare in comparison? Figure 6.2 shows how performance related to choice of change strategy and illustrates principles of maintaining or regaining enhanced performance.

These principles are: Fine Tuning is not a viable change strategy in the current environment; Corporate Transformation (using a directive/coercive style) is the most common change strategy used when an organization needs to radically regain 'fit' with a changed environment. There were two groups of

Scale of change

Style of change management	Fine tuning	Incremental adjustment	Modular trans-formation	Corporate trans-formation
Collaborative				
Consultative	Lower performers	Maintaining fit-medium to high performers		
Directive				Regaining fit by corporate turnaround
Coercive				

Figure 6.2   The change model and corporate performance

organizations in this category: the first group were previously medium per-formers, where, because of radical legislative changes in the financial services and airlines industries, the executives took radical action to transform their organizations in order to survive in the dramatically new conditions. The second group were extremely low performers before the study, unlikely to survive in the new competitive environment created by changed legislation. In all cases, new chief executives were appointed to re-shape the organizations, resulting in major re-positioning of each organization within its environment. So high per-formance can be maintained by either a Consultative or a Directive corporate leadership style, and by Incremental Adjustment or Modular Transformation.

Case Examples

We present four summary case studies, each is representative of one of the four major change strategies defined by the contingency matrix (see Figure 6.1) to indicate how each strategy can be effectively used, in specific circumstances, to maintain high performance.

Macquarie Bank: Successful Participative Evolution

Much of the traditional OD literature has been concerned with Type 1, 'Participative Evolution', and its prescriptions are valid for conditions more prevalent in times of stability or steady economic growth. However, our study showed that continuous incremental (evolutionary) change combined with flexible, far-sighted change leadership can maintain high performance even in a rapidly changing industry environment. Macquarie Bank was the one organiza-tion which had continued to be highly profitable using an incremental change strategy. Macquarie is a niche merchant bank with an impressive growth and performance record. Over the period 1984–88, its total revenue rose from A$46 million to A$198 million. Its high performance has continued; in 1990, it became the only Australian bank to receive an upgrade of its credit rating (from A– to A+ on its international rating by Standard and Poors).

Under the leadership of David Clarke (Chairman) and Tony Berg (MD), the bank developed a strategy of continuously proactive innovation. One executive remarked: 'We never stay still, but we don't change in quantum leaps – our corporate culture would preclude that – running a business on partnership concepts means that policy decisions are not dramatic, they evolve.' Macquarie met banking deregulation in the 1980s by diversification into high valued-added specialist markets like foreign exchange, bullion, and commodities and later making carefully chosen acquisitions. Internal change was managed by developing an increasing number of relatively autonomous business units (30 by 1988) and solving coordination problems, not by establishing additional control systems, but by developing a strongly held set of corporate values. The management style was a collegial style seen as consultative by the executive but, on balance, seen as more directive by first line and middle level managers. These lower level managers all rated a directive style as appropriate; 'we need strength and decisiveness at the top', one commented.

Macquarie Bank's strategies were successful because of its relatively small size relative to other banks and its development of innovative niche-oriented business strategies combined with a continuously adaptive loose-coupled flexible organization. There can be a place for evolutionary change strategies in a turbulent environment, provided that environmental scanning is effective, relevant organizational changes are made continually, and the style of executive change management is flexible rather than stereotyped.

Westpac Bank: Successful Charismatic Transformation

We have one case of successful Charismatic Transformation – the Westpac Banking Group. In the early 1980s, the merger of two different banks created the largest financial institution in Australia. The period leading up to the merger represented a period of corporate transformation; a major organizational change program was mounted to back up an aggressive market strategy for the new institution. This first wave of change was heavily sponsored from the top, by the MD, Bob White. The change program was focused on goal setting, team building, appraisal, and management development. The bank was renamed, a new product divisional structure created, and there were several major corporate restructures.

The second wave of change was still consultative in style but focused on change at the divisional level. As the largest Australian bank, Westpac was responding to new levels of competition from domestic and foreign financial institutions. In addition, many leading Australian corporations were internationalizing their operations. This meant that major Australian banks needed to offer international services to their Australian client base. To achieve its aim of becoming an internationally recognized financial intermediary, Westpac embarked (in 1983–87) on an aggressive strategy of diversification into related financial services by developing business in profitable market niches (e.g., insurance) and by acquisition. It entered a phase of almost continual structural change at Divisional level. Over the 1978–88 period we see, therefore, a move from corporate transformation to modular transformation in the scale of change and a move from a consultative change style to a directive change style by 1988. The increase in directive leadership at the corporate level represents a move to achieve greater accountability and a sharpened focus on results in the face of a tougher, more competitive economic environment. Westpac lifted its revenue from approximately A\$4,500 million in 1983 to just over A\$9,000 million in 1987. Its profit (before tax) in the same period rose from A\$412 million to A\$849 million. Charismatic Transformation is a change method widely advocated by behavioral scientists in the U.S. (e.g., Kanter, 1983; Schein, 1985), but it is interesting that executives 'toughened' their style from consultative to directive when faced with the task of managing a larger, more diversified organization in a more competitive environment.

Advance Bank: Successful Forced Evolution

Advance Bank is typical of several medium-sized Australian financial institutions which have changed markedly in the period of financial deregulation. In 1985–86 the former building society became a bank, moving through a transitional period of directive transformation before settling down into ongoing change of Type 3 Forced Evolution. Following the period of Directive Transformation initiated by its dynamic new CEO John Thame, the bank repositioned its corporate strategy by diversification and geographical extension from NSW to other Australian states. Thame's leadership represented a major shift from the Fine Tuning consensus style approach of the previous CEO who ran the organization as a NSW-centered building society. The current strategy has proved effective in maintaining high performance for a localized niche bank with a specialist focus on property financing and commercial transactions in the small to medium end of the financial market. There was growth in 1984–88 in total revenue from A\$233 million to A\$597 million, of profit before tax from A\$22 to A\$57 and in total assets from A\$1,899 million to A\$4,556.

MLC Life: Successful Dictatorial Transformation

In our study, MLC Life Ltd is an example of Dictatorial Transformation being an effective means of regaining high profitability. MLC Life went through cataclysmic transformative change subsequent to its takeover in 1983 by Lend Lease Corporation, one of Australia's most successful building construction companies. Pettigrew and Whipp (1991) have pointed out that 'a crisis provides the space and legitimacy to effect major strategic re-orientations' (p. 174).

MLC Life was a traditional insurance company that had failed to adjust its culture to a series of major industry changes beginning in the mid-1970s and intensifying in the 1980s. As a result, it was rapidly becoming unprofitable and losing market share. Under two successive chief executives from Lend Lease (John Morschel and Ian Crow), a new focused business strategy was chosen which targeted superannuation and products designed for middle socio-economic consumers. As a result, the organization was dramatically downsized, with reductions of up to 40% in some areas. A new business-driven, externally-oriented culture was built around concepts of accountability, initiative, and high performance. This culture was underpinned by a leaner, flatter organization driven by well-defined objectives. By 1988, Corporate Transformation had given way to Modular Transformation and a Coercive change management style had given way to a Consultative style (as seen by senior executives) or a Directive style (as seen by supervisors and middle managers).

In business terms, the change strategy was highly successful. MLC's revenue rose from A$243 million in 1983 to A$453 million in 1987; its pre-tax profit rose from $133 million to $249 million. In 1993, MLC Life remains one of the most profitable companies in the Australian insurance industry. Its market share position increased from number 25 at the time of acquisition to number 3 in 1988. Directive/Dictatorial Transformation (Change Strategy Type 4) becomes more common in a turbulent business environment in which global business re-definition, social change, new technologies, and political intervention all have marked effects on the organization. At such times, major organizational restructuring is needed, may run counter to the entrenched interests of some key stakeholder groups, and there may be few rewards to offer them for changing. In such circumstances, force (authoritative direction or coercion) may become the only available means to ensure organizational survival. In the Australian public sector, governments have used commissions of inquiry, replacement of 'permanent' heads, and efficiency audits to bring government organizations into line with changed definitions of function and reductions in resources. In the private sector, boards of management have removed CEOs and senior executives, and individual entrepreneurs have used takeovers and mergers to initiate organization-wide transformation.

Conclusion

A more comprehensive approach to organizational change management and consultancy is needed which finds a place for transformation as well as incrementalism and which accommodates the use of directive/coercive as well as participative means of achieving change. The revised Dunphy/Stace model reconciles the views of the major and often opposing theoretical traditions in the organization behavior area, as they apply to the management of organizational change. These are the 'tender-minded' tradition of the 'human relations/human resource' theorists whose theories underlie OD strategies, and the 'tough-minded' tradition of the pluralistic power perspective theorists and economic rationalists. Rather than evolution and transformation being incompatible strategies, and collaboration and coercion being incompatible modes, they are in fact complementary, their usefulness depending on the particular circumstances.

The situational model for planned change strategies described here allows managers and consultants to go beyond personal value preference as the major selection criterion for an organizational change strategy. The model suggests that for most organizations undergoing transformational change at the corporate level, a directive management style is needed to begin the process of repositioning the organization. However, it goes on to suggest that once this basis for organizational renewal is in place, there is a choice to be made at the corporate level as to the mix of directive and consultative strategies needed to keep up the momentum of change. If the change program is to be successful, there must also be a predominance of consultative practices at the business unit level in order to win commitment at that level to the implementation of change. Effective organizational change therefore demands that managers and consultants give up rigid reflexive responses in designing organizational change programs in favor of a mindful flexibility of choice.

Appendix A Defining the Scale of Change

Scale Type 1: Fine Tuning. Organizational change which is an ongoing process characterized by fine tuning of the 'fit' or match between the organization's strategy, structure, people, and processes. Such effort is typically manifested at departmental/divisional levels and deals with one or more of the following:

- Refining policies, methods, and procedures.
- Creating specialist units and linking mechanisms to permit increased volume and increased attention to unit quality and cost.
- Developing personnel especially suited to the present strategy (improved training and development; tailoring award systems to match strategic thrusts).
- Fostering individual and group commitment to the company mission and the excellence of one's own department.
- Promoting confidence in the accepted norms, beliefs, and myths.
- Clarifying established roles (with their associated authorities and powers), and the mechanisms for allocating resources.

Scale Type 2: Incremental Adjustment. Organizational change which is characterized by incremental adjustments to the changing environment. Such change involves distinct modifications (but not radical change) to corporate business strategies, structures, and management processes, for example:

- Expanding sales territory.
- Shifting the emphasis among products.
- Improved production process technology.
- Articulating a modified statement of mission to employees.
- Adjustments to organizational structures within or across divisional boundaries to achieve better links in product/service delivery.

Scale Type 3: Modular Transformation. Organizational change which is characterized by major realignment of one or more departments/divisions. The process of radical change is focused on these subparts rather than on the organization as a whole, for example:

- Major restructuring of particular departments/divisions.
- Changes in key executives and managerial appointments in these areas.
- Work and productivity studies resulting in significantly reduced or increased workforce numbers.
- Reformed departmental/divisional goals.
- Introduction of significantly new process technologies affecting key departments or divisions.

Scale Type 4: Corporate Transformation. Organizational change which is corporation-wide, characterized by radical shifts in business strategy, and revolutionary changes throughout the whole organization involving many of the following features:

- Reformed organizational mission and core values.
- Altered power and status affecting the distribution of power in the organization.
- Reorganization – major changes in structures, systems, and procedures across the organization.
- Revised interaction patterns – new procedures, work flows, communication networks, and decision making patterns across the organization.
- New executives in key managerial positions from outside the organization.

Appendix B Styles of Change Leadership

Type 1: Collaborative. This involves widespread participation by employees in important decisions about the organization's future, and about the means of bringing about organizational change.

Type 2: Consultative. This style of leadership involves consultation with employees, primarily about the means of bringing about organizational change, with their possible limited involvement in goal setting relevant to their area of expertise or responsibility.

Type 3: Directive. This style of leadership involves the use of managerial authority and direction as the main form of decision making about the organization's future, and about the means of bringing about organizational change.

Type 4: Coercive. This style of leadership involves managers/executives or outside parties forcing or imposing change on key groups in the organization.

References

Bartunek, J. M. and Louis, M. L. (1988) 'The interplay of organizational development and organizational transformation', *Research in Organizational Change and Development,* vol. 2, pp. 97–134.

Beer, M. and Walton, A. E. (1987) 'Organizational change and development', *Annual Review of Psychology,* vol. 38, pp. 339–67.

Dunphy, D. C. and Stace, D. A. (1988) 'Transformational and Coercive strategies for planned organizational change: Beyond the OD model', *Organizational Studies,* vol. 9, no. 3, pp. 339–55.

Eldon, M. (1987) 'Sociotechnical systems in Norway: Empowering participation through worker managed change', *Journal of Applied Behavioral Science*, vol. 23, no. 3, pp. 339–55.

Golembiewski, R. T. (ed.) (1979) *Approaches to Planned Change Parts I & II*, New York, Marcel Dekker.

Harris, P. R. (1985) *Management in Transition*, San Francisco, CA, Jossey-Bass.

Haveman, H. A. (1992) 'Between a rock and a hard place: Organizational change and performance under conditions of fundamental environmental transformation', *Administrative Science Quarterly*, vol. 37, pp. 48–75.

Kanter, R. M. (1983) *The Change Masters: Innovation and Entrepreneurship in the American Corporation*, New York, Simon and Schuster.

Kanter, R. M., Stein, B. A. and Jick, T. D. (1992) *The Challenge of Organizational Change: How Companies Experience It and Guide It*, New York, Free Press, MacMillan.

Kimberley, J. and Quinn, R. E. (1984) *Managing Organizational Transitions*, New York, Dow-Jones-Irwin.

Mason, R. O. and Mitroff, R. (1981) *Challenging Strategic Planning Assumptions*, New York, Wiley Interscience.

Miller, D. (1982) 'Evolution and revolution: A quantum view of structural change in organizations', *Journal of Management Studies*, vol. 19, no. 2, pp. 131–51.

Miller, D. and Friesen, P. H. (1984) *Organizations: A Quantum View*, New Jersey, Prentice Hall.

Mirvis, P. H. (1988) 'Organization development: Part 1 – An evolutionary perspective', *Research in Organizational Change and Development*, vol. 2, pp. 1–57.

Mirvis, P. H. (1990) 'Organization development: Part 2 – A revolutionary perspective', *Research in Organizational Change and Development*, vol. 4, pp. 1–66.

Muczuk, J. P. and Reimann, B. C. (1987) 'The case for directive leadership', *Academy of Management Executive*, vol. 1, no. 3, pp. 301–11.

Neumann, J. E. (1989) 'Why people don't participate in organizational change' in Woodman, R. W. and Pasmore, W. A. (eds) *Research in Organizational Change and Development* (Vol. 3), Greenwich, JAI Press.

Peters, J. (1988) *Thriving on Chaos: A Handbook for a Management Revolution*, New York, Alfred A Knoff.

Pettigrew, A. and Whipp, R. (1991) *Managing Change for Competitive Success*, Oxford, Blackwell.

Porras, J. I. and Silvers, R. C. (1991) 'Organization development and transformation', *Annual Review of Psychology*, vol. 42, pp. 51–78.

Quinn, J. B. (1980) *Strategies for Change: Logical Incrementalism*, New York, Irwin.

Salancik, B. R. and Pfeffer, J. (1978) *The External Control of Organizations: A Resource Dependence Perspective*, New York, Harper and Row.

Schein, E. (1985) *Organizational Culture and Leadership: A Dynamic View*, San Francisco, CA, Jossey-Bass.

Shaskin, M. (1984) 'Participative management is an ethical imperative', *Organizational Dynamics*, vol. 1, pp. 62–75.

Part III
Managing Change

Introduction

Thus far in this book we have worked inwards from the environmental drivers for change, down to the types of change we may need to think about within the context of an organisation. In Part III we will move on to the practical side of managing change; that is, what we actually have to do in order to achieve our objectives.

The first paper we consider is John Kotter's Harvard Business Review classic entitled 'Leading Change: Why Transformation Efforts Fail'. This paper is based on Kotter's own experience of organisations. He uses this experience to create a rubric for change, a set of rules which help to guide people through the process of change. Although Kotter notes that the model is limited; change is far more complex, multifaceted and political than could be accounted for in a single model of change, he presents his series of guidelines as 'a relatively simply vision' to help people steer themselves through the process.

In the next paper entitled 'Quality Management in the Twenty-First Century-Implementing Successful change', Oakland and Tanner have framed their practical consideration of change under the umbrella of quality management. It can be argued that most change management is in some way related to quality management, be that through improvements to products or services, by solving an organisational problem or by taking advantage of an environmental opportunity. Having extract five key themes of change management from the literature, Oakland and Tanner then use primary research to test the importance of these approaches. The conclusions they drew from their research led them to construct a double loop framework for change. The framework connects the key themes from the literature in an integrative framework which demonstrates the importance of the relationship between managing the organisations readiness for change and the processes of implementation.

The last paper in this part is a very practical paper which outlines a project management type approach to the management of organisational change. The paper, produced by the Victorian Quality Council, maps out a project management type approach to managing change. Aimed at people with little experience of leading or directing change within an organisational context, the paper presents some guiding principles and a number of key issues for consideration. Finally the paper presents a list of tips to help the first line manager to steer the changes successfully through.

Leading Change: Why Transformation Efforts Fail

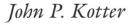

John P. Kotter

Over the past decade, I have watched more than 100 companies try to remake themselves into significantly better competitors. They have included large organizations (Ford) and small ones (Landmark Communications), companies based in the United States (General Motors) and elsewhere (British Airways), corporations that were on their knees (Eastern Airlines), and companies that were earning good money (Bristol-Myers Squibb). These efforts have gone under many banners: total quality management, reengineering, right sizing, restructuring, cultural change, and turnaround. But, in almost every case, the basic goal has been the same: to make fundamental changes in how business is conducted in order to help cope with a new, more challenging market environment.

A few of these corporate change efforts have been very successful. A few have been utter failures. Most fall somewhere in between, with a distinct tilt toward the lower end of the scale. The lessons that can be drawn are interesting and will probably be relevant to even more organizations in the increasingly competitive business environment of the coming decade.

The most general lesson to be learned from the more successful cases is that the change process goes through a series of phases that, in total, usually require a considerable length of time. Skipping steps creates only the illusion of speed and never produces a satisfying result. A second very general lesson is that critical mistakes in any of the phases can have a devastating impact, slowing momentum and negating hard-won gains. Perhaps because we have relatively little experience in renewing organizations, even very capable people often make at least one big error.

Kotter, J.P. (1995) 'Leading change: Why transformation efforts fail', *Harvard Business Review*, March–April, pp. 56–67.

Error #1: Not Establishing a Great Enough Sense of Urgency

Most successful change efforts begin when some individuals or some groups start to look hard at a company's competitive situation, market position, technological trends, and financial performance. They focus on the potential revenue drop when an important patent expires, the five-year trend in declining margins in a core business, or an emerging market that everyone seems to be ignoring. They then find ways to communicate this information broadly and dramatically, especially with respect to crises, potential crises, or great opportunities that are very timely. This first step is essential because just getting a transformation program started requires the aggressive cooperation of many individuals. Without motivation, people won't help and the effort goes nowhere.

Compared with other steps in the change process, phase one can sound easy. It is not. Well over 50% of the companies I have watched fail in this first phase. What are the reasons for that failure? Sometimes executives underestimate how hard it can be to drive people out of their comfort zones. Sometimes they grossly over-estimate how successful they have already been in increasing urgency. Sometimes they lack patience: 'Enough with the preliminaries; let's get on with it.' In many cases, executives become paralyzed by the downside possibilities. They worry that employees with seniority will become defensive, that morale will drop, that events will spin out of control, that short-term business results will be jeopardized, that the stock will sink, and that they will be blamed for creating a crisis.

A paralyzed senior management often comes from having too many managers and not enough leaders. Management's mandate is to minimize risk and to keep the current system operating. Change, by definition, requires creating a new system, which in turn always demands leadership. Phase one in a renewal process typically goes nowhere until enough real leaders are promoted or hired into senior-level jobs.

Transformations often begin, and begin well, when an organization has a new head who is a good leader and who sees the need for a major change. If the renewal target is the entire company, the CEO is key. If change is needed in a division, the division general manager is key. When these individuals are not new leaders, great leaders, or change champions, phase one can be a huge challenge.

Bad business results are both a blessing and a curse in the first phase. On the positive side, losing money does catch people's attention. But it also gives less maneuvering room. With good business results, the opposite is true: convincing people of the need for change is much harder, but you have more resources to help make changes.

But whether the starting point is good performance or bad, in the more successful cases I have witnessed, an individual or a group always facilitates a frank discussion of potentially unpleasant facts: about new competition, shrinking margins, decreasing market share, flat earnings, a lack of revenue growth, or other relevant indices of a declining competitive position. Because there seems to be an almost universal human tendency to shoot the bearer of bad news, especially if the head of the organization is not a change champion, executives in these companies often rely on outsiders to bring unwanted information. Wall Street analysts, customers, and consultants can all be helpful in this regard. The purpose of all this activity, in the words of one former CEO of a large European company, is 'to make the status quo seem more dangerous than launching into the unknown'.

In a few of the most successful cases, a group has manufactured a crisis. One CEO deliberately engineered the largest accounting loss in the company's history, creating huge pressures from Wall Street in the process. One division president commissioned first-ever customer-satisfaction surveys, knowing full well that the results would be terrible. He then made these findings public. On the surface, such moves can look unduly risky. But there is also risk in playing it too safe: when the urgency rate is not pumped up enough, the transformation process

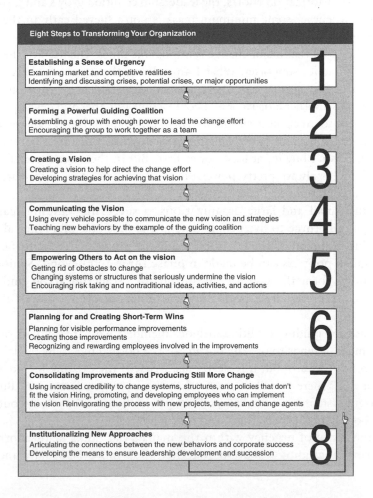

Eight Steps to Transforming Your Organization

1   **Establishing a Sense of Urgency**
Examining market and competitive realities
Identifying and discussing crises, potential crises, or major opportunities

2   **Forming a Powerful Guiding Coalition**
Assembling a group with enough power to lead the change effort
Encouraging the group to work together as a team

3   **Creating a Vision**
Creating a vision to help direct the change effort
Developing strategies for achieving that vision

4   **Communicating the Vision**
Using every vehicle possible to communicate the new vision and strategies
Teaching new behaviors by the example of the guiding coalition

5   **Empowering Others to Act on the vision**
Getting rid of obstacles to change
Changing systems or structures that seriously undermine the vision
Encouraging risk taking and nontraditional ideas, activities, and actions

6   **Planning for and Creating Short-Term Wins**
Planning for visible performance improvements
Creating those improvements
Recognizing and rewarding employees involved in the improvements

7   **Consolidating Improvements and Producing Still More Change**
Using increased credibility to change systems, structures, and policies that don't fit the vision Hiring, promoting, and developing employees who can implement the vision Reinvigorating the process with new projects, themes, and change agents

8   **Institutionalizing New Approaches**
Articulating the connections between the new behaviors and corporate success
Developing the means to ensure leadership development and succession

cannot succeed and the long-term future of the organization is put in jeopardy.

When is the urgency rate high enough? From what I have seen, the answer is when about 75% of a company's management is honestly convinced that business-as-usual is totally unacceptable. Anything less can produce very serious problems later on in the process.

Error #2: Not Creating a Powerful Enough Guiding Coalition

Major renewal programs often start with just one or two people. In cases of successful transformation efforts, the leadership coalition grows and grows over time. But whenever some minimum mass is not achieved early in the effort, nothing much worthwhile happens.

It is often said that major change is impossible unless the head of the organization is an active supporter. What I am talking about goes far beyond that. In successful transformations, the chairman or president or division general manager, plus another 5 or 15 or 50 people, come together and develop a shared commitment to excellent performance through renewal. In my experience, this group never includes all of the company's most senior executives because some people just won't buy in, at least not at first. But in the most successful cases, the coalition is always pretty powerful – in terms of titles, information and expertise, reputations and relationships.

In both small and large organizations, a successful guiding team may consist of only three to five people during the first year of a renewal effort. But in big companies, the coalition needs to grow to the 20 to 50 range before much progress can be made in phase three and beyond. Senior managers always form the core of the group. But sometimes you find board members, a representative from a key customer, or even a powerful union leader.

Because the guiding coalition includes members who are not part of senior management, it tends to operate outside of the normal hierarchy by definition. This can be awkward, but it is clearly necessary. If the existing hierarchy were working well, there would be no need for a major transformation. But since the current system is not working, reform generally demands activity outside of formal boundaries, expectations, and protocol.

A high sense of urgency within the managerial ranks helps enormously in putting a guiding coalition together. But more is usually required.

Someone needs to get these people together, help them develop a shared assessment of their company's problems and opportunities, and create a minimum level of trust and communication. Off-site retreats, for two or three days, are one popular vehicle for accomplishing this task. I have seen many groups of 5 to 35 executives attend a series of these retreats over a period of months.

Companies that fail in phase two usually underestimate the difficulties of producing change and thus the importance of a powerful guiding coalition. Sometimes they have no history of teamwork at the top and therefore undervalue the importance of this type of coalition. Sometimes they expect the team to be led by a staff executive from human resources, quality, or strategic planning instead of a key line manager. No matter how capable or dedicated the staff head, groups without strong line leadership never achieve the power that is required.

Efforts that don't have a powerful enough guiding coalition can make apparent progress for a while. But, sooner or later, the opposition gathers itself together and stops the change.

Error #3: Lacking a Vision

In every successful transformation effort that I have seen, the guiding coalition develops a picture of the future that is relatively easy to communicate and appeals to customers, stockholders, and employees. A vision always goes beyond the numbers that are typically found in five-year plans. A vision says something that helps clarify the direction in which an organization needs to move. Sometimes the first draft comes mostly from a single individual. It is usually a bit blurry, at least initially. But after the coalition works at it for 3 or 5 or even 12 months, something much better emerges through their tough analytical thinking and a little dreaming. Eventually, a strategy for achieving that vision is also developed.

In one midsize European company, the first pass at a vision contained two-thirds of the basic ideas that were in the final product. The concept of global reach was in the initial version from the beginning. So was the idea of becoming preeminent in certain businesses. But one central idea in the final version – getting out of low value-added activities – came only after a series of discussions over a period of several months.

Without a sensible vision, a transformation effort can easily dissolve into a list of confusing and incompatible projects that can take the organization in the wrong direction or nowhere at all. Without a sound vision, the reengineering project in the accounting department, the new 360-degree performance appraisal from the human resources department, the plant's quality program, the cultural change project in the sales force will not add up in a meaningful way.

In failed transformations, you often find plenty of plans and directives and programs, but no vision. In one case, a company gave out four-inch-thick notebooks describing its change effort. In mind-numbing detail, the books spelled out procedures, goals, methods, and deadlines. But nowhere was there a clear and compelling statement of where all this was leading. Not surprisingly, most of the employees with whom I talked were either confused or alienated. The big, thick books did not rally them together or inspire change. In fact, they probably had just the opposite effect.

In a few of the less successful cases that I have seen, management had a sense of direction, but it was too complicated or blurry to be useful. Recently, I asked an executive in a midsize company to describe his vision and received in return a barely comprehensible 30-minute lecture. Buried in his answer were the basic elements of a sound vision. But they were buried–deeply.

A useful rule of thumb: if you can't communicate the vision to someone in five minutes or less and get a reaction that signifies both understanding and interest, you are not yet done with this phase of the transformation process.

Error #4: Undercommunicating the Vision by a Factor of Ten

I've seen three patterns with respect to communication, all very common. In the first, a group actually does develop a pretty good transformation vision and then proceeds to communicate it by holding a single meeting or sending out a single communication. Having used about 0.0001% of the yearly intracompany communication, the group is startled that few people seem to understand the new approach. In the second pattern, the head of the organization spends a considerable amount of time making speeches to employee groups, but most people still don't get it (not surprising, since vision captures only 0.0005% of the total yearly communication). In the third pattern, much more effort goes into newsletters and speeches, but some very visible senior executives still behave in ways that are antithetical to the vision. The net result is that cynicism among the troops goes up, while belief in the communication goes down.

Transformation is impossible unless hundreds or thousands of people are willing to help, often to the point of making short-term sacrifices. Employees will not make sacrifices, even if they are unhappy with the status quo, unless they believe that useful change is possible. Without credible communication, and a lot of it, the hearts and minds of the troops are never captured.

This fourth phase is particularly challenging if the short-term sacrifices include job losses. Gaining understanding and support is tough when downsizing is a part of the vision. For this reason, successful visions usually include new growth possibilities and the commitment to treat fairly anyone who is laid off.

Executives who communicate well incorporate messages into their hour-by-hour activities. In a routine discussion about a business problem, they talk about how proposed solutions fit (or don't fit) into the bigger picture. In a regular performance appraisal, they talk about how the employee's behavior helps or undermines the vision. In a review of a division's quarterly performance, they talk not only about the numbers but also about how the division's executives are contributing to the transformation. In a routine Q&A with employees at a company facility, they tie their answers back to renewal goals.

In more successful transformation efforts, executives use all existing communication channels to broadcast the vision. They turn boring and unread company newsletters into lively articles about the vision. They take ritualistic and tedious quarterly management meetings and turn them into exciting discussions of the transformation. They throw out much of the company's generic management education and replace it with courses that focus on business problems and the new vision. The guiding principle is simple: use every possible channel, especially those that are being wasted on nonessential information.

Perhaps even more important, most of the executives I have known in successful cases of major change learn to 'walk the talk'. They consciously attempt to become a living symbol of the new corporate culture. This is often not easy. A 60-year-old plant manager who has spent precious little time over 40 years thinking about customers will not suddenly behave in a customer-oriented way. But I have witnessed just such a person change, and change a great deal. In that case, a high level of urgency helped. The fact that the man was a part of the guiding coalition and the vision-creation team also helped. So did all the communication, which kept reminding him of the desired behavior, and all the feedback from his peers and subordinates, which helped him see when he was not engaging in that behavior.

Communication comes in both words and deeds, and the latter are often the most powerful form. Nothing undermines change more than behavior by important individuals that is inconsistent with their words.

Error #5: Not Removing Obstacles to the New Vision

Successful transformations begin to involve large numbers of people as the process progresses. Employees are emboldened to try new approaches, to develop new ideas, and to provide leadership. The only constraint is that the actions fit within the broad parameters of the overall vision. The more people involved, the better the outcome.

To some degree, a guiding coalition empowers others to take action simply by successfully communicating the new direction. But communication is never sufficient by itself. Renewal also requires the removal of obstacles. Too often, an employee understands the new vision and wants to help make it happen. But an elephant appears to be blocking the path. In some cases, the elephant is in the person's head, and the challenge is to convince the individual that no external obstacle exists. But in most cases, the blockers are very real.

Sometimes the obstacle is the organizational structure: narrow job categories can seriously undermine efforts to increase productivity or make it very difficult even to think about customers. Sometimes compensation or performance-appraisal systems make people choose between the new vision and their own self-interest. Perhaps worst of all are bosses who refuse to change and who make demands that are inconsistent with the overall effort.

One company began its transformation process with much publicity and actually made good progress through the fourth phase. Then the change effort ground to a halt because the officer in charge of the company's largest division was allowed to undermine most of the new initiatives. He paid lip service to the process but did not change his behavior or encourage his managers to change. He did not reward the unconventional ideas called for in the vision. He allowed human resource systems to remain intact even when they were clearly inconsistent with the new ideals. I think the officer's motives were complex. To some degree, he did not believe the company needed major change. To some degree, he felt personally threatened by all the change. To some degree, he was afraid that he could not produce both change and the expected operating profit. But despite the fact that they backed the renewal effort, the other officers did virtually nothing to stop the one blocker. Again, the reasons were complex. The company had no history of confronting problems like this. Some people were afraid of the officer. The CEO was concerned that he might lose a talented executive. The net result was disastrous. Lower level managers concluded that senior management had lied to them about their commitment to renewal, cynicism grew, and the whole effort collapsed.

In the first half of a transformation, no organization has the momentum, power, or time to get rid of all obstacles. But the big ones must be confronted and removed. If the blocker is a person, it is important that he or she be treated fairly and in a way that is consistent with the new vision. But action is essential, both to empower others and to maintain the credibility of the change effort as a whole.

Error #6: Not Systematically Planning For and Creating Short-Term Wins

Real transformation takes time, and a renewal effort risks losing momentum if there are no short-term goals to meet and celebrate. Most people won't go on the long march unless they see compelling evidence within 12 to 24 months that the journey is producing expected results. Without short-term wins, too many people give up or actively join the ranks of those people who have been resisting change.

One to two years into a successful transformation effort, you find quality beginning to go up on certain indices or the decline in net income stopping. You find some successful new product introductions or an upward shift in market share. You find an impressive productivity improvement or a statistically higher customer-satisfaction rating. But whatever the case, the win is unambiguous. The result is not just a judgment call that can be discounted by those opposing change.

Creating short-term wins is different from hoping for short-term wins. The latter is passive, the former active. In a successful transformation, managers actively look for ways to obtain clear performance improvements, establish goals in the yearly planning system, achieve the objectives, and reward the people involved with recognition, promotions, and even money. For example, the guiding coalition at a U.S. manufacturing company produced a highly visible and successful new product introduction about 20 months after the start of its renewal effort. The new product was selected about six months into the effort because it met multiple criteria: it could be designed and launched in a relatively short period; it could be handled by a small team of people who were devoted to the new vision; it had upside potential; and the new product-development team could operate outside the established departmental structure without practical problems. Little was left to chance, and the win boosted the credibility of the renewal process.

Managers often complain about being forced to produce short-term wins, but I've found that pressure can be a useful element in a change effort.

When it becomes clear to people that major change will take a long time, urgency levels can drop. Commitments to produce short-term wins help keep the urgency level up and force detailed analytical thinking that can clarify or revise visions.

Error #7: Declaring Victory Too Soon

After a few years of hard work, managers may be tempted to declare victory with the first clear performance improvement. While celebrating a win is fine, declaring the war won can be catastrophic. Until changes sink deeply into a company's culture, a process that can take five to ten years, new approaches are fragile and subject to regression.

In the recent past, I have watched a dozen change efforts operate under the reengineering theme. In all but two cases, victory was declared and the expensive consultants were paid and thanked when the first major project was completed after two to three years. Within two more years, the useful changes that had been introduced slowly disappeared. In two of the ten cases, it's hard to find any trace of the reengineering work today.

Over the past 20 years, I've seen the same sort of thing happen to huge quality projects, organizational development efforts, and more. Typically, the problems start early in the process: the urgency level is not intense enough, the guiding coalition is not powerful enough, and the vision is not clear enough. But it is the premature victory celebration that kills momentum. And then the powerful forces associated with tradition take over.

Ironically, it is often a combination of change initiators and change resistors that creates the premature victory celebration. In their enthusiasm over a clear sign of progress, the initiators go overboard. They are then joined by resistors, who are quick to spot any opportunity to stop change. After the celebration is over, the resistors point to the victory as a sign that the war has been won and the troops should be sent home. Weary troops allow themselves to be convinced that they won. Once home, the foot soldiers are reluctant to climb back on the ships. Soon thereafter, change comes to a halt, and tradition creeps back in.

Instead of declaring victory, leaders of successful efforts use the credibility afforded by short-term wins to tackle even bigger problems. They go after systems and structures that are not consistent with the transformation vision and have not been confronted before. They pay great attention to who is promoted, who is hired, and how people are developed. They include new reengineering projects that are even bigger in scope than the initial ones. They understand that renewal efforts take not months but years. In fact, in one of the most successful transformations that I have ever seen, we quantified the amount of change that occurred each year over a seven-year period. On a scale of one (low) to ten (high), year one received a two, year two a four, year three a three, year four a seven, year five an eight, year six a four, and year seven a two. The peak came in year five, fully 36 months after the first set of visible wins.

Error #8: Not Anchoring Changes in the Corporation's Culture

In the final analysis, change sticks when it becomes 'the way we do things around here', when it seeps into the bloodstream of the corporate body. Until new behaviors are rooted in social norms and shared values, they are subject to degradation as soon as the pressure for change is removed.

Two factors are particularly important in institutionalizing change in corporate culture. The first is a conscious attempt to show people how the new approaches, behaviors, and attitudes have helped improve performance. When people are left on their own to make the connections, they sometimes create very inaccurate links. For example, because results improved while charismatic Harry was boss, the troops link his mostly idiosyncratic style with those results instead of seeing how their own improved customer service and productivity were instrumental. Helping people see the right connections requires communication. Indeed, one company was relentless, and it paid off enormously. Time was spent at every major management meeting to discuss why performance was increasing. The company newspaper ran article after article showing how changes had boosted earnings.

The second factor is taking sufficient time to make sure that the next generation of top management really does personify the new approach. If the requirements for promotion don't change, renewal rarely lasts. One bad succession decision at the top of an organization can undermine a decade of hard work. Poor succession decisions are possible when boards of directors are not an integral part of the renewal effort. In at least three instances I have seen, the champion for change was the retiring executive, and although his successor was not a resistor, he was not a change champion. Because the boards did not understand the transformations in any detail, they could not see that their choices were not good fits. The retiring executive in one case tried unsuccessfully to talk his board into a less seasoned candidate who better personified the transformation. In the other two cases, the CEOs did not resist the boards' choices, because they felt the transformation could not be undone by their successors. They were wrong. Within two years, signs of renewal began to disappear at both companies.

There are still more mistakes that people make, but these eight are the big ones. I realize that in a short article everything is made to sound a bit too simplistic. In reality, even successful change efforts are messy and full of surprises. But just as a relatively simple vision is needed to guide people through a major change, so a vision of the change process can reduce the error rate. And fewer errors can spell the difference between success and failure.

Quality Management in the 21st Century – Implementing Successful Change

John S. Oakland and Steve J. Tanner

Introduction

Brown and Eisenhardt (1998) noted that developing technology, the changing needs of stakeholders and economic pressures all contribute to the need for organisations worldwide to significantly modify the way they do things. Major organisational change requires huge investments in energy, time and resources, but our own experience has shown that many change programmes fail to meet expectations. Published estimates of success levels can be as low as 10%, although other authors often quote a 30% success rate as an average from organisations' experiences (Higgs and Rowland, 2000; Smith, 2003).

The literature is full of models and frameworks offering solutions. Research by Bain and Company revealed that, having employed more than three new tools or techniques annually for the previous 5 years, the typical company was planning to adopt another 3.7 in the coming 12 months (Ghoshal and Bartlett, 1997). As succinctly put by Schaffer and Thompson (1992), 'Most improvement efforts have as much impact on company performance as a rain dance has on the weather'.

In a business environment, where the average tenure of the Chief Executive is reducing on a year on year basis, never has there been a time when the management of change has been so critical. This pressure has not been reserved

Oakland J. S. and Tanner S. J. (2006) 'Quality management in the 21st century – implementing successful change', *International Journal of Productivity and Quality Management*, vol. 1, no. 1–2, pp. 69–87.

for just private sector organisations; public sector management is also feeling the force of change. The research reported in this paper had the aim of identifying the critical factors reported by organisations in their quest to manage change successfully.

The Aspects of Successful Business Change

Our review of the literature examining the drivers of successful change identified five main themes. These were leadership, project management, processes, people and learning.

The Role of Leadership in Change

Leadership has a key role to play, both in setting direction, inspiring change throughout the organisation and ensuring that change is implemented. Many authors have noted that leadership is so important (e.g. Beer and Nohria, 2000; Collins, 2001; Guha et al., 1997; Jones, 2004; Kotter, 1995; Martin and Cheung, 2002; Senge et al., 1999). In achieving world-class performance, leaders have a role developing a number of critical competencies related to helping to focus individual attention on organisational mind-sets, facilitating strategy implementation and building change capability (Higgs and Rowland, 2000).

An important ingredient in the right cultural mix for successful change is an atmosphere of open communication, participation, and cross-training (Guha et al., 1997; Martensen and Dahlgaard, 1999), which is driven by the leadership style. Executive and departmental (or business-unit) levels should be aligned in support of the change. There appear to be two focal points of power and leadership that need to coordinate their efforts: the executive leadership at the enterprise level and the middle rank of leadership at the department, division, or business unit level. Executives control strategy and resources, while middle management coordinates deployment of the resources to accomplish the strategic objectives (Smith, 2003).

To quell likely pockets of resistance, an organisation's 'vision' for change must be embraced throughout all levels of the organisation, especially by those functional and middle-level managers affected by the process change (Kaplan and Norton, 2001). To achieve this requires continuous articulation and communication of the value of reporting results and how each individual contributing and accountable to the overall company's change effort (Guha et al., 1997).

The role of the sponsor is pivotal (Martin and Cheung, 2002; Smith, 2003). The sponsor should be versed in developing support for the change among key executives, organising the project's infrastructure (for example, appointing a capable and dedicated project team), positioning the change initiative with stakeholders, protecting project commitments from other organisational priorities, and demonstrating continued support for the effort in ways that are visible to stakeholders.

Communication throughout the project is critical to developing and maintaining stakeholder support. As mentioned previously, the sponsor needs to communicate his or her support for the change, and progress should be tracked and publicised. It is also important that people understand what they had to do to make the change successful. Conversely, failed efforts were characterised by vague goals and poor communication (Smith, 2003).

There tend to be strategic 'stimuli' ranging from financial pressures, continued market leaderships, customer dissatisfaction and/or organisation inefficiencies that trigger firms to undertake business change (Guha et al., 1997). The stimulus itself is not necessarily a determinant of success, but organisations attempting to change performance radically seem to require some 'sense of urgency' in their business situation, which translates in turn into a compelling vision that is espoused throughout the organisation.

Project Management

Second, and related to leadership, is the need to identify and define the change that is required. This is often linked to financial pressure. A project management approach is the most successful approach when implementing such change (Martin and Cheung, 2002; Smith, 2003; Turner and Peymai, 1995), with a need to define clear success measures being important.

Given the dismal rate of success, it seems reasonable to provide for the contingency of recovering from barriers that stymie a project. Tactics for revitalising stalled projects should be defined. Planning should emphasise keeping the change manageable. The challenge is to achieve the change objectives without jeopardising other strategic interests. There are tactics to accomplish this, such as:

- phasing the change effort across business units
- cascading the change down the management hierarchy
- successive approximations whereby the change is viewed as a learning curve with intermediate targets that gradually lead to the desired end state (Smith, 2003).

Incremental process change can work but this appears to be appropriate when risk aversion is lower and environmental conditions less dire (Guha et al., 1997). Execution is the real difference between success and failure (Paper et al., 2001). The implementation plan should provide for replacement of key players given the time span associated with process change and the normal turnover rates for senior and middle managers (Smith, 2003).

Processes

Measurement is key to success (Oakland, 2003; Tanner and Oakland, 2005). A well-defined process management approach should include a documented methodology of change, use objective and quantified metrics showing the value of change, continuously communicate process metrics to senior management, and possess a well-documented rollout of the new process design. (Guha et al., 1997).

Process mapping is the mechanism used to map and understand complex business processes (Oakland, 2003; Tanner and Oakland, 2005). The systematic nature of the process mapping methodology keeps people focused and acts as a rallying point. Moreover, process mapping provides a common language for everyone involved in the project (Paper et al., 2001).

Process improvements should be aligned with business objectives and focussed on what the business needs to change to become more successful. In this case, effective communication of ideas from top management throughout the enterprise is imperative. In addition, organisations should be wary of the 'I've arrived' syndrome. Change is continuous and is never over (Paper et al., 2001).

People

Managing change also has its softer side. People are the essential contributors to successful change, and managing change within the culture of an organisation is important. As already noted, good communication is also vital (Guha et al., 1997; Smith, 2003).

Once a team perceives that they 'own' a project, they tend to want to make it work. It becomes 'their' project. In addition, management should encourage people to be dissatisfied with the way things are currently done. However, punishing people for complaining about ineffective work processes is an effective way to promote the status quo (Paper et al., 2001).

While support from the top is critical, actual implementation should be carried out from the bottom up. The idea of empowerment is to push decisions down to where the work is actually done. Process mapping o systematic and proven methodologies that help support empowered teams. Business processes are complex, but process mapping offers a comprehensive blueprint of the existing state. The blueprint enables systematic identification of opportunities for improvement. People are unpredictable. They cannot be modelled or categorised universally. However, people do the work and therefore must be trained, facilitated, and nurtured. Balanced consideration of the social, technical, and business value elements should be maintained throughout the project (Guha et al., 1997).

Successful change projects establish an objective and unbiased team or individual that continues to push the organisation and line functions to find new innovative processes. These 'challengers' must be empowered to implement the changes without barriers from functional managers (Guha et al., 1997).

Learning

Organisational learning is key to managing change successfully (Senge, 1999; Senge et al., 1999). Some organisations see the involvement of external consultants to be important when managing chance. They provide industry expertise, skilled resource, and change management knowledge and experience to the project (Guha et al., 1997; Martin and Cheung, 2002). Once the change has been completed, organisations also capture the learning both at a project and at an organisational level (Young, 1998).

Successful change projects are enabled in organisations that: have a propensity to learn from best practice and customer needs; exhibit deutero learning whereby employees individually and collectively reflect on their past experiences, modify their course when necessary, and discover new opportunities (Guha et al., 1997).

Summary of the Aspects of Successful Business Change

These five areas, leadership, project management, processes, people and learning, formed a basic framework for our research. The main aim of the research was to identify the factors that were reported as being critical to managing change successfully within both public and private sector organisations. The research addressed strategic change, step change and continuous improvement approaches, identifying the barriers to change and how to overcome them.

Methodology

The aim of the research called for the collection of factors that had led to successful change in organisations. Senior managers, typically at board level, or their direct reports, were approached in 34 organisations and invited to participate in the research. The sample was selected on a convenience basis (Moser and Kalton, 1971) by choosing a cross section of European-based organisations that were known to us as being role models for managing change successfully.

Twenty-eight organisations agreed to participate, representing an 82% response rate. The breakdown of these organisations has been given in Figure 8.1.

Interviews, which typically lasted for 1 hour, were conducted face-to-face or over the telephone. Data was collected using a semi-structured questionnaire, the basic structure of which is given in Table 8.1.

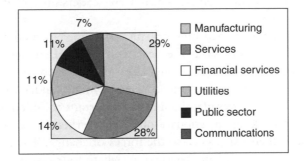

Figure 8.1 Breakdown of participating organizations

Table 8.1 Components of the questionnaire

Questionnaire section	Main contents
Introduction	Background information such the respondents' name and position
Drivers for change	The context of the change being described
	The need for the change
Preparing for change	Leadership and strategic alignment
	Planning for change
	Controlling change
	Managing stakeholders
	Using external support
	Establishing success measures
Implementing change	Maturity of process management
	Organisational structure
	Training and development
	Managing cultural changes
	Monitoring behaviours
	Performance measurement and benefits evaluation
	Risk management
	Managing communications
	Learning
Forces of change	Practices supporting the change
	Practices hindering the change
	Future perspective

Analysis of the Responses

The results have been presented in order of three broad themes. Firstly, organisations were asked to identify the triggers for change. Secondly, the way that the organisation prepared for change was examined, which led to the identification of two sub-themes, which were leadership and direction, and planning for change.

The third theme examined how organisations implemented change. A key finding was that processes sit at the heart of successful change programmes. In addition, consideration was given to the organisation's structure and its resources, as well as its systems and controls. Finally, under this theme, the behaviour of the people was identified as an important consideration.

In addition to asking questions around these themes, respondents were asked to identify their experience of the forces of change. Their responses are summarised in the last part of this section, where four common factors were identified.

Triggers for Change

We focused on a particular change programme in the organisation and asked respondents to identify the major drivers of the change. These fell into two categories: external drivers and internal drivers for change, as shown in Table 8.2.

The first impression from the list of drivers in Table 8.2 was that there are two different agendas for change. But on reflection, the internal drivers were considered to be a manifestation of external drivers for change. For example, if customers are becoming more demanding then, internally, there will be a need to improve the quality of products and services, or improve the innovation process.

The conclusion was that organisations in the research were all driven to change due to external, strategic drivers. But at the same time there was an operational context that had to be taken into account. A consequence of this

Table 8.2 Main drivers for change

External drivers	Internal drivers
Customer requirements	Improving operational efficiency
Demand from other stakeholders, such as the government	Need to improve the quality of products and services
Regulatory demand	Process improvement
Market competition	
Shareholders/city	

conclusion is that to manage change successfully, there is a need for a focus on both strategic and operational issues, with both being closely linked.

Preparing for Change

The previous section noted a first finding from the research, which was that successful change focuses on both strategic and operational issues. Under the umbrella of preparing for change two more themes emerged from the research. These were the role that leaders play in establishing direction and the way organisations plan for change.

Leadership and Direction

Respondents were asked how senior managers identify and select priorities for change. Perhaps surprisingly, identification and selection of priorities for change were based mainly on cost/financial considerations, with improving efficiency with respect to customers and operations coming a poor second.

Before making a decision, leaders were found to develop alternative scenarios and not just go with their first idea. Once the decision was made to change something, leaders stayed with the decision, accepting the risks associated with it. They also set clear success criteria on which to direct and evaluate the project.

In terms of the project management and governance for the change programme in question:

- projects tend to be led from the top and carried out by team members from a variety of hierarchies and functions
- sponsors, executive boards, steering committees and project teams were the norm
- progress reporting based on measurable outputs was used most often.

An interesting result was that, besides leadership support for change programmes, the data indicates equal importance being given to the need for project teams and the inclusion of employees. This reflects the balance that needs to be made between 'Project Hierarchy' and 'Functional Hierarchy' when managing change (Turner, 1993).

The majority of the organisations consult and communicate regularly with key stakeholders, as shown by the data in Figure 8.2. Storytelling was a common approach to aid the communication of the change with the organisation's people. The focus of most of this communication was found to be top-down, with executive boards and steering committees being central to communication. This top-down preference may be a consequence of the stronger focus on cost and financial considerations when selecting priorities for change.

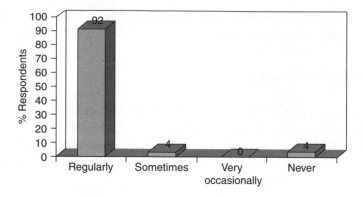

Figure 8.2   Communications with key stakeholders

Almost all organisations used external support at some point in their change or improvement programme and most external support was highly regarded. The analysis indicates that consultants are used in a wide variety of roles, with training and technical support being the main ones.

Preparing for Change

Most organisations were found to specify clear targets in their project plan and, where targets are broad, this is often intentional or unavoidable – not too convincing when we recognise the high levels of failures in change programmes. Figure 8.3 provides the responses to the question regarding the inclusion of targets in the project plan.

The expected objectives and benefits of the change programme are interesting. Expected long-term objectives and benefits are strongly related to the drivers of change and, therefore, evolve around cost reduction, cultural alignment, better customer relationship and operational effectiveness and efficiency. Short-term objectives and benefits lie in operational improvements. Others include better communication and cultural aspects. Some organisations do not state short-term objectives and benefits.

Most metrics and targets put in place to measure the success of the change relate back to the drivers and expected benefits. The main success measures include cost, operational effectiveness/efficiency and various customer measures.

Less than half of the organisations either run a pilot implementation or do some feasibility testing (Figure 8.4). Where this did not occur, it was often stated to be not appropriate or applicable.

When asked, 'Did you review previous change initiatives to learn from them and aid this change programme?' some organisations conduct at least some review and learn from previous change initiatives, but a worrying 25% did not (Figure 8.5).

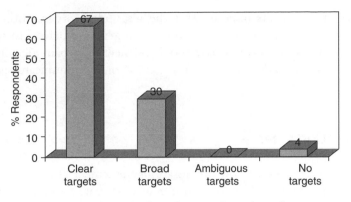

Figure 8.3   Inclusion of targets in project plans

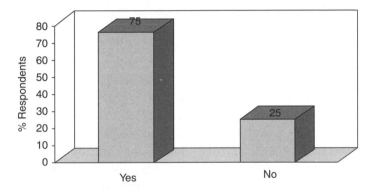

Figure 8.4   Pilot implementation experience

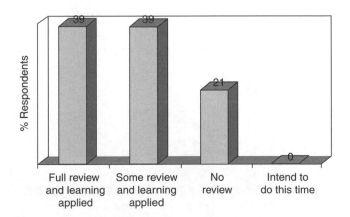

Figure 8.5   Review and learning from previous change programmes

Analysis of the results indicates that the respondent organisations understand well the importance of relating project targets and drivers to measures and most organisations do not have problems meeting project deadlines, but only some always meet deadlines. Many organisations communicate results and learning.

Implementing Change

The third theme considers how organisations implement change successfully. One of the major findings from the research was that it was common for organisations to do this through a process-centred approach. It was also found that there was a need to consider the impact of the change on the organisation and resources, the systems and controls, and finally the behaviours of the actors in the changed organisation.

Processes at the Centre of the Change

As shown in Figure 8.6, respondent organisations claim to define and document all or most of their new processes. The majority have fully established process ownership and governance (Figure 8.7).

Organisations were found to use a variety of means for process deployment, including workshops, the intranet, training sessions, and one-to-one coaching. Frequently, people directly involved in improving the processes are responsible for their deployment. The results also show support for the importance of people involvement in change management – communication and information are regarded as highly important.

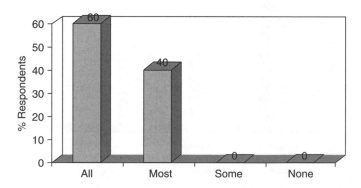

Figure 8.6   Degree to which new processes are defined and documented

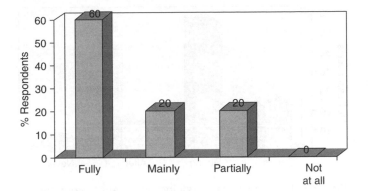

Figure 8.7   Degree of process ownership and governance

When asked about evaluating and mitigating for the risks associated with the change, the responses suggested that risk assessment was considered at the planning stage of a project. There was recognition that risks had to be managed throughout the project. Generally, a fairly robust approach seems to have been adopted in most cases with some organisations having developed alternative solutions when evaluating and mitigating for the risks.

Organisation and Resource

It was interesting to understand how new organisation structures, developed during the change programme, enable efficient and effective end-to-end process operation. Not many organisations appear to restructure as part of their change management programmes. It was found that most enabling factors relate to putting measures in place that directly relate to the drivers and expected benefits of the programme or outputs from the new processes. However, how people's competencies are identified and matched to new roles fitted into three categories:

- some organisations try to match process needs with people's competencies
- skills matrix and gap analysis assessment can lead to subsequent training in some cases
- frequently, there were no new roles created as a result of the change/ improvement programme.

Most organisations do training before or during the change programme, but some respondents do training throughout the programme (Figure 8.8).

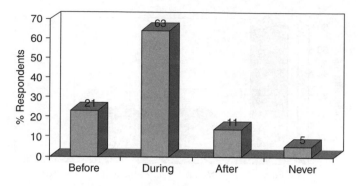

Figure 8.8 Occurrence of training due change programmes

Systems and Controls

When asked about how any new policies were defined and deployed, there seemed to be some confusion between policies, processes and procedures. Several change/improvement programmes did not result in new policies. As an example, where the Six Sigma DMAIC system had been part of the change programme, consideration of new systems and policies was evident in the 'improve' and 'control' phases. Some respondents claimed that new policies were mainly defined and deployed via computer systems and management systems. Training was occasionally used.

In terms of performance measures being defined and measured:

- for Six Sigma, this was done in the Analyse part of DMAIC
- some organisations define key performance indicators at the outset of the project
- measures are based mainly on drivers for the change programme i.e. cost and operational measures
- some performance measures related to key outputs of the process.

The realisation of the expected outcomes/benefits of the change programme was perceived as either very well or well. All organisations conducted or intend to conduct a post-completion review that included a review of benefits achieved. As Figure 8.9 shows, most organisations interviewed had seen substantial or some measurable improvement to core business results, but for others it was too early to be able to comment on the level of benefits achieved.

Behaviours

Respondents were asked how they assessed, communicated and implemented necessary changes in behaviour. This seems to be an area lacking focus/attention

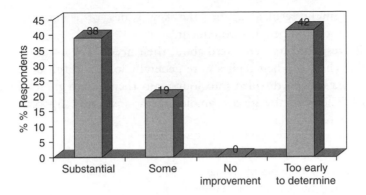

Figure 8.9   Measurable improvement to core business results

Table 8.3   Common enablers and barriers to change

Practices helping change	Practices hindering change
Data-led analysis (hard facts) is an important aspect	Changes in the organisation, e.g. re-design, departure of MD
Cross functional teams with high performers and the right skills	Lack of communication
Disciplined project management	General issues based on resistance to change and project management issues i.e. silo-thinking, delays etc.
Clear accountability and goals	Too little top management involvement
Stakeholder management	
Process thinking	
Communication	
Staff involvement	
Senior management commitment	

in some organisations, whilst others use many forms of communication, formally as well as informally, involving as many employees as possible. The results generally indicate strong support for communication to all people in the organisation.

Enablers and Barriers to Change

Organisations were asked what practices significantly *helped* or *hindered* the change programme. Table 8.3 summarises the responses.

Encouragingly results support the key issues of change management communication and people involvement.

Finally, respondents were asked about their needs now in terms of delivering lasting change. Their replies were generally long and full of feeling. The responses have been distilled into four main themes and these are given in Table 8.4. The table also gives examples of responses that support the themes identified, which were:

- extending or completing the change
- evaluating the benefits of change
- maximising the benefits of change
- approach to managing future change.

Table 8.4 Future needs to deliver lasting change

Theme	Example evidence to support theme
Extending or completing the change	The change is reasonably self-sufficient; but we need an on-going emphasis on improving what's in place and a wider roll out/implementation to other areas.
	A full roll out is now required. The plan for this will be put together after the final review of the pilot programme.
	Buy-in from Senior Executive Team. Buy-in from staff at all levels. Sufficient time and space to go through a change programme of this size.
	Currently at the beginning of the process – perception it will take 2–3 years to get embedded. Need to get to critical mass of advocates – need to get to position where it doesn't rely on 2–3 individuals to move forward and rollout. Need to get to self-sustaining position.
	Programme is over the peak and need to wind down to the finish.
	Culture and attitude improvement is imperative.
	Continuity, and access to people. Support from senior team.
Evaluating the benefits change Maximising of change	Put in place regular management information flows and a 'business as usual' team to monitor the benefits after the dedicated project team have disbanded.
	Clear, measurable review process established.
	Stability to allow the organisation to see the real impact and benefits from the changes (with respect to costs).
	Evaluate where to use the new techniques in the business and what to do with the internal experts that have been developed in the business.

Continued

	Table 8.4 Continued
Theme	**Example evidence to support theme**
	The programme provides a framework for the foreseeable future, in terms of: processes/operational, cultural/human performance, customers. Need to carry on driving the benefits out from it after the 2 years.
	Focus on where we are going; clear understanding of goal. Carry on doing what we're doing.
	Keep the momentum going – holding a reunion event next week; plan to have 2–3 a year for the next couple of years to reinforce the learning and the networking.
	Full involvement of managers to run the new systems when they are rolled out.
	Celebrating success to reinforce benefits.
	Continue to follow through the benefits realisation for some years.
	HR need to hand hold some companies/businesses where there is resistance, to reinforce the new ways.
Approach to managing future change	Key message (and challenge) is that change is the beginning of everlasting change.
	Still need an agreed and integrated approach to change to enable both radical and incremental change to be coordinated and efficient.
	Continuous improvement of the process and the IT systems. Also continuous alignment with the organisation's strategy.
	More commercial focus in the organisation.
	Invest time to plan projects properly and manage formerly.
	Get programme resources sufficient to implement the programme in the correct time frame – utilise expertise within the force, plus consultants.

Identifying the Drivers of Successful Change

A number of key insights have been identified from this research and each of these is discussed in turn.

The Agenda for Change is Driven by External Events

All the organisations interviewed were reacting to shifts in their external environment when introducing their change programme. Many of these could be traced to an external event, such as a regulatory change or increased competition. Even when internal reasons were given for the need to change, these could be related to some form of external pressure on the organisation.

In some cases, the changes made by the organisation were proactive in that action was being taken to prevent a future performance problem. But it was more common that the organisation's reaction was playing 'catch-up'. Scanning the external environment and taking action in advance to be 'ahead of the game' could possibly improve an organisation's ability to implement improvements.

Leaders Set a Clear Direction and Manage Risks

The research indicated that leaders identify and select priorities for change. One feature of successful change programmes was that before making the decision alternatives were considered, but in the end leaders made a definite decision to change something and stuck with it, accepting that there were risks associated with any decision. Once the decision was made leaders set success criteria and communicated the need for the change, often using storytelling as an approach.

The Need for Change must be Aligned to the Operational Issues

The External event that triggers the change forms part of the strategic context of the change. But the need must be translated into an operational context so people in the organisation understand how they will be affected and what must be done to address the challenge. As an example, if there is a need to become more competitive or react to a government initiative, the strategic need can be translated into quantifiable efficiency and effectiveness improvements that are understood at an operational level. This link is a central role of the leadership of the organisation as they set direction. If the link is broken between the strategic and operational issues there is a risk of misdirected effort leading to no or limited bottom-line benefits or the change will never get off the starting blocks.

A Process Approach is Central to Successful Change

The previous observation, the need for leaders to translate the high level strategic change into operational terms, explains why process management sits at the heart of a successful change programme. Process thinking is a vehicle to understand and review the work actually performed within the organisation. It also enables full participation in the change process and a way of establishing current and future performance levels. In essence, process thinking provides a hands-on well proven approach to deliver improvement. The processes need to be understood, measured and improved.

Performance Measurement has a Key Role in Supporting Change

Four sub-themes were identified from the 'implementing the change' theme in the research. These were processes at the centre of the change, organisation and resource, systems and controls, and behaviours. The first of these sub-themes, processes, has just been discussed. A second component identified from the systems and controls sub-theme that played a critical role was performance measurement. Performance measurement was seen as critical to assessing the levels of performance both before and after the change, and to providing a control during the change. Good performance measurement also allows target areas for improvement to be identified and has a key role in communication.

A Project-Based Approach Increases the Chance of Success

A common theme was the use of project management to deliver change. Project management includes the activities of planning, communication, establishing targets and learning from the change. The research indicated that this is an area where there is scope for improvement within many organisations. In particular the area of setting clear measurable objectives for the change and evaluating their achievement may be singled out for attention. Two other areas were learning from change and the need stability and to keep a focus on the project right through to completion so that all the potential benefits are delivered.

External Support Adds Value in Managing Change and the Transfer of Knowledge

One of the beliefs changed as a result of the research related to the use of external support. Before the research was conducted it was perceived that organisations would avoid using external consultants unless absolutely necessary. But the research indicated that it was generally recognised that lack of technical and project management expertise proved to be barriers to successful change. Several organisations had realised that the only way to gain access to such expertise was through the use of consultants. Consultants had to be selected wisely, however, only choosing consultants who were prepared to transfer their knowledge to the organisation during the duration of the programme.

Aligning the Culture to Support Changes in Peoples' Behaviour

At the end of most change programmes, there is a need for people to do things differently. The final insight relates to the change to the behaviour of the people, which impacts the culture of the organisation. This was most effective where the proposed change was aligned to the existing culture. For example, where there was a need to improve customer service in a customer focused organisation. Organisations reported the need to identify those aspects of the culture that reinforced the change and use these as key enablers. Similarly where the culture was judged to a barrier to the change, steps were taken to try and minimise resistance, for example, though the use of internal marketing and though the action of leaders.

Continuous Review

Successful change requires leaders to continually negotiate all aspects of the change approach. For example, they need to challenge the priorities, structure and programme metrics to ensure they are driving the desired behaviours and delivering the required benefits.

In Summary

In summary, the analysis of the responses provided support for the main themes that were identified from the literature review, these being:

- the triggers for change
- preparing for change
- implementing change.

A number of insights have been identified from the research, and these are the basis of the organisational change framework. Given the common nature of the themes that were identified during the research it is believed that this will provide a valuable framework for organisations that are undertaking, or plan to undertake, either an incremental or large-scale change programme. It identifies two main constructs of change management consistent with the thoughts of others, which can be better understood within the overall framework for change as shown in Figure 8.10.

Based on the results of our research, the change framework has two interacting cycles (Carnall, 1994): 'readiness for change', and 'implementing change'.

The experiences of many organisations that have launched change programmes, such as six sigma, is that the first part – readiness – is not at all well understood or developed. This often results in a rush into implementation, with huge emphases on training programmes and projects. Even managers in the General Electric, who are famed for their six-sigma programme, have admitted that they have found themselves going round and round the lower circle without engaging the strategic alignment offered by the upper one.

To break into the top circle we need to start with the *Drivers of Change* – it is important to understand what are the key drivers for change inside or outside the organisation, in order that the *Need for Change* may be understood and articulated to focus the stakeholders' desire for change. This is where leaders give meaning to the change, without which, as many organisations later discover, initial enthusiasm and energy quickly dissolves. For example, what are the drivers for the introduction of digital technology into BBC World Service – reduced

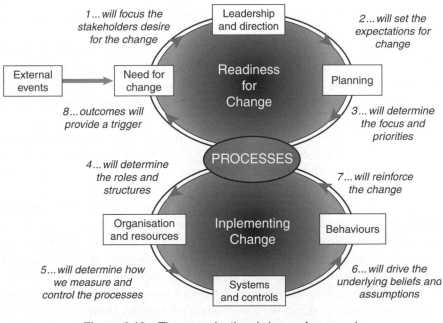

Figure 8.10 The organisational change framework

costs, better programme reception, more effective programme making? Clarity on this is key, as from it derives clear and consistent *Leadership and Direction* to turn the need into expectations – values, aims, measured objectives and targets. Robust *Planning* then allows the priorities to emerge and focuses people's minds on the strategic objectives.

The implementation of change is a rich tapestry of potential failure – a minefield for the unsuspecting. Worse than that, most managers tend to find they have entered the minefield at the wrong point. Trying to change behaviours, for example, is a frequent starting point for many 'programmes'. These programmes include such matters as attitudes and empowerment, without bedding these things in the reality of the business.

Following clarity on need, clear and unambiguous leadership, direction and good detailed planning, the first port of call must be the organisational *Processes* in which people live and work. Whether we like it or not, and whether we have worked them out or not, the processes drive the way the *Organisation & Resources* work – the structure, roles, competencies and resources deployed. Performance measures and technology then support the organisation's *Systems and Controls*. This is where *Behaviour* comes in – all of the above drives behaviour – the way the organisation is structured, who my boss is, how I am measured, the processes and systems – good or bad – that I live and work in. When managers talk about attitudes of the people it might be interesting for them to understand where these come from. Attitudes stem from beliefs and values, both of which are management's responsibility to influence. Most people start work for an organisation with positive attitudes and behaviours and it is frequently the systems and environment that cause problems and deterioration.

The 'figure of eight' closes when we return to the process for it is our behaviour that makes the processes work or not, resulting in achievements in quality and on time delivery, or not. Taking another trip round the figure of eight will verify the change protocols and ensure that anchorage to the strategies is maintained.

World-class organisations, of which there need to be more in most countries, are doing *all* of these things. They have implemented their version of the framework and are achieving world-class performance and results. What this requires first, of course, is world-class leadership and commitment.

It is often difficult for managers to stand back and view their work on change in a holistic fashion. Personal agendas can lead to a push on human resource or information technology issues, preventing the holistic view. This is where an external view can be so helpful. An output of the 'leadership' box may be scenarios for reacting to the need for change … there's usually more than one way to address the need and managers often benefit from external support in asking the questions that lead to alternative routes to change.

Conclusions

The research described in this paper set out to identify the factors contributing to successful change in organisations. The five themes identified from the literature review were supported by the empirical data collected through the 28 interviews conducted. The analysis led to the development of an organisational change framework, which proposes a two-cycle approach with the readiness for change centred on the top cycle, and implementing change on the bottom cycle. The two cycles are linked through processes. The organisational change framework has practical implications for all organisations.

References

Beer, M. and Nohria, N. (2000) *Breaking the Code of Change,* Boston, MA, Harvard Business School Press.

Brown, S.L. and Eisenhardt, K.M. (1998) *Competing on the Edge,* Boston, MA, Harvard Business School Press.

Carnall, C. (1994) *Managing Change,* London, Prentice Hall.

Collins, J. (2001) *Good to Great,* New York, HarperBusiness.

Ghoshal, S. and Bartlett, C.A. (1997) *The Individualized Corporation,* London, Heinemann.

Guha, S., Grover, V., Kettinger, W.J. and Teng, J.T.C. (1997) 'Business process change and organizational performance: exploring an antecedent model', *Journal of Management Information Systems,* vol. 14, no. 1, pp. 119–56.

Higgs, M. and Rowland, D. (2000) 'Building change leadership capability', Henley Working Paper Series (HWP 2000/04), p. 22.

Jones, G. (2004) 'High-performance leadership: turning pressure to advantage', *Strategy Magazine,* vol. 3, pp.18–21.

Kaplan, R.S. and Norton, D.P. (2001) *The Strategy Focused Organisation,* Boston, MA, Harvard Business School Press.

Kotter, J.P. (1995) 'Leading change: why transformation efforts fail', *Harvard Business Review,* vol. 73.

Martensen, A. and Dahlgaard, J.J. (1999) 'Integrating business excellence and innovation management: developing vision, blueprint and strategy for innovation in creative and learning organizations', *Total Quality Management,* vol. 10, nos 4/5.

Martin, I. and Cheung, Y. (2002) 'Change management at Mobil Oil Australia', *Business Process Management Journal,* vol. 8, no. 5, pp. 447–62.

Moser, C.A. and Kalton, G. (1971) *Survey Methods in Social Investigation,* Aldershot, Dartmouth.

Oakland, J.S. (2003) *Total Organizational Excellence,* Oxford, Butterworth-Heinemann.

Paper, D.J., Rodger, J.A. and Pendharker, P.C. (2001) 'A BPR case study at Honeywell', *Business Process Management Journal,* vol. 7, no. 2, pp. 85–100.

Schaffer, R.H. and Thompson, H.A. (1992) 'Successful change programs begin with results', *Harvard Business Review,* vol. 70, no. 1, pp. 80–89.

Senge, P.M. (1999) 'It's the learning: the real lesson of the quality movement', *The Journal for Quality & Participation,* pp. 34–40.

Senge, P.M., Kleiner, A., Roberts, C., Ross, R., Roth, G. and Smith, B. (1999) *The Dance of Change,* London, Nicholas Brealey Publishing.

Smith, M. (2003) 'Business process design: correlates of success and failure', *The Quality Management Journal,* vol. 10, no. 2, pp. 38–50.

Tanner, S.J. and Oakland, J.S. (2005) *How to Measure and Manage Performance,* London, British Quality Foundation.

Turner, J.R. (1993) *The Handbook of Project-Based Management,* Maidenhead, McGraw-Hill.

Turner, R. and Peymai, R. (1995) 'Process management: the versatile approach to achieving quality in project based organisations', Henley Working Paper Series (HWP 9425).

Young, T.L. (1998) *The Handbook of Project Management,* London, Kogan Page.

Successfully Implementing Change

Victorian Quality Council

Successfully Implementing Change

Change is a fundamental component of continuous quality improvement. Any improvement methodology involves introducing change and measuring its impact. In health care there has been recognition of the need for system change to support the delivery of safe, quality care. As Berwick stated 'every system is perfectly designed to achieve exactly the results it gets.' This focus on system change has been associated with the development of a number of tools and improvement strategies. Health services are also implementing system change in response to risk areas identified through review of adverse events.

This paper is designed to assist the beginner in project management who, although enthusiastic, may be unprepared for some of the barriers that are normal to confront during the change process. It is not enough to provide the tools and strategies with which to improve safety and quality of health care and expect success. There is a need to be aware of what to expect when introducing change, how to engage staff and to make change sustainable. Knowledge or awareness of change processes may assist in ensuring success of a project.

Successful implementation of system change is essential in the provision of safe, quality care to consumers. Implementation of improvement projects and sustaining the resulting change can be a difficult process. It has been stated all too often that quality improvement projects fail on a regular basis. The individual or the teams introducing change have a challenging task. Change management is one component of a successful project; the need for project planning and the use of quality improvement tools are also critical. (Appendix 1)

This paper will discuss some issues that are common to confront when introducing change, and outlines some strategies that may improve the likelihood of success.

Engaging Others in Improvement

It is important to consider how people will personally be affected by the change process, 'change requires that people do something they have not done before' (Galvin 2003). People are generally the most critical resource, supporter, barrier and risk when managing change. The uncertainty of change can provoke strong emotions, with most people experiencing some sense of grief and loss as they let go of the old and move towards the new. A range of emotions may be displayed by those affected by the change process: frustration, anger, despair, acceptance, enthusiasm and elation. Which emotion is encountered will depend on whether staff make the change willingly or unwillingly, the level of consultation that occurred and the support provided by leadership. Awareness of the range of reactions to change will help the leader of the change process respond appropriately to concerns that are expressed. Understanding why these emotions occur may assist the leader to introduce change in a manner that anticipates, acknowledges and responds to concerns.

Staff may:

- not be aware of the reasons why change is necessary
- feel that there are other more important issues to be dealt with
- not agree with the proposed change, or feel that there is a better way to achieve the outcome
- disagree about how the change should be implemented
- feel there is a criticism about the way they do things implied in the change process
- feel that they have done this before and nothing changed
- feel that there will be extra work for them as a result of the changes. (NHS *Managing the human dimensions of change*, 2005)

How can the leader of the change process use this knowledge to improve the likelihood of success of their project? Since improvement depends on the actions of people, ultimately it comes down to winning hearts and minds. Staff will not respond well to just being told to change, nor can the project leader stand over staff to ensure compliance. To be successful, a change management process must include an effective communication strategy. All stakeholders must have opportunities to express their views and attitudes as part of the planning process. A lot of improvement is about changing mindsets. It is about having the tools, techniques and confidence to work with colleagues to try something that is different. It is about understanding the possibilities of thinking differently and aiming to make practical improvements for patients and staff.

Guiding Principles

Some guiding principles in planning a change include:

- having a plan for the project implementation but being prepared to adapt this if the outcomes at different stages show this to be necessary
- having Executive (or senior) support which is essential for the success of a project, but recognising that change will come from bottom up
- setting objectives and congratulating the team when each objective is achieved, but remembering that improvement is an ongoing process
- recognising that a plan for introducing change and monitoring the effects of the change is important, but gaining commitment of people is vital in the success of a project. (NHS *Managing the human dimensions of change*, 2005)

Communication

Communication should take place in some form with all those affected by the proposed change, staff, consumers, internal and external stakeholders. Early communication and consultation, while the change implementation is still in the planning stage, will assist in getting people interested and prepared to participate in the change process. They will have some ownership of the project and an interest in its success.

Stakeholders will have different levels of involvement. At various stages of the implementation they can be informed, consulted, collaborated with or be active participants. Stakeholders should be provided with as much information as possible, including baseline data, the objectives of the change, and should be involved in anticipating problems and determining solutions.

Implementing change in healthcare requires commitment from the people who will be affected by the proposed changes. Two important aspects are motivation and resistance.

Motivation

Change will be more successful, and more people will be committed to the change, if they believe it will improve things. The 'What's in it for me?' test helps to identify useful motivators. The best scenario is to have a 'win-win' situation for all, where the change management will have a positive outcome for all.

Encouraging debate and discussion about the need for change through data presentation can help to create a sense of urgency. People tend to move away from a problem and towards an improved state. Clinical leaders can influence this process and create a positive planning environment and encourage staff to contribute creativity and innovation to the change.

Health professional teams have been found to work most effectively when there is:

- influential and high level endorsement and support
- recognition of different values and skills within the team
- effective leadership, which bridges the gap between management and staff
- training in communication and team processes
- appropriate infrastructure and resources
- opportunity to reflect and evaluate.

Resistance

'Resistance is a natural, universal, inevitable human response to a change that someone else thinks is a good idea, and resisting change or improvement does not make someone bad or narrow-minded.' (NHS *Managing the human dimensions of change*, 2005)

Evaluation

Evaluation is an important component of any change process. As part of the project planning a decision needs to be made about measures that will be used to determine if the planned change leads to an improvement. (Appendix 1)

Using a Pilot

It is often a good idea to begin with a pilot, a small trial of the proposed option or solution, which can be undertaken in an area that is keen to be involved. Using people in an area who are enthusiastic about implementing the change will increase the chances of success and pave the way for a positive broader rollout. This pilot may be a particular unit, medical specialty or a specific group of patients.

The pilot or trial can highlight any barriers to change as well as provide valuable learning in successful change strategies. The information and outcomes achieved from a pilot can re-define the approach used in implementing change. The purpose of conducting a pilot project should be clarified with stakeholders. Generally a pilot project is run to assess the best method of implementation, not to determine if the project will go ahead.

Sharing the Results

Dissemination of the evaluation is important and consideration of the audience, the method and format of communicating the feedback should be undertaken. Present the final package containing all the planning, data, outcomes and learning to staff and stakeholders. If this evaluation is shared, and the emphasis is on learning in a non-punitive environment, then it can become a benchmark (or standard) for implementing change.

Even a small change benefits from an evaluation, as sharing of the outcomes and lessons learned will bring attention to the activity. Evaluation of many small change implementations can provide a valuable accumulation of information about what works within that organisation or health care in general.

Celebrate success – what worked, be open and honest about what didn't work, the lessons learned and recommendations for the future. The evaluation needs to show the improvement in the light of the stakeholder and organisation values that were identified in the planning stage.

Tips

- Have a defined communication strategy
- Be consistent about sharing information
- Consider using a variety of media to reach people
- Involve stakeholders in the planning process
- Support staff with training and opportunities to practice
- Listen and act on questions, feedback and concerns
- Celebrate ideas, achievements and successes
- Have a clear reason for implementing change
- Have a shared vision about what the change will achieve
- Learn about the target population
- When developing strategies, consider the barriers to implementing change and cater for them within the strategy development
- Remember that resistance is a natural response to change that is introduced by somebody else

- Identify the change champions, the innovators; these are the people who will be prepared to introduce change
- Be aware of the different rate of uptake of change (see below)
- Provide feedback of progress to stakeholders

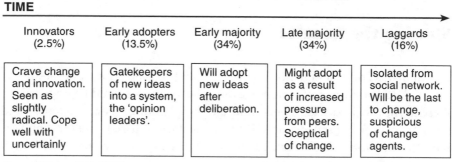

TIME

Innovators (2.5%)	Early adopters (13.5%)	Early majority (34%)	Late majority (34%)	Laggards (16%)
Crave change and innovation. Seen as slightly radical. Cope well with uncertainly	Gatekeepers of new ideas into a system, the 'opinion leaders'.	Will adopt new ideas after deliberation.	Might adopt as a result of increased pressure from peers. Sceptical of change.	Isolated from social network. Will be the last to change, suspicious of change agents.

Source: Rogers E.M. (1995).

Conclusion

The key to implementing change and continuous improvement is the effective exchange of information between people and process, a combination of business and human dimensions towards a shared objective. Case studies are presented in Appendix 2.

Appendix 1

Model for improvement

Planning for 'how are we going to achieve the change' should be done at the same time as planning 'who or what is involved'. During planning, the indicators of success should answer the question – 'How will we know it worked?' As well as showing the intended and unintended impact of the change, it can demonstrate if the resources, time and energy invested represent value for money. Ongoing evaluation can demonstrate the extent to which changes have been sustained. (NHS *Managing the human dimensions of change, 2005*.)

A commonly used model for improvement is the IHI model, also known as the Nolan model and modified from quality improvement leaders including Deming and Juran.

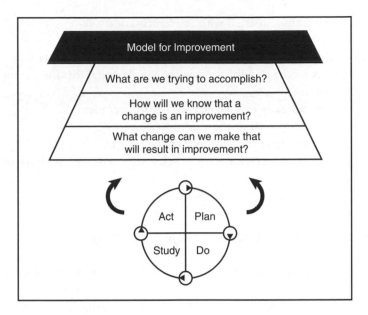

Figure 9.A1   Model for improvement

Source: Langley G., Nolan R., Nolan T., Norman C. Provost L. (1996) *The Improvement Guile a Practical Approach to Enhancing Organizational Performance*, San Francisco, CA, Jossey Bass Publishers.

Appendix 2

Case Studies

VQC Hand Hygiene Pilot Project

A VQC Hand Hygiene pilot project was conducted in 2004, with the aim of developing a practical model for sustained improvement in hand hygiene practices, to reduce the risk of healthcare-acquired infections. The model developed will be rolled out to all Victorian health services. The participating pilot sites trialled the model on a select number of wards, and the following data was collected and analysed on a regular basis:

1. Accurate and sustainable measurement of clinical MRSA infections
2. Assessment of HH compliance per sentinel wards
3. Hand hygiene solutions used by participating wards

Participating pilot sites noted a number of features of the project, which assisted with implementing practice change:

■ Use of posters, brochures to promote the practice change
■ Gantt chart to assist with project planning

- Realistic time frames assisted with implementation
- Identification of champions in each clinical area
- Launch with Executive support (wearing promotional T shirt)
- Use of various media to publicise project, e.g. hospital intranet, competition to decide slogan
- Identification and early involvement of key stakeholders
- Regular feedback to staff of audit results
- Policy change to reflect the objective of the project
- Barriers to project implementation acknowledged and addressed in the education program
- Adequate resource allocation

VQC Pressure Ulcer Prevention Project (PUPPs)

In 2004 the VQC reported on data collected in the first statewide pressure ulcer point prevalence survey (PUPPS Report, 2004). A range of recommendations was developed to assist acute and subacute public health services with pressure ulcer prevention and management. A second statewide pressure ulcer prevalence survey was conducted to ascertain the scope and severity of this known problem area in Victoria's health services, and to review changes made since PUPPS 1.

PUPPS 2 tracked the level of improvement in pressure ulcer prevalence, and management since the release of the first report. The findings of PUPPS 2 indicated that significant improvement had occurred, but that more needs to be done.

A number of lessons were learnt throughout these projects about implementing practice change:

- Use best practise clinical guidelines
- Practice change is facilitated by environmental change, e.g. provision of appropriate equipment such as pressure reduction foam mattress
- Executive support
- Education program
- Agreed targets, measures
- Feedback to staff results of data collection
- Integrate with associated programs
- Support of multidisciplinary committee
- Identify staff resources e.g. wound management staff
- Articulate the aim of the project and the benefits to patients/staff
- Use a multifactorial approach
- Focus on high risk areas
- Include patient information/education
- Ensure practise change is supported by change in organisational policies

References

Berwick D. (2000) 'Institute of Medicine 2000 Annual Meeting', www.jom.edu/ObjectFile/Master/7/695/berwickppt

Bevan H. and Pisek P. (2003) 'Achieving change in large health organisations' Presentation at Asia Pacific Quality Improvement Conference, Auckland.

Bridges W. (1998) *Managing Transitions – Making the Most of Change*, Reading, MA, Addison-Wesley Publishing Company.

Department of Human Services (2003) 'Metropolitan health strategy', www.health.vic.gov.au/metrohealthstrategy/strategy.htm

Grol R. (1997) 'Beliefs and evidence in changing clinical practice', *British Medical Journal*, vol. 315, pp. 418–21.

NHS Modernisation Agency (2005) 'Improvement Leaders Guide, Managing the human dimensions of change', London, *Department of Health Publications*, www.modern.nhs.uk Institute for Healthcare Improvement, www.jhi.org/IHI/Topics/ImprovementMethods/HowToImprove/

NHS Modernisation Agency (2005) 'Improvement Leaders Guide, Evaluating Improvement', London, *Department of Health Publications*, www.modern.nhs.uk

Roger E.M. (2000) 'Effecting and leading change in health care organisations', *The Joint Commission Journal on Quality Improvement*, July 2000, pp. 388–98.

Victorian Quality Council (2003) 'Better Quality, Better Health Care – a safety and quality improvement framework for Victorian health services', *Department of Human Services*, 2003 www.health.vic.gov.au/qualitycouncil

Victorian Quality Council (2004) 'VQC State – wide PUPPs Report – 2003 Pressure Ulcer Point Prevalence Survey', *Department of Human Services*, 2004 www.health.vic.gov.au/qualitycouncil

Part IV
Resisting Change

Introduction

In Part IV of this book we develop the theme of the practical implications of managing change by considering the issue of resistance. In their 1979 article entitled 'Choosing Strategies for Change', Kotter and Schlesinger recognise that it is perfectly reasonable for people to fear organisational change. It introduces ambiguity and uncertainty to a part of their lives with which they were previously comfortable and confident. However, as the pace of environmental change increases and organisations are required to respond more rapidly and in ever more radical ways, so the need to efficiently bring about the required changes increases.

Kotter and Schlesinger note that before you can overcome resistance to change, it is useful to consider why people are resistant. This has two advantages. First you might discover new information that forces you to doubt the viability of the plan for change that you have devised. Resistance is justified and the plan for change needs to change. Second, only by recognising the basis for that resistance can you construct a clear and targeted plan for overcoming this whilst still meeting the demands of a wide group of stakeholders.

In the next paper in this part, entitled 'Managing the Human Side of Change', Rosabeth Moss Kanter highlights another important reason for trying to overcome resistance to change. Rather than seeing resistance simply as something which prevents the achievement of the overall objectives for change, she notes the ways in which resistance can create short term inefficiencies in the day-to-day running of the organisation. As such, if small change processes bring about a reduction in effectiveness, how much more problematic will large change processes be? Basing her consideration on the experiences of a consulting firm, she has produced a list of the ten most common reasons why managers face resistance to change. The solution offered is useful, in that she suggests that resistance can be overcome by building commitment to the change, however, within an organisational context there needs to be some consideration of the short term potential for losses. It could be argued that time spent persuading people to change is time not spent changing.

The last paper in the part takes a more psycho-social perspective on the reasons for resistance to change. In his paper 'Minds, Hearts and Deeds: Cognitive, Affective and Behavioural Responses to Change' Roy Kark Smollen considers the levels on which people are affected by change. Whereas the previous papers promote a well-reasoned cognitive perspective of resistance, Smollen draws on the emotional and behavioural aspects of change. Not only does he consider these from the perspective of the employee subject to the process of change, but he also considers the relevance of such factors for those leading or managing the change. Whilst the Smollen paper doesn't offer any convenient taxonomies to frame change or guidelines for success, it does offer a useful and thought provoking way of thinking about resistance to change.

Choosing Strategies for Change

10

John P. Kotter and Leonard A. Schlesinger

'From the frying pan into the fire', 'let sleeping dogs lie', and 'you can't teach an old dog new tricks' are all well-known sayings born of the fear of change. When people are threatened with change in organizations, similar maxims about certain people and departments are trotted out to prevent an alteration in the status quo. Fear of change is understandable, but because the environment changes rapidly, and it has been doing so increasingly, organizations cannot afford not to change. One major task of a manager, then, is to implement change, and that entails overcoming resistance to it. In this article, the authors describe four basic reasons people resist change. They also describe various methods for dealing with the resistance and provide a guide to what kinds of approaches will work when the different types of resistance occur.

'It must be considered that there is nothing more difficult to carry out, nor more doubtful of success, nor more dangerous to handle, than to initiate a new order of things.'[1]

In 1973, The Conference Board asked 13 eminent authorities to speculate what significant management issues and problems would develop over the next 20 years. One of the strongest themes that runs through their subsequent reports is a concern for the ability of organizations to respond to environmental change. As one person wrote: 'It follows that an acceleration in the rate of change will result in an increasing need for reorganization. Reorganization is usually feared, because it means disturbance of the status quo, a threat to people's vested interests in their jobs, and an upset to established ways of doing things. For these reasons, needed reorganization is often deferred, with a resulting loss in effectiveness and an increase in costs.'[2]

Subsequent events have confirmed the importance of this concern about organizational change. Today, more and more managers must deal with new government regulations, new products, growth, increased competition, technological developments, and a changing work force. In response, most companies or divisions of major corporations find that they must undertake moderate

Kotter, J.P and Schlesinger, L.A. (1979) 'Choosing strategies for change', *Harvard Business Review*, March–April, pp. 106–14.

organizational changes at least once a year and major changes every four or five.[3]

Few organizational change efforts tend to be complete failures, but few tend to be entirely successful either. Most efforts encounter problems, they often take longer than expected and desired, they sometimes kill morale, and they often cost a great deal in terms of managerial time or emotional upheaval. More than a few organizations have not even tried to initiate needed changes because the managers involved were afraid that they were simply incapable of successfully implementing them.

In this article, we first describe various causes for resistance to change and then outline a systematic way to select a strategy and set of specific approaches for implementing an organizational change effort. The methods described are based on our analyses of dozens of successful and unsuccessful organizational changes.

Diagnosing Resistance

Organizational change efforts often run into some form of human resistance. Although experienced managers are generally all too aware of this fact, surprisingly few take time before an organizational change to assess systematically who might resist the change initiative and for what reasons. Instead, using past experiences as guidelines, managers all too often apply a simple set of beliefs – such as 'engineers will probably resist the change because they are independent and suspicious of top management'. This limited approach can create serious problems. Because of the many different ways in which individuals and groups can react to change, correct assessments are often not intuitively obvious and require careful thought.

Of course, all people who are affected by change experience some emotional turmoil. Even changes that appear to be 'positive' or 'rational' involve loss and uncertainty.[4] Nevertheless, for a number of different reasons, individuals or groups can react very differently to change – from passively resisting it, to aggressively trying to undermine it, to sincerely embracing it.

To predict what form their resistance might take, managers need to be aware of the four most common reasons people resist change. These include: a desire not to lose something of value, a misunderstanding of the change and its implications, a belief that the change does not make sense for the organization, and a low tolerance for change.

Parochial Self-Interest

One major reason people resist organizational change is that they think they will lose something of value as a result. In these cases, because people focus on their own best interests and not on those of the total organization, resistance often results in 'politics' or 'political behavior'.[5] Consider these two examples:

After a number of years of rapid growth, the president of an organization decided that its size demanded the creation of a new staff function – New Product Planning and Development – to be headed by a vice president. Operationally, this change eliminated most of the decision-making power that the vice presidents of marketing, engineering, and production had over new products. Inasmuch as new products were very important in this organization, the change also reduced the vice presidents' status which, together with power, was very important to them.

During the two months after the president announced his idea for a new product vice president, the existing vice presidents each came up with six or seven reasons the new arrangement might not work. Their objections grew louder and louder until the president shelved the idea.

A manufacturing company had traditionally employed a large group of personnel people as counselors and 'father confessors' to its production employees. This group of counselors tended to exhibit high morale because of the professional satisfaction they received from the 'helping relationships' they had with employees. When a new performance appraisal system was installed, every six months the counselors were required to provide each employee's supervisor with a written evaluation of the employee's 'emotional maturity', 'promotional potential', and so forth.

As some of the personnel people immediately recognized, the change would alter their relationships from a peer and helper to more of a boss and evaluator with most of the employees. Predictably, the personnel counselors resisted the change. While publicly arguing that the new system was not as good for the company as the old one, they privately put as much pressure as possible on the personnel vice president until he significantly altered the new system.

Political behavior sometimes emerges before and during organizational change efforts when what is in the best interests of one individual or group is not in the best interests of the total organization or of other individuals and groups.

While political behavior sometimes takes the form of two or more armed camps publicly fighting things out, it usually is much more subtle. In many cases, it occurs completely under the surface of public dialogue. Although scheming and ruthless individuals sometimes initiate power struggles, more often than not those who do are people who view their potential loss from change as an unfair violation of their implicit, or psychological, contract with the organization.[6]

Misunderstanding and Lack of Trust

People also resist change when they do not understand its implications and perceive that it might cost them much more than they will gain. Such situations often occur when trust is lacking between the person initiating the change and the employees.[7] Here is an example:

When the president of a small midwestern company announced to his managers that the company would implement a flexible working schedule for all employees, it never occurred to him that he might run into resistance. He had been introduced to the concept at a management seminar and decided to use it to make working conditions at his company more attractive, particularly to clerical and plant personnel.

Shortly after the announcement, numerous rumors begin to circulate among plant employees – none of whom really knew what flexible working hours meant and many of whom were distrustful of the manufacturing vice president. One rumor, for instance, suggested that flexible hours meant that most people would have to work whenever their supervisors asked them to – including evenings and weekends. The employee association, a local union, held a quick meeting and then presented the management with a nonnegotiable demand that the flexible hours concept be dropped. The president, caught completely by surprise, complied.

Few organizations can be characterized as having a high level of trust between employees and managers; consequently, it is easy for misunderstandings to develop when change is introduced. Unless managers surface misunderstandings and clarify them rapidly, they can lead to resistance. And that resistance can easily catch change initiators by surprise, especially if they assume that people only resist change when it is not in their best interest.

Different Assessments

Another common reason people resist organizational change is that they assess the situation differently from their managers or those initiating the change and see more costs than benefits resulting from the change, not only for themselves but for their company as well. For example:

The president of one moderate-size bank was shocked by his staff's analysis of the bank's real estate investment trust (REIT) loans. This complicated analysis suggested that the bank could easily lose up to $10 million, and that the possible losses were increasing each month by 20%. Within a week, the president drew up a plan to reorganize the part of the bank that managed REITs. Because of his concern for the bank's stock price, however, he chose not to release the staff report to anyone except the new REIT section manager.

The reorganization immediately ran into massive resistance from the people involved. The group sentiment, as articulated by one person, was: 'Has he gone mad? Why in God's name is he tearing apart this section of the bank? His actions have already cost us three very good people [who quit], and have crippled a new program we were implementing [which the president was unaware of] to reduce our loan losses.'

Managers who initiate change often assume both that they have all the relevant information required to conduct an adequate organization analysis and that those who will be affected by the change have the same facts, when neither assumption is correct. In either case, the difference in information that groups work with often leads to differences in analyses, which in turn can lead to resistance. Moreover, if the analysis made by those not initiating the change is more accurate than that derived by the initiators, resistance is obviously 'good' for the organization. But this likelihood is not obvious to some managers who assume that resistance is always bad and therefore always fight it.[8]

Low Tolerance for Change

People also resist change because they fear they will not be able to develop the new skills and behavior that will be required of them. All human beings are limited in their ability to change, with some people much more limited than others.[9] Organizational change can inadvertently require people to change too much, too quickly.

Peter F. Drucker has argued that the major obstacle to organizational growth is managers' inability to change their attitudes and behavior as rapidly as their organizations require.[10] Even when managers intellectually understand the need for changes in the way they operate, they sometimes are emotionally unable to make the transition.

It is because of people's limited tolerance for change that individuals will sometimes resist a change even when they realize it is a good one. For example, a person who receives a significantly more important job as a result of an organizational change will probably be very happy. But it is just as possible for such a person to also feel uneasy and to resist giving up certain aspects of the current situation. A new and very different job will require new and different behavior, new and different relationships, as well as the loss of some satisfactory current activities and relationships. If the changes are significant and the individual's tolerance for change is low, he might begin actively to resist the change for reasons even he does not consciously understand.

People also sometimes resist organizational change to save face; to go along with the change would be, they think, an admission that some of their previous decisions or beliefs were wrong. Or they might resist because of peer group pressure or because of a supervisor's attitude. Indeed, there are probably an endless number of reasons why people resist change.[11]

Assessing which of the many possibilities might apply to those who will be affected by a change is important because it can help a manager select an appropriate way to overcome resistance. Without an accurate diagnosis of possibilities of resistance, a manager can easily get bogged down during the change process with very costly problems.

Dealing with Resistance

Many managers underestimate not only the variety of ways people can react to organizational change, but also the ways they can positively influence specific individuals and groups during a change. And, again because of past experiences, managers sometimes do not have an accurate understanding of the advantages and disadvantages of the methods with which they *are* familiar.

Education and Communication

One of the most common ways to overcome resistance to change is to educate people about it beforehand. Communication of ideas helps people see the need for and the logic of a change. The education process can involve one-on-one discussions, presentations to groups, or memos and reports. For example:

As a part of an effort to make changes in a division's structure and in measurement and reward systems, a division manager put together a one-hour audiovisual presentation that explained the changes and the reasons for them. Over a four-month period, he made this presentation no less than a dozen times to groups of 20 or 30 corporate and division managers.

An education and communication program can be ideal when resistance is based on inadequate or inaccurate information and analysis, especially if the initiators need the resistors' help in implementing the change. But some managers overlook the fact that a program of this sort requires a good relationship between initiators and resistors or that the latter may not believe what they hear. It also requires time and effort, particularly if a lot of people are involved.

Participation and Involvement

If the initiators involve the potential resistors in some aspect of the design and implementation of the change, they can often forestall resistance. With a participative change effort, the initiators listen to the people the change involves and use their advice. To illustrate:

The head of a small financial services company once created a task force to help design and implement changes in his company's reward system. The task force was composed of eight second- and third-level managers from different parts of the company. The president's specific charter to them was that they recommend changes in the company's benefit package. They were given six months and asked to file a brief progress report with the president once a month. After they had made their recommendations, which the president largely accepted, they were asked to help the company's personnel director implement them.

We have found that many managers have quite strong feelings about participation – sometimes positive and sometimes negative. That is, some managers feel that there should always be participation during change efforts, while others feel this is virtually always a mistake. Both attitudes can create problems for a manager, because neither is very realistic.

When change initiators believe they do not have all the information they need to design and implement a change, or when they need the whole-hearted commitment of others to do so, involving others makes very good sense. Considerable research has demonstrated that, in general, participation leads to commitment, not merely compliance.[12] In some instances, commitment is needed for the change to be a success. Nevertheless, the participation process does have its drawbacks. Not only can it lead to a poor solution if the process is not carefully managed, but also it can be enormously time consuming. When the change must be made immediately, it can take simply too long to involve others.

Facilitation and Support

Another way that managers can deal with potential resistance to change is by being supportive. This process might include providing training in new skills, or giving employees time off after a demanding period, or simply listening and providing emotional support. For example:

Management in one rapidly growing electronics company devised a way to help people adjust to frequent organizational changes. First, management staffed its human resource department with four counselors who spent most of their time talking to people who were feeling 'burnt out' or who were having difficulty adjusting to new jobs. Second, on a selective basis, management offered people four-week minisabbaticals that involved some reflective or educational activity away from work. And, finally, it spent a great deal of money on in-house education and training programs.

Facilitation and support are most helpful when fear and anxiety lie at the heart of resistance. Seasoned, tough managers often overlook or ignore this kind of resistance, as well as the efficacy of facilitative ways of dealing with it. The basic drawback of this approach is that it can be time consuming and expensive and still fail.[13] If time, money, and patience just are not available, then using supportive methods is not very practical.

Negotiation and Agreement

Another way to deal with resistance is to offer incentives to active or potential resistors. For instance, management could give a union a higher wage rate in return for a work rule change; it could increase an individual's pension benefits in return for an early retirement. Here is an example of negotiated agreements:

In a large manufacturing company, the divisions were very interdependent. One division manager wanted to make some major changes in his organization. Yet, because of the interdependence, he recognized that he would be forcing some inconvenience and change on other divisions as well. To prevent top managers in other divisions from under-mining his efforts, the division manager negotiated a written agreement with each. The agreement specified the outcomes the other division managers would receive and when, as well as the kinds of cooperation that he would receive from them in return during the change process. Later, whenever the division managers complained about his changes or the change process itself, he could point to the negotiated agreements.

Negotiation is particularly appropriate when it is clear that someone is going to lose out as a result of a change and yet his or her power to resist is significant. Negotiated agreements can be a relatively easy way to avoid major resistance, though, like some other processes, they may become expensive. And once a manager makes it clear that he will negotiate to avoid major resistance, he opens himself up to the possibility of blackmail.[14]

Manipulation and Co-Optation

In some situations, managers also resort to covert attempts to influence others. Manipulation, in this context, normally involves the very selective use of information and the conscious structuring of events.

One common form of manipulation is co-optation. Co-opting an individual usually involves giving him or her a desirable role in the design or implementation of the change. Co-opting a group involves giving one of its leaders, or someone it respects, a key role in the design or implementation of a change. This is not a form of participation, however, because the initiators do not want the advice of the co-opted, merely his or her endorsement. For example:

One division manager in a large multibusiness corporation invited the corporate human relations vice president, a close friend of the president, to help him and his key staff diagnose some problems the division was having. Because of his busy schedule, the corporate vice president was not able to do much of the actual information gathering or analysis himself, thus limiting his own influence on the diagnoses. But his presence at key meetings helped commit him to the diagnoses as well as the solutions the group designed. The commitment was subsequently very important because the president, at least initially, did not like some of the proposed changes. Nevertheless, after discussion with his human relations vice president, he did not try to block them.

Under certain circumstances co-optation can be a relatively inexpensive and easy way to gain an individual's or a group's support (cheaper, for example, than negotiation and quicker than participation). Nevertheless, it has its drawbacks. If people feel they are being tricked into not resisting, are not being treated equally, or are being lied to, they may respond very negatively. More than one manager has found that, by his effort to give some subordinate a sense of participation through co-optation, he created more resistance than if he had done nothing. In addition, co-optation can create a different kind of problem if those co-opted use their ability to influence the design and implementation of changes in ways that are not in the best interests of the organization.

Other forms of manipulation have drawbacks also, sometimes to an even greater degree. Most people are likely to greet what they perceive as covert treatment and/or lies with a negative response. Furthermore, if a manager develops a reputation as a manipulator, it can undermine his ability to use needed approaches such as education/communication and participation/involvement. At the extreme, it can even ruin his career.

Nevertheless, people do manipulate others successfully – particularly when all other tactics are not feasible or have failed.[15] Having no other alternative, and not enough time to educate, involve, or support people, and without the power or other resources to negotiate, coerce, or co-opt them, managers have resorted to manipulating information channels in order to scare people into thinking there is a crisis coming which they can avoid only by changing.

Explicit and Implicit Coercion

Finally, managers often deal with resistance coercively. Here they essentially force people to accept a change by explicitly or implicitly threatening them

Exhibit 10.1 Methods for dealing with resistance to change

Approach	Commonly used in situations	Advantages	Drawbacks
Education + communication	Where there is a lack of information or inaccurate information and analysis.	Once persuaded, people will often help with the implementation of the change.	Can be very time-consuming if lots of people are involved.
Participation + involvement	Where the initiators do not have all the information they need to design the change, and where others have considerable power to resist.	People who participate will be committed to implementing change, and any relevant information they have will be integrated into the change plan.	Can be very time-consuming if participators design an inappropriate change.
Facilitation + support	Where people are resisting because of adjustment problems.	No other approach works as well with adjustment problems.	Can be time-consuming, expensive, and still fail.
Negotiation + agreement	Where someone or some group will clearly lose out in a change, and where that group has considerable power to resist.	Sometimes it is a relatively easy way to avoid major resistance.	Can be too expensive in many cases if it alerts others to negotiate for compliance.
Manipulation + co-optation	Where other tactics will not work, or are too expensive.	It can be a relatively quick and inexpensive solution to resistance problems.	Can lead to future problems if people feel manipulated.
Explicit + implicit coercion	Where speed is essential, and the change initiators possess considerable power.	It is speedy, and can overcome any kind of resistance.	Can be risky if it leaves people mad at the initiators.

(with the loss of jobs, promotion possibilities, and so forth) or by actually firing or transferring them. As with manipulation, using coercion is a risky process because inevitably people strongly resent forced change. But in situations where speed is essential and where the changes will not be popular, regardless of how they are introduced, coercion may be the manager's only option.

Successful organizational change efforts are always characterized by the skillful application of a number of these approaches, often in very different combinations. However, successful efforts share two characteristics: managers employ the approaches with a sensitivity to their strengths and limitations (see Exhibit 10.1 on preceding page) and appraise the situation realistically.

The most common mistake managers make is to use only one approach or a limited set of them *regardless of the situation*. A surprisingly large number of managers have this problem. This would include the hard-boiled boss who often coerces people, the people-oriented manager who constantly tries to involve and support his people, the cynical boss who always manipulates and co-opts others, the intellectual manager who relies heavily on education and communication, and the lawyerlike manager who usually tries to negotiate.[16]

A second common mistake that managers make is to approach change in a disjointed and incremental way that is not a part of a clearly considered strategy.

Choice of Strategy

In approaching an organizational change situation, managers explicitly or implicitly make strategic choices regarding the speed of the effort, the amount of preplanning, the involvement of others, and the relative emphasis they will give to different approaches. Successful change efforts seem to be those where these choices both are internally consistent and fit some key situational variables.

The strategic options available to managers can be usefully thought of as existing on a continuum (see Exhibit 10.2).[17] At one end of the continuum, the change strategy calls for a very rapid implementation, a clear plan of action, and little involvement of others. This type of strategy mows over any

---

Exhibit 10.2 Strategic continuum

Fast	Slower
Clearly planned.	Not clearly planned at the beginning.
Little Involvement of others.	Lots of involvement of others.
Attempt to overcome any resistance.	Attempt to minimize any resistance.

Key situational variables

The amount and type of resistance that is anticipated.

The position of the initiators vis-à-vis the resistors (in terms of power, trust, and so forth).

The locus of relevant data for designing the change, and of needed energy for implementing it.

The stakes involved (e.g., the presence or lack of presence of a crisis, the consequences of resistance and lack of change).

resistance and, at the extreme, would result in a fait accompli. At the other end of the continuum, the strategy would call for a much slower change process, a less clear plan, and involvement on the part of many people other than the change initiators. This type of strategy is designed to reduce resistance to a minimum.[18]

The further to the left one operates on the continuum in Exhibit 10.2, the more one tends to be coercive and the less one tends to use the other approaches – especially participation; the converse also holds.

Organizational change efforts that are based on inconsistent strategies tend to run into predictable problems. For example, efforts that are not clearly planned in advance and yet are implemented quickly tend to become bogged down owing to unanticipated problems. Efforts that involve a large number of people, but are implemented quickly, usually become either stalled or less participative.

Situational Factors

Exactly where a change effort should be strategically positioned on the continuum in Exhibit 10.2 depends on four factors:

1. The amount and kind of resistance that is anticipated. All other factors being equal, the greater the anticipated resistance, the more difficult it will be simply to overwhelm it, and the more a manager will need to move toward the right on the continuum to find ways to reduce some of it.[19]
2. The position of the initiator vis-à-vis the resistors, especially with regard to power. The less power the initiator has with respect to others, the more the initiating manager *must* move to the left on the continuum.[20] Conversely, the stronger the initiator's position, the more he or she can move to the right.
3. The person who has the relevant data for designing the change and the energy for implementing it. The more the initiators anticipate that they will need information and commitment from others to help design and implement the change, the more they must move to the right.[21] Gaining useful information and commitment requires time and the involvement of others.
4. The stakes involved. The greater the short-run potential for risks to organizational performance and survival if the present situation is not changed, the more one must move to the left.

Organizational change efforts that ignore these factors inevitably run into problems. A common mistake some managers make, for example, is to move too quickly and involve too few people despite the fact that they do not have all the information they really need to design the change correctly.

Insofar as these factors still leave a manager with some choice of where to operate on the continuum, it is probably best to select a point as far to the right as possible for both economic and social reasons. Forcing change on people can have just too many negative side effects over both the short and the long term. Change efforts using the strategies on the right of the continuum can often help develop an organization and its people in useful ways.[22]

In some cases, however, knowing the four factors may not give a manager a comfortable and obvious choice. Consider a situation where a manager has a weak position vis-à-vis the people whom he thinks need a change and yet is faced with serious consequences if the change is not implemented immediately. Such a manager is clearly in a bind. If he somehow is not able to increase his power in the situation, he will be forced to choose some compromise strategy and to live through difficult times.

Implications for Managers

A manager can improve his chance of success in an organizational change effort by:

1. Conducting an organizational analysis that identifies the current situation, problems, and the forces that are possible causes of those problems. The analysis should specify the actual importance of the problems, the speed with which the problems must be addressed if additional problems are to be avoided, and the kinds of changes that are generally needed.
2. Conducting an analysis of factors relevant to producing the needed changes. This analysis should focus on questions of who might resist the change, why, and how much; who has information that is needed to design the change, and whose cooperation is essential in implementing it; and what is the position of the initiator vis-à-vis other relevant parties in terms of power, trust, normal modes of interaction, and so forth.
3. Selecting a change strategy, based on the previous analysis, that specifies the speed of change, the amount of preplanning, and the degree of involvement of others; that selects specific tactics for use with various individuals and groups; and that is internally consistent.
4. Monitoring the implementation process. No matter how good a job one does of initially selecting a change strategy and tactics, something unexpected will eventually occur during implementation. Only by carefully monitoring the process can one identify the unexpected in a timely fashion and react to it intelligently.

Interpersonal skills, of course, are the key to using this analysis. But even the most outstanding interpersonal skills will not make up for a poor choice of strategy and tactics. And in a business world that continues to become more and more dynamic, the consequences of poor implementation choices will become increasingly severe.

Notes

1. Niccolò Machiavelli, *The Prince.*
2. Bower, Marvin and Walton, C. Lee Jr (1973) 'Gearing a business to the future' in *Challenge to Leadership*, New York, The Conference Board, p. 126.
3. For recent evidence on the frequency of changes, see Allen, Stephen A. (1978) 'Organizational choice and general influence networks for diversified companies', *Academy of Management Journal,* September, p. 341.
4. For example, see Luke, Robert A. Jr (1973) 'A structural approach to organizational change', *Journal of Applied Behavioral Science,* September–October, p. 611.
5. For a discussion of power and politics in corporations, see Zaleznik, Abraham and Manfred F.R. Kets de Vries (1975) *Power and the Corporate Mind*, Boston, MA, Houghton Mifflin, chapter 6; and Miles, Robert H. (1978) *Macto Organizational Behavior*, Pacific Palisades, CA, Goodyear, chapter 4.
6. See Schein, Edgar H. (1965) *Organizational Psychology*, Englewood Cliffs, NJ, Prentice-Hall, p. 44.
7. See Argyris, Chris (1970) *Intervention Theory and Method*, Reading, MA, Addison-Wesley, p. 70.
8. See Lawrence, Paul R. (1954) 'How to deal with resistance to change', HBR May–June, p. 49; reprinted as HBR Classic, January–February 1969, p. 4.
9. For a discussion of resistance that is personality based, see Watson, Goodwin (1969) 'Resistance to change' in Bennis, Warren C., Benne, Kenneth F. and Chin, Robert (eds) *The Planning of Change,* New York, Holt, Rinchart, and Winston, p. 489.
10. Drucker, Peter F. (1954) *The Practice of Management*, New York, Harper and Row.
11. For a general discussion of resistance and reasons for it, see chapter 3 in Zaltman, Gerald and Duncan, Robert (1977) *Strategies for Planned Change*, New York, John Wiley.
12. See, for example, Marrow, Alfred J., Bowers, David F. and Seashore, Stanley E. (1967) *Management by Participation*, New York, Harper and Row.
13. Zaltman and Duncan, *Strategies for Planned Change,* chapter 4.
14. For an excellent discussion of negotiation, see Nierenberg, Gerald I. (1968) *The Art of Negotiating*, Birmingham, Cornerstone.
15. See Kotter, John P. (1977) 'Power, dependence, and effective management', HBR July–August, p. 125.
16. Ibid., p. 135.
17. See Greiner, Larry E. (1967) 'Patterns of organization change', HBR May–June, p. 119; and Greiner, Larry E. and Barnes, Louis B. (1970) 'Organization change and development' in Dalton, Gene W. and Lawrence, Paul R. (eds) (1970) *Organizational Change and Development,* Homewood, IL, Irwin, p. 3.
18. For a good discussion of an approach that attempts to minimize resistance, see Tagiuri, Renato (1979) 'Notes on the management of change: implication of postulating a need for competence' in Kotter, John P., Sathe, Vijay and Schlesinger, Leonard A. (eds) *Organization*, Homewood, IL, Irwin.
19. Lorsch, Jay W. (1976) 'Managing change' in Lawrence, Paul R., Barnes, Louis B. and Lorsch, Jay W. (eds) *Organizational Behavior and Administration,* Homewood, IL, Irwin, p. 676.
20. Ibid.
21. Ibid.
22. Beer, Michael (1979) *Organization Change and Development: A Systems View*, Pacific Palisades, CA, Goodyear.

Managing the Human Side of Change

11

Rosabeth Moss Kanter

This is a time of historically unprecedented change for most corporations. The auto and steel industries are in turmoil because of the effects of foreign competition. Financial services are undergoing a revolution. Telecommunications companies are facing profound and dramatic changes because of the breakup of AT&T and greater competition from newly organized longdistance carriers. Health care organizations are under pressure to cut costs and improve services in the face of government regulation and the growth of for-profit hospital chains.

Change, and the need to manage it well, has always been with us. Business life is punctuated by necessary and expected changes: the introduction of new toothpastes, regular store remodellings, changes in information systems, reorganizations of the office staff, announcements of new benefits programs, radical rethinking of the fall product line, or a progression of new senior vice-presidents.

But as common as change is, the people who work in an organization may still not like it. Each of those 'routine' changes can be accompanied by tension, stress, squabbling, sabotage, turnover, subtle undermining, behind-the-scenes footdragging, work slowdowns, needless political battles, and a drain on money and time – in short, symptoms of that ever-present bugaboo, resistance to change.

If even small and expected changes can be the occasion for decrease in organizational effectiveness, imagine the potential for disaster when organizations try to make big changes, such as developing a new corporate culture, restructuring the business to become more competitive, divesting losing operations and closing facilities, reshuffling product divisions to give them a market orientation, or moving into new sales channels.

Moss Kanter, R. (1985) 'Managing the Human Side of Change', *Management Review*, vol. 74, no. 4.

Because the pace of change has speeded up, mastering change is increasingly a part of every manager's job. All managers need to know how to guide people through change so that they emerge at the other end with an effective organization. One important key is being able to analyze the reasons people resist change. Pinpointing the source of the resistance makes it possible to see what needs to be done to avoid resistance, or convert it into commitment to change.

As a consulting firm, Goodmeasure has worked with the change-related problems of over a hundred major organizations. We have distilled a list of the ten most common reasons managers encounter resistance to change, and tactics for dealing with each.

Loss of Control

How people greet a change has to do with whether they feel in control of it or not. Change is exciting when it is done *by us,* threatening when it is done *to us.*

Most people want and need to feel in control of the events around them. Indeed, behind the rise of participative management today is the notion that 'ownership' counts in getting commitment to actions, that if people have a chance to participate in decisions, they feel better about them. Even involvement in details is better than noninvolvement. And the more choices that are left to people, the better they feel about the changes. If all actions are imposed upon them from outside, however, they are more likely to resist.

Thus, the more choices we can give people the better they'll feel about the change. But when they feel out of control and powerless, they are likely not only to feel stress, but also to behave in defensive, territorial ways. I proposed in my 1977 *Men and Women of the Corporation* that, in organizations at least, it is *powerlessness* that 'corrupts', not power. When people feel powerless, they behave in petty, territorial ways. They become rules-minded, and they are over-controlling, because they're trying to grab hold of some little piece of the world that they *do* control and then overmanage it to death. (One way to reassert control is to resist everyone else's new ideas.) People do funny things when they feel out of control, but giving people chances for involvement can help them feel more committed to the change in question.

Excess Uncertainty

A second reason people resist change is what I call the 'Walking Off A Cliff Blindfolded Problem' – too much uncertainty. Simply not knowing enough about what the next step is going to be or feel like makes comfort impossible.

If people don't know where the next step is going to take them, whether it is the organizational equivalent of off a cliff or under a train, change seems dangerous. Then they resist change, because they reason, 'It's safer to stay with the devil you know than to commit yourself to the devil you don't.'

Managers who do not share enough information with their employees about exactly what is happening at every step of a change process, and about what they anticipate happening next, and about when more information will be coming, make a mistake, because they're likely to meet with a great deal of resistance. Information counts in building commitment to a change, especially step-by-step scenarios with timetables and milestones. Dividing a big change into a number of small steps can help make it seem less risky and threatening. People can focus on one step at a time, but not a leap off the cliff; they know what to do next.

Change requires faith that the new way will indeed be the right way. If the leaders themselves do not appear convinced, then the rest of the people will not budge. Another key to resolving the discomfort of uncertainty is for leaders to demonstrate their commitment to change. Leaders have to be the first over the cliff if they want the people they manage to follow suit. Information, coupled with the leaders' actions to make change seem safer, can convert resistance to commitment.

Surprise, Surprise!

A third reason people resist change is the surprise factor. People are easily shocked by decisions or requests suddenly sprung on them without groundwork or preparation. Their first response to something totally new and unexpected, that they have not had time to prepare for mentally, is resistance.

Companies frequently make this mistake when introducing organizational changes. They wait until all decisions are made, and then spring them on an unsuspecting population. One chemical company that has had to reorganize and frequently lay people off is particularly prone to this error. A manager might come into work one day to find on her desk a list of people she is supposed to inform, immediately, that their jobs are changing or being eliminated. Consequently, that manager starts to wonder whether she is on somebody *else's* list, and she feels so upset by the surprise that her commitment to the organization is reduced. The question. 'Why couldn't they trust me enough to even hint that this might happen?' is a legitimate one.

Decisions for change can be such a shock that there is no time to assimilate or absorb them, or what might be good about those changes. All we can do is feel threatened and resist – defend against the new way or undermine it.

Thus, it is important to not only provide employees with information to build a commitment to change, but also to arrange the *timing* of the information's release. Give people advance notice, a warning, and a chance to adjust their thinking.

The 'Difference' Effect

A fourth reason people resist change is the effect of 'difference' – the fact that change requires people to become conscious of, and to question, familiar routines and habits.

A great deal of work in organizations is simply habitual. In fact, most of us could not function very well in life if we were not engaged in a high proportion of 'mindless' habitual activities – like turning right when you walk down the corridor to work, or handling certain forms, or attending certain meetings. Imagine what it would be like if, every day you went to work, your office was in an entirely different place and the furniture was rearranged. You would stumble around, have trouble finding things, feel uncomfortable, and need to expend an additional amount of physical and emotional energy. This would be exhausting and fatiguing. Indeed, rapidly growing high-technology companies often present people with an approximation of this new-office-every-day nightmare, because the addition of new people and new tasks is ubiquitous, while established routines and habitual procedures are minimal. The over work syndrome and 'burn-out' phenomenon are accordingly common in the industry.

One analogy comes from my work on the introduction of a person who is 'different' (an 'O') in a group formerly made up of only one kind of person (the 'X's'), the theme of Goodmeasure's production. *A Tale of 'O'*. When a group of X's has been accustomed to doing things a certain way, to having habits and modes of conversation and jokes that are unquestioned, they are threatened by the presence of a person who seems to require operating in a different way. The X's are likely to resist the introduction of the O, because the difference effect makes them start feeling self-conscious, requires that they question even the habitual things that they do, and demands that they think about behavior that used to be taken for granted. The extra effort required to 'reprogram' the routines is what causes resistance to the change.

Thus, an important goal in managing change is to minimize or reduce the number of 'differences' introduced by the change, leaving as many habits and routines as possible in place. Sometimes managers think they should be doing just the opposite – changing everything else they can think of to symbolize that the core change is really happening. But commitment to change is more likely to occur when the change is not presented as a wild difference but rather as continuous with tradition. Roger Smith, the chairman of General Motors, launched what I consider one of the most revolutionary periods of change in the company's history by invoking not revolution, but tradition: 'I'm going to take this company back to the way Alfred Sloan intended it to be managed.'

Not only do many people need or prefer familiar routines, they also like familiar surroundings. Maintaining some familiar sights and sounds, the things that make people feel comfortable and at home, is very important in getting employees' commitment to a change.

Loss of Face

If accepting a change means admitting that the way things were done in the past was wrong, people are certain to resist. Nobody likes losing face or feeling embarassed in front of their peers. But sometimes making a commitment to a new procedure, product, or program carries with it the implicit assumption that the 'old ways' must have been wrong, thereby putting all the adherents of the 'old ways' in the uncomfortable position of either looking stupid for their past actions or being forced to defend them – and thereby arguing against any change.

The great sociologist Erving Goffman showed that people would go to great lengths to save face, even engaging in actions contrary to their long-term interest to avoid embarassment.

I have seen a number of new chief executives introduce future strategies in ways that 'put down' the preceding strategies, thus making automatic enemies of the members of the group that had formulated and executed them. The rhetoric of their speeches implies that the new way gains strength only in contrast to the failures and flaws of the old way – a kind of Maoist 'cultural revolution' mentality in business. 'The way we've been managing is terrible', one CEO says routinely. He thus makes it hard for people who lived the old ways to shed them for the new, because to do so is to admit they must have been 'terrible' before. While Mao got such confessions, businesses do not.

Instead, commitment to change is ensured when past actions are put in perspective – as the apparently right thing to do then, but now times are different. This way people do not lose face for changing; just the opposite. They look strong and flexible. They have been honored for what they accomplished under the old conditions, even if it is now time to change.

Building Commitment to Change

- ■ Allow room for participation in the planning of the change.
- ■ Leave choices within the overall decision to change.
- ■ Provide a clear picture of the change, a 'vision' with details about the new state.

→

Building Commitment to Change Continued

$\longrightarrow$

- Share information about change plans to the fullest extent possible.
- Divide a big change into more manageable and familiar steps; let people take a small step first.
- Minimize surprises; give people advance warning about new requirements.
- Allow for digestion of change requests – a chance to become accustomed to the idea of change before making a commitment.
- Repeatedly demonstrate your own commitment to the change.
- Make standards and requirements clear – tell exactly what is expected of people in the change.
- Offer positive reinforcement for competence; let people know they can do it.
- Look for and reward pioneers, innovators, and early successes to serve as models.
- Help people find or feel compensated for the extra time and energy change requires.
- Avoid creating obvious 'losers' from the change. (But if there are some, be honest with them – early on.)
- Allow expressions of nostalgia and grief for the past – then create excitement about the future.

Rosabeth Moss Kanter and the staff of Goodmeasure, Inc.

Concerns about Future Competence

Sometimes people resist change because of personal concerns about their future ability to be effective after the change: Can I do it? How will I do it? Will I make it under the new conditions? Do I have the skills to operate in a new way? These concerns may not be expressed out loud, but they can result in finding many reasons why change should be avoided.

In local telephone companies, employees have been told for years that they would be promoted for one set of reasons, and the workers had developed one set of skills and competencies. It is very threatening for many employees to be told that, all of a sudden, the new world demands a new set of competencies, a new set of more market-oriented entrepreneurial skills. Nobody likes to look inadequate. And nobody, especially people who have been around a long time, wants to feel that he or she has to 'start over again' in order to feel competent in the organization.

It is essential, when managing a change, to make sure that people *do* feel competent, that there is sufficient education and training available so that people understand what is happening and know that they can master it – that they *can* indeed do what is needed. Positive reinforcement is even more important in managing change than it is in managing routine situations.

In addition to education and training, people also need a chance to practice the new skills or actions without feeling that they are being judged or that they are going to look foolish to their colleagues and peers. They need a chance to get comfortable with new routines or new ways of operating without feeling stupid because they have questions to ask. Unfortunately, many corporations I know have spent a lot of time making executives and managers feel stupid if they have questions; they're the ones that are supposed to have the *answers*.

We have to be sensitive enough in the management of change to make sure that nobody feels stupid, that everyone can ask questions, and that everybody has a chance to be a learner, to come to feel competent in the new ways.

Ripple Effects

People may resist change for reasons connected to their own activities. Change does sometimes disrupt other kinds of plans or projects, or even personal and family activities that have nothing to do with the job, and anticipation of those disruptions causes resistance to change.

Changes inevitably send ripples beyond their intended impact. The ripples may also negate promises the organization has made. Plans or activities seemingly unrelated to the core of the change can be very important to people. Effective 'change masters' are sensitive to the ripples changes cause. They look for the ripples and introduce the change with *flexibility* so that, for example, people who have children can finish out the school year before relocating, or managers who want to finish a pet project can do so, or departments can go through a transition period rather than facing an abrupt change. That kind of sensitivity helps get people on board and makes them feel committed, rather than resistant, to the change.

More Work

One reasonable source of resistance to change is that change is simply *more work*. The effort it takes to manage things under routine circumstances needs to be multiplied when things are changing. Change requires more energy, more time, and greater mental preoccupation.

Members of project teams creating innovation put in a great deal of overtime on their own, because of the demands – and the lure – of creating something new. During the breakup of the Bell System, many managers worked 60 or 70 hour weeks during the process, not seeing their families, simply because of the work involved in moving such a large system from one state to another. And the pattern is repeated in corporation after corporation.

Change does require above-and-beyond effort. It cannot be done automatically, it cannot be done without extra effort, and it takes time. There is ample reason to resist change, if people do not want to put in the effort. They need support and compensation for the extra work of change in order to move from resistance to commitment.

Managers have options for providing that support. They can make sure that families are informed and understanding about the period of extra effort. They can make sure that people are given credit for the effort they are putting in and rewarded for the fact that they are working harder than ever before – rewards ranging from cash bonuses to special trips or celebrations. They can recognize that the extra effort is voluntary and not take it for granted, but thank people by providing recognition, as well as the additional support or facilities or comfort they need. While an employee is working harder, it certainly helps to know that your boss is acknowledging that extra effort and time.

Past Resentments

The ninth reason people resist change is negative, but it is a reality of organizational life – those cobwebs of the past that get in the way of the future. Anyone who has ever had a gripe against the organization is likely to resist the organization telling them that they now have to do something new.

The conspiracy of silence, that uneasy truce possible as long as everything remains the same and people can avoid confrontations, is broken when you ask for change. Unresolved grievances from the past rise up to entangle and hamper the change effort. One new plant manager at Honeywell was surprised by resistance to a quality-of-work-life program, which he thought the workers would like because of the direct benefits to them. Then he discovered that the workers were still angry at management for failing to get them a quiet air-conditioning system despite years of complaints about summer noise levels in the factory. Until be listened to them and responded to their grievance, he could not get their commitment to his change plans.

Sweeping away the cobwebs of the past is sometimes a necessity for overcoming resistance to change. As long as they remain aggrieved, people will not want to go along with something *we* want. Going forward can thus mean first going back – listening to past resentments and repairing past rifts.

Sometimes the Threat Is Real

The last reason people resist change is, in many ways, the most reasonable of all: *Sometimes the threat posed by the change is a real one.*

Sometimes a change does create winners and losers. Sometimes people do lose status, clout, or comfort because of the change. It would be naive to imagine otherwise. In fact, managing change well means recognizing its political realities.

The important thing here is to avoid pretense and false promises. If some people *are* going to lose something, they should hear about it early, rather than worrying about it constantly and infecting others with their anxiety or antagonism. And if some people are going to be let go or moved elsewhere, it is more humane to do it fast.

We all know the relief that people feel, even people who are being told the worst, at finally knowing that the thing they have feared is true. Now they can go ahead and plan their life. Thus, if some people are threatened by change because of the realities of their situations, managers should not pretend this is not so. Instead, they should make a clean break or a clean cut – as the first step in change, rather than leaving it to the end.

Of course, we all lose something in change, even the winners. Even those of us who are exhilarated about the opportunity it represents, or who are choosing to participate in a new era that we think is going to be better for our careers, more productive and technologically exciting, as many of the changes in American corporations promise to be.

Change is never entirely negative; it is also a tremendous opportunity. But even in that opportunity there is some small loss. It can be a loss of the past, a loss of routines, comforts, and traditions that were important, maybe a loss of relationships that became very close over time. Things will not, in fact, be the same any more.

Thus, we all need a chance to let go of the past, to 'mourn' it. Rituals of parting help us say goodbye to the people we have been close to, rather than just letting those relationships slip away. 'Memorial services', 'eulogies', or events to honor the past help us let go. Unfortunately, those kinds of ceremonies and rituals are not legitimate in some companies. Instead, people are in one state, and the next day they have to move to another state without any acknowledgement of the loss that is involved. But things like goodbye parties or file-burning ceremonies or tacking up the company's history on bulletin boards are not just frills or luxuries; they are rituals that make it easier for people to move into the future because their loss is acknowledged and dealt with.

Resistance to change is not irrational; it stems from good and understandable concerns. Managers who can analyze the sources of resistance are in the best position to invent the solutions to it – and to manage change smoothly and effectively.

There may be no skill more important for the challenging times ahead.

Minds, Hearts and Deeds: Cognitive, Affective and Behavioural Responses to Change

Roy Kark Smollan

Introduction

Leaders of change will hope, if not expect, that organisational members will comply with the change initiative, and preferably enthusiastically support it with appropriate action (Piderit, 2000). Duck (1993) suggests that organisations that introduce change need to gain the hearts and minds of their members if the change is to be successful. A number of researchers into organisational behaviour have criticised the neglect of emotion, both by managers and fellow researchers (e.g. Ashforth and Humphrey, 1995; Fisher and Ashkanasy, 2000). Studies of organisational change in particular have also been criticised for excluding the affective domain and focussing on cognitive and behavioural aspects (Mossholder et al., 2000). Since change is often an 'affective event' (Weiss and Cropanzano, 1996; Basch and Fisher, 2000) analysing its emotional impacts is critical.

Gersick (1991) has distinguished between incremental and radical change and points to the resulting positive and negative emotions. While she did not differentiate between the emotions that are likely under different types of change it seems logical that radical change will produce more emotional reaction than incremental change, since the ramifications of the former are much

Smollan, R.K. (2006) 'Minds, hearts and deeds: Cognitive, affective and behavioural responses to change', *Journal of Change Management*. Vol. 6, no. 2, pp. 143–58.

greater. It must also be noted that change is often a process that unfolds over time, sometimes years (Piderit, 2000; Isabella, 1990; Paterson and Cary, 2002), and that the human responses will be as dynamic as the changes themselves. Changes of greater complexity are likely to generate more negative and more intense emotions (Kiefer, 2004) and more resistance (George and Jones, 2001), and therefore require more careful and sustained management. However, it will be suggested in this article, that no matter what type of change is contemplated, leaders will need to gauge how employees might respond on all three levels.

In this article I will review literature on the relationship between cognition and emotion in the context of change, present a model of cognitive, affective and behavioural responses to change, analyse the variables that mediate and moderate these responses, and derive a related set of propositions that can be tested empirically.

Cognition and Emotion in the Context of Change

The relationship between emotion and cognition has been debated for centuries by philosophers, psychologists, novelists and organisational theorists, with a number of different conclusions – emotion is the opposite of reason (Weber, 1946), emotion is deeply interwoven with reason (Ashforth and Humphrey, 1995), emotion can occur independently of reason (Zajonc, 1980; Izard, 1992).

Cognition is a process of thought in which a person first becomes aware of stimuli, appraises the significance of those stimuli and then considers possible behavioural responses (Scherer, 1999). Emotions are immediate responses to environmental stimuli that are important to the individual and tend to be short in duration (Frijda, 1988; Gray and Watson, 2001). Emotion needs to be distinguished from moods, which are more diffuse in nature, not specifically linked to events or objects, lower in intensity and longer lasting (Gray and Watson, 2001; Weiss and Cropanzano, 1996), and from temperament, which is a facet of disposition and is a relatively stable and biologically rooted pattern of individual differences (Bates, 2000). Affect comprises emotion, mood and temperament. Circumplex models of affect have analysed its dimensions along two main axes, pleasantness (positive and negative emotions) and arousal or activation (high and low) (Tellegen et al., 1999; Russell and Carroll, 1999).

Lazarus (1991) suggests that the relationship between cognition and emotion is bidirectional – emotion influences cognition, cognition elicits emotion. He asserts that while cognition does not necessarily lead to emotion, emotion cannot occur without cognition. Emotion alerts the individual to factors in the environment which are potentially significant. For example, a feeling of anxiety may heighten awareness of the need to take action, while guilt and anger produce thoughts that may lead to redress of an injustice.

In the context of organisational change employees become aware of change through a variety of mechanisms, from formal communication, peer discussion and other observable cues. Through primary appraisal (Lazarus, 1999) employees evaluate the significance of the change event for themselves (Weiss and Cropanzano, 1996) and can extend this to the impact on others and the organisation itself. Secondary appraisal focuses on the causes and agents of change, and on possible coping strategies (Lazarus, 1999; Scherer, 1999; Paterson and Hartel, 2002; Jordan et al., 2002). George and Jones' (2001) model of resistance to change delineates the steps that occur when employees use a combination of cognitive and affective processes to make sense of the impending changes, particularly when the existing schemata (cognitive frameworks that help people to understand events) are challenged.

Cognitive and affective responses create attitudes to change that may contain positive and negative elements (Piderit, 2000) and will be influenced by a range of factors, including perceived favourability of outcomes and fairness of outcomes, processes of decision making and communication (Weiss et al., 1999; Paterson and Hartel, 2002; Matheny and Smollan, 2005).

The question that now arises is to what extent cognitive and affective processes predict behavioural responses. Do employees follow their minds *and* their hearts when deciding how to respond to organisational stimuli, and specifically in the context of this article, change events? The model presented below depicts the nature of the responses and the factors that affect them.

A Model of Cognitive, Affective and Behavioural Responses to Change

Figure 12.1 shows that organisational change triggers cognitive responses (positive, negative, neutral or mixed evaluations) which are mediated by perceptions of the favourability of the outcomes, and the justice, scale, pace and timing of change. Cognitive responses impact on, and are impacted by, affective responses (positive, negative, neutral or mixed emotions) (Lazarus, 1991). Before behaviour occurs (positive, negative, neutral or mixed – from the view of the organisation), people usually consider the implications of behavioural choices. Piderit (2000), for example, suggests that employees rarely engage in resistant behaviour without considering the possible personal consequences. Some, however, may be moved to act on affective impulses without considering the ramifications of their actions. Cognitive, affective and behavioural responses are moderated by factors within the individual (emotional intelligence, disposition, previous experience of change, change and stressors outside the workplace); factors within the change manager/s (leadership ability, emotional intelligence and trustworthiness); and within the organisation (culture and context). Employee responses may alter some aspect of the change programme, highlighting the dynamic and circular nature of the process. The model is applicable to a wide spectrum of change events but the nature of the change will clearly have differing impacts on employees. An organisational restructuring to accommodate growth, accompanied by the recruitment and promotion of staff, will naturally evoke different emotions from one that results in downsizing. The concept of the change context will be revisited towards the end of the paper as a moderating variable to cognitive, affective and behavioural responses.

Positive responses: Employees may believe that the changes will be beneficial, to the organisation, some of its external stakeholders, to groups of employees or the individual employee. Positive cognitions should lead to positive emotions that could range in intensity from exhilaration and enthusiasm to pleasure and contentment (French, 2001; Antonacopoulou and Gabriel, 2001). On the behavioural level employees willingly engage in the tasks expected of them and may even attempt to exceed performance expectations. Organisational Citizenship Behaviours (Organ, 1988; Spector and Fox, 2002), which encompass a range of pro-social behaviours, such as helping others, showing initiative, altruistic actions, loyalty and increased effort, may result.

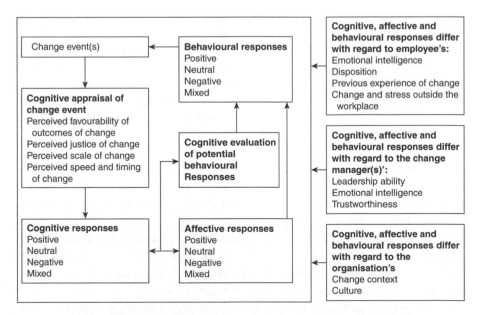

Figure 12.1 Model of responses to organisational change

Neutral responses: The changes may have little perceived impact on some employees including little, if any, emotional arousal. They are likely to demonstrate acquiescence or submissive collaboration (Bacharach et al., 1996).

Negative responses: Employees who experience strong cognitive reactions, accompanied by strong negative emotions, such as fear or anger, will be likely to reject the changes (Kiefer, 2004). Rejection is a term that encompasses but is not confined to the term resistance, and manifests itself in many ways: disloyalty, neglect, exit or intention to quit (Turnley and Feldman, 1999), lower trust (Kiefer, 2004; Brockner et al., 1997), active campaigning against the change (Mishra and Spreitzer, 1998), deception (Shapiro et al., 1995), sabotage (La Nuez and Jermier, 1994; Spector and Fox, 2002), violence and aggression (Spector and Fox, 2002; Fox et al., 2001; Neuman and Baron, 1998), industrial action, such as strikes, go-slows and refusal to work or complete certain tasks (Skarlicki et al., 1999). Researchers have used the terms Organisational Resistance Behaviours (Skarlicki et al., 1999) and Counterproductive Work Behaviours (Spector and Fox, 2002) to categorise a number of dysfunctional and anti-social behaviours, some of which are targeted at organisational members, and some at the organisation itself. It should also be noted that negative cognitive and affective responses are often well-intentioned (Piderit, 2000). They may result in action construed as appropriate, and which lead to further discussion and the implementation of more acceptable, and possibly more beneficial, organisational outcomes.

The term resistance to change has been criticised by Dent and Goldberg (1999) and Piderit (2000). They allege that it is overused and inaccurately used. Resistance is often seen as refusal to engage in the change or subverting it, but can also be conceptualised as reluctance (Piderit, 2000) or inertia (George and Jones, 2001). Anticipated resistance becomes a self-fulfilling prophecy whereby managers have been educated and trained to see resistance as inevitable, negative and largely due to the ignorance or wilfulness of recalcitrant employees. Resistance is not always confined to 'workers' – managers themselves are often sources of resistance too (Spreitzer and Quinn, 1996; La Nuez and Jermier, 1994).

Mixed responses: Employees who have mixed cognitive evaluations of different aspects of change, mixed positive and negative emotions, or, say, a positive cognition but a negative emotion, may demonstrate positive, negative, neutral or mixed behaviours. For example, employees could consider an extended work schedule to be in the interests of the customers, and therefore the organisation, but not believe that all employees should be required to work inconvenient shifts, and feel anxiety and anger if they are forced to do so. The behavioural outcome could be to persuade management to change the schedule or a colleague to change shifts. An employee may however simply accept new methods of record keeping that accompany the change, and comply with them, yet simultaneously experience happiness in dealing with different customers and perform at a high level. Piderit (2000) notes the ambivalence within and among the three dimensions of attitudes to change. Behavioural responses in particular, can be contradictory, for example overt support for the change, accompanied by a covert rejection by means of an anonymous submission to a suggestion box. The need for a specific change might be accepted on a cognitive level but there could be emotional resistance. The nature of the behavioural response is therefore not a simple outcome of cognitive and affective reactions. There are a number of forces at work that prevent what would seem a logical, if not preferred, response (Piderit, 2000). Research propositions cannot automatically state, for example, that negative cognitive and emotional responses to change will lead to negative behavioural responses.

Variables Mediating Cognitive Responses to Change

Before a judgement takes place (a cognitive evaluation), people use a number of lenses through which they view the changes.

Perceived Favourability of Outcomes

Employees will analyse the favourability of outcomes for themselves, others and for the organisation, and there may be differing outcomes for various stakeholders (Paterson and Cary, 2002). For example, Matheny and Smollan (2005) found that individuals saw different outcomes for themselves, for others and for the organisation. Where employees find it difficult to predict outcomes their responses will remain either neutral or ambivalent. Disposition (which will be considered in more depth later) can play a significant role, with optimists and pessimists experiencing opposite forms of anticipation (Wanberg and Banas, 2000).

Proposition 1: Cognitive responses to change are mediated by the perceived favourability of the outcomes of change.

Perceived Justice of Change

Employees' cognitive and affective responses to change are tempered by their perceptions of fairness (Cobb et al., 1995; Skarlicki et al., 1999). A considerable body of research on organisational justice has identified distinctive elements. Distributive justice refers to the fairness of outcomes (Homans, 1961).

Procedural justice relates to perceptions of the fairness by which decisions are made (Thibaut and Walker, 1975; Leventhal, 1980; Tyler and Lind, 1992). This includes interactional justice (Bies and Moag, 1986), divided into inter-personal justice and informational justice (Greenberg, 1993), and is manifested in the ways in which managers communicate outcomes and procedures to staff. Systemic justice (Sheppard et al., 1992; Harlos and Pinder, 2000) is an over-arching term for the perceived fairness of a wide variety of practices over time, and is a facet of the organisational culture. In the context of organisa-tional change employees may view announced changes against the backdrop of historical practices, including previous change initiatives.

While perceptions of each form of justice have their own distinctive impact (Paterson and Cary, 2002; Matheny and Smollan, 2005) Lind's (2001) Fairness Heuristic Theory suggests that people take a holistic view of events and issues when making fairness judgements. While perceptions of justice would tend to produce positive emotions, perceptions of injustice will lead to more intense negative emotions (Mikula et al., 1998; Weiss et al., 1999). Negative perceptions and feelings are likely to lead to negative behavioural responses.

Violations of the psychological contract (Rousseau, 1988; Robinson and Rousseau, 1989) also produce a sense of injustice and strong emotional reactions. The psychological contract, an employee perception of mutual obligations of employer and employee, is a distinct construct to that of organ-isational justice but there are considerable overlaps (Cropanzano and Prehar, 2001). Violations of the psychological contract lead to various negative behavioural responses, such as intentions to quit, neglect and a decrease in Organisational Citizenship Behaviours (Turnley and Feldman, 1999; Kickul et al., 2002).

Proposition 2: Cognitive responses to change are mediated by employees' perceptions of justice.

The Scale of the Change

Cognitive reactions to change will be influenced by the scale of the change (Mossholder et al., 2000). Dirks et al. (1996) propose that individuals with a strong sense of psychological ownership of some aspect of their jobs will find revolutionary change threatening, and tend to resist it. George and Jones (2001) argue that changes to existing schemata will have a more profound impact on people than changes within the schemata themselves, a point also made by Gersick (1991). While welcome change outcomes may engender pos-itive reactions (French, 2001) the sheer scale of the change or too many new events occurring simultaneously (Blount and Janicik, 2001; Kiefer, 2004) may trigger negative reactions.

Proposition 3: Cognitive responses to change will be affected by the perceived scale of the change.

Perceived Speed and Timing of the Change

There is little management literature dealing with individual responses to the speed of change. Most research has focussed on organisational pacing from a strategic and tactical perspective (e.g. Gersick, 1994; Sastry, 1997) or the extent to which an individual's work pace is affected by schedule changes. For example, Blount and Janicik (2001) propose that an unwanted schedule delay will be viewed particularly negatively if it is unexpected, if the period of delay is unknown, and if impatience is a dispositional influence. Conversely, if the pace of change is deemed too fast employees may believe they cannot take the necessary steps in time, or do so with severe disruption to normal routines, and they are likely to react negatively (Blount and Janicik, 2001; Huy, 2001).

Huy (2001) provides a useful model of how different styles of management intervention impact on different types of change. For example, more radical forms of change require a longer time frame for implementation. Since using an inappropriate approach creates negative employee perceptions he urges managers to be aware of individual responses to not only the pacing, but also the timing and sequencing of organisational changes. The introduction of a major change at the busiest time of the year or month, or the announcement of a new executive bonus scheme following downsizing, are bound to be perceived negatively by many employees.

Proposition 4: Cognitive responses to change are mediated by the perceived speed and timing of the change.

Variables Moderating Cognitive, Affective and Behavioural Responses to Change

A cognitive response triggers an affective response although the impact has also been considered bi-directional (Lazarus, 1991). Perceived favourability of outcomes, justice, scale, and speed and timing of change, all have affective elements.

There are a number of variables that moderate cognitive, affective and behavioural responses. Some of the moderators lie within the individual, and some within the manager(s) leading or implementing the change, and some within the broader context of the organisation itself.

Variables within the Employee

Employees' Emotional Intelligence (EI)

Competing models of emotional intelligence have focussed on EI as ability (Salovey and Mayer, 1990) and on EI as a combination of ability and disposition (Goleman, 1998; Bar-On, 1997). Goleman (1998), for example, identifies empathy and integrity as key characteristics of EI. Focussing on the ability model emotional intelligence is seen as the ability to accurately perceive the emotions of oneself and others, to regulate one's emotions and respond appropriately to the emotions of others (Mayer and Salovey, 1997). In the context of organisational change employees who are high in EI are able to discern and control the feelings they experience. Employees high in EI will be aware of the potential impact of their behaviour on their peers and managers and moderate their words and actions. Cognitive processes are thus embedded in the affective processes and the two promote or constrain behaviour. For example, Jordan et al. (2002) propose that employees with high EI are able to cognitively and affectively process issues pertaining to job insecurity, and devise appropriate coping strategies.

Proposition 5: Cognitive, affective and behavioural responses to change are moderated by employees' emotional intelligence.

Disposition of Employees

It is commonly believed by lay people that the way in which employees respond to organisational change is directly related to disposition (Wanous et al., 2000). Change often involves uncertainty and those who have what French (2001, p. 482) refers to as negative capability are able to 'tolerate ambiguity and paradox' since they have the 'capacity to integrate mental and emotional states' and consequently adapt their behaviour. Watson and Clark (1997) specifically identified a predilection for change in various facets of life as representative of people with high positive affectivity, a characteristic which will also be found in organisational contexts (Spector and Fox, 2002).

In an empirical study Judge et al. (1999) found seven personality factors predicted reactions to change, which they grouped into two main categories. Positive self-concept included locus of control, self-efficacy, self-esteem, and positive affectivity, while risk tolerance included openness to experience, tolerance of ambiguity and risk aversion. In particular, tolerance for ambiguity and positive affectivity were strongly correlated to self-reported ability to deal with change. Wanberg and Banas (2000) revealed that self-esteem, optimism and perceived control were related to acceptance of change.

Jimmieson et al. (2004) reported change-related efficacy to be a significant variable in determining responses to organisational change. In developing and testing a scale to measure dispositional reactions to change, Oreg (2003) found four major relevant personality factors: need for routine, emotional responsiveness, short-term focus on outcomes and cognitive rigidity. In a number of empirical studies he found that disposition predicted reaction to change, regardless of context.

Proposition 6: Cognitive, affective and behavioural responses to change are moderated by employee disposition.

Employees' Previous Experience of Change

Previous experience of change has the potential of producing two opposing responses to a newly announced change. An employee who has previously experienced a positive change, or who has coped well with a negative change, may respond positively, while an employee with a negative experience would view the new change with unease. Past failures in organisational change breed cynicism, which, according to Wanous et al. (2000), becomes a self-fulfilling prophecy. In this context the employees are pessimistic about outcomes, attribute blame to management (Wanous et al., 2000), and their lack of commitment can undermine the changes (Abraham, 2000). Even if previous initiatives have been successful frequent changes will trigger negative reactions (Kiefer, 2004).

Proposition 7: Cognitive, affective and behavioural responses to change are moderated by employees' previous experience of change.

Change and Stress Producing Events Outside the Workplace

An organisational change impacts on one part of an employee's life. The manner in which an employee reacts to the change depends on the broader context of his/her life. The Holmes-Rahe Social Readjustment Rating scale, developed in 1967, and other instruments that have followed, have over the years demonstrated high correlations between recent life changes and physical and psychological symptoms (Rahe et al., 2000). An individual faced with a major change outside of work, or a number of minor changes, may react negatively – on cognitive, affective and behavioural levels – to an organisational change. Any stress-inducing issue outside of work can trigger negative responses to change at work, as employees' coping resources are depleted. Employee disposition is a related factor – those with higher resilience are better able to cope with additional demands (Wanberg and Banas, 2000).

Proposition 8: Employees responses to organisational change are moderated by changes and any stress-producing event outside of work.

Variables within the Change Manager(s)

Two or more levels of management may be involved in designing and implementing organisational change and the perceptions of employees of the contributions of different managers will produce different evaluations.

Leadership Ability of Change Manager(s)

The links between leadership and successful organisational change have been documented in many works (e.g. Eisenbach et al., 1999). Two major types of leadership have been associated with change, transformational leadership (Bass, 1999; Yukl, 1999) and charismatic leadership (Conger et al., 2000; Yukl, 1999). These literatures have emphasised the ability of leaders to drive change and motivate followers to higher levels of performance. While there are many other types of leadership successful change managers have to adopt styles that engage followers (Huy, 2001). Participative forms of leadership (Kotter and Schlesinger, 1979; Chawla and Kelloway, 2004) have long been considered to have considerable impact in overcoming resistance to change and simultaneously affecting perceptions of organisational justice (Thibaut and Walker, 1975).

Proposition 9: Cognitive, affective and behavioural responses to change are moderated by the leadership ability of the change manager(s).

Emotional Intelligence of Change Manager(s)

Transformational leadership has been associated with emotional intelligence (Ashkanasy and Tse, 2000). Leaders with high EI demonstrate both empathy and integrity (Parry and Proctor-Thomson, 2002) which are key qualities in developing employee trust since leaders are able to influence people on both the cognitive and affective levels (George, 2000; Ashkanasy and Tse, 2000). Leaders need to be particularly adept at discerning the emotional reactions of employees to change and providing the necessary support, especially given the uncertainty and negative emotions that accompany many changes (Kiefer, 2004).

Proposition 10: Cognitive, affective and behavioural responses of employees to change are moderated by the emotional intelligence of the change manager(s).

Perceived Trustworthiness of the
Change Manager(s)

Perceptions of the trustworthiness of the managers will also influence employees' responses to change. Leventhal (1980) and Tyler and Lind (1992) noted trust to be a significant factor in the formation of employee perceptions of procedural justice and that this impacts directly on their choice of behaviour. Brockner et al. (1997) demonstrated empirically that employees' trust in managers derives from perceptions of procedural justice and has a significant impact on their acceptance of changes, particularly when the outcomes are unfavourable, a link which was confirmed by Paterson and Cary (2002) in a study on downsizing. Chawla and Kelloway (2004) found trust to be related to procedural and informational justice during a merger. Parry and Proctor-Thomson (2002) discovered that integrity contributes strongly to transformational leadership ability, while Conger et al. (2000) found a similar relationship with charismatic leadership. Kiefer (2004) demonstrated that negative emotions during periods of change lead to reduced trust in leaders.

Proposition 11: Cognitive, affective and behavioural responses to change are moderated by employees' perceptions of the trustworthiness of the change manager(s).

Variables within the Context
of the Organisation

Organisational Culture

The ways in which individuals interpret organisational events, including change events, depend to a large extent on their previous history with the organisation. An organisation where speedy response to change is a major driver will encounter different individual responses to one that is more bureaucratic and less agile. Paradoxically, an organisation that seldom consults staff may find that a unilateral change, even an unpalatable one, is accepted as the norm, whereas an organisation that invites participation as general rule, but fails to do so during a change, may find a surprised and somewhat hostile reception. Perceived systemic injustice (Sheppard et al., 1992; Harlos and Pinder, 2000) will nevertheless lend weight to views that an announced change is unfair.

Where the culture itself is the object of change, there may be more resistance as the 'deep structure' (Gersick, 1991) or schemata (Bartunek and Moch, 1987; George and Jones, 2001) are dismantled, and the implications and mechanisms are complex (Porras and Robertson, 1992). There is a strong emotional undertone to organisational culture (Porras and Robertson, 1992) and if this is damaged the consequences can be severe (Huy, 2001).

In an empirical study Kabanoff et al. (1995) found that organisations with different value structures depicted and communicated change differently, but the authors did not specifically address individual responses. Turnbull (2002), however, studied the ways individuals responded to an organisation's attempts to deliberately change its culture to one of trust, openness, innovation and loyalty, in workshops laden with emotional appeals. She found that employees did experience both cognitive and affective reactions, but often in unintended ways, with mistrust, anger and embarrassment often eventuating. Employees reported the need to hide their feelings and in many cases pretended to comply with the changes.

Proposition 12: Cognitive, affective and behavioural responses to change are moderated by organisational culture.

Organisational Change Context

To return to a point made during the introduction of the model, the context of the change underpins many of the responses. The mostly frequently cited example of negative change is downsizing, which has a profound affect on victims (Paterson and Cary, 2002) and a lesser, but noticeably significant, impact on survivors (O'Neill and Lenn, 1995; Armstrong-Stassen, 1998). A merger (even without any redundancies) may create winners and losers, as some people are given greater responsibilities and more status while others may experience the opposite (Kiefer, 2002). Office relocations may also produce perceived winners and losers (Daley and Geyer, 1994). An expansion programme will generally produce positive reactions. Naturally, with any change there is the possibility of mixed responses within individuals. A person who gains promotion from a change, or a bigger department to manage, or who may need to travel more, will consider the extra demands that these changes will bring. Heightened anxiety and a sense of regret may exist alongside the more joyous outcomes.

Proposition 13: Cognitive, affective and behavioural responses to change are moderated by the change context.

Conclusion

Change is a potentially affective event (Weiss and Cropanzano, 1996) and the model and propositions advanced above extend the literature on organisational change, and in particular, the impact of cognitive and affective reactions on behaviour. Testing of these propositions by means of quantitative and qualitative research will uncover the complexities of these relationships and the myriad of variables involved, and add to knowledge of how organisational change can be better understood and managed.

References

Abraham, R. (2000) 'Organizational cynicism: bases and consequences', *Genetic, Social and General Psychology Monographs*, vol. 126, no. 3, pp. 269–92.

Antonacopoulou, E. P. and Gabriel, Y. (2001) 'Emotion, learning and organizational change: towards an integration of psychoanalytic and other perspectives', *Journal of Organizational Change Management*, vol. 14, no. 5, pp. 435–51.

Armstrong-Stassen, M. (1998) 'The effect of gender and organizational level on how survivors appraise and cope with organizational downsizing', *Journal of Applied Behavioral Science*, vol. 34, no. 2, pp. 125–42.

Ashforth, B. E. and Humphrey, R. H. (1995) 'Emotion in the workplace: a reappraisal', *Human Relations*, vol. 48, no. 2, pp. 97–125.

Ashkanasy, N. M. and Tse, B. (2000) 'Transformational leadership as management of emotion: a conceptual review' in Ashkanasy, N. M. et al. (eds) *Emotions in the Workplace: Research, Theory and Practice*, Westport, CT, Quorum Books, pp. 221–35.

Bacharach, S. et al. (1996) 'The organizational transformation process: dissonance reduction and logics of action in the aftermath of deregulation', *Administrative Science Quarterly*, vol. 41, no. 3, pp. 477–506.

Bar-On, R. (1997) *The Emotional Quotient Inventory (EQ-I) Technical Manual*, Toronto, Multi-Health Systems.

Bartunek, J. M. and Moch, M. K. (1987) 'First-order, second-order and third-order change and organization development interventions; a cognitive approach', *Journal of Applied Behavioral Science*, vol. 23, no. 4, pp. 483–500.

Basch, J. and Fisher, C. D. (2000) 'Affective events-emotions matrix: classification of work events and associated emotions' in Ashkanasy, N. M. et al. (eds) *Emotions in the Workplace: Research, Theory and Practice*, Westport, CT, Quorum Books, pp. 36–48.

Bass, B. M. (1999) 'Two decades of research and development in transformational leadership', *European Journal of Work and Organizational Psychology*, vol. 8, no. 1, pp. 9–32.

Bates, J. E. (2000) 'Temperament as an emotion construct: theoretical and practical issues' in Lewis, M. and Haviland-Jones, J. M. (eds) *Handbook of Emotions* (2nd edn), New York, The Guilford Press, pp. 382–96.

Bies, R. J. and Moag, J. S. (1986) 'Interactional justice: communication criteria of fairness' in Lewicki, R. J. et al. (eds) *Research on Negotiation in Organizations*, Greenwich, CT, JAI Press, pp. 43–55.

Brockner, J. et al. (1997) 'When trust matters: the moderating effect of outcome favourability', *Administrative Science Quarterly*, vol. 42, no. 3, pp. 558–83.

Blount, S. and Janicik, G. A. (2001) 'When plans change: examining how people evaluate timing changes in work organization', *Academy of Management Review*, vol. 26, no. 4, pp. 566–85.

Chawla, A. and Kelloway, E. K. (2004) 'Predicting openness and commitment to change', *The Leadership and Organizational Development Journal*, vol. 25, no. 6, pp. 485–98.

Cobb, A. T. et al. (1995) 'The role justice plays in organizational change', *Public Administration Quarterly*, 1992, pp. 135–51.

Conger, J. A. et al. (2000) 'Charismatic leadership and follower effects', *Journal of Organizational Behavior*, vol. 21, no. 7, pp. 747–67.

Cropanzano, R. and Prehar, C. (2001) 'Emerging justice concerns in an era of changing psychological contracts' in Cropanzano, R. (ed.) *Justice in the Workplace: From Theory to Practice*, 2, Mahwah, NJ, Lawrence Erlbaum and Associates, pp. 245–69.

Daley, J. P. and Geyer, P. D. (1994) 'The role of fairness in implementing large-scale change: employee evaluations of process and outcome in seven facility relocations', *Journal of Organizational Behavior*, vol. 15, pp. 623–28.

Dent, E. B. and Goldberg, S. G. (1999) 'Challenging "resistance to change"', *Journal of Applied Behavioral Science*, vol. 35, no. 1, pp. 25–41.

Dirks, K. T. et al. (1996) 'Psychological ownership in organizations' in Woodman, R. W. and Passmore, W. A. (eds) *Research in Organizational Change and Development*, 9, Greenwich, CT, JAI Press, pp. 1–23.

Duck, J. D. (1993) 'Managing change: The art of balancing', *Harvard Business Review*, vol. 71, no. 6, pp. 109–18.

Eisenbach, R. et al. (1999) 'Transformational leadership in the context of organizational change', *Journal of Organizational Change Management*, vol. 12, no. 2, pp. 80–88.

Fisher, C. D. and Ashkanasy, N. M. (2000) 'The emerging role of emotions in work life: an introduction', *Journal of Organizational Behavior*, vol. 21, pp. 123–29.

Fox, S. et al. (2001) 'Counterproductive Work Behaviour (CWB) in response to job stressors and organizational justice: Some mediator and moderator tests for autonomy and emotions', *Journal of Vocational Behavior*, vol. 59, pp. 291–309.

French, R. (2001) '"Negative capability": Managing the confusing uncertainties of change', *Journal of Organizational Change Management*, vol. 14, no. 5, pp. 480–92.

Frijda, N. (1988) 'The laws of emotion', *American Psychologist*, vol. 43, no. 5, pp. 349–58.

George, J. M. (2000) 'Emotions and leadership: The role of emotional intelligence', *Human Relations*, vol. 53, no. 8, pp. 1027–55.

George, J. M. and Jones, G. R. (2001) 'Towards a process model of individual change in organizations', *Human Relations*, vol. 54, no. 4, pp. 419–44.

Gersick, C. J. G. (1991) 'Revolutionary change theories: a multilevel exploration of the punctuated equilibrium paradigm', *Academy of Management Review*, vol. 16, no. 1, pp. 10–36.

Gersick, C. J. G. (1994) 'Pacing strategic change: The case of a new venture', *Academy of Management Journal*, vol. 37, no. 1, pp. 9–45.

Goleman, D. (1998) *Working with Emotional Intelligence*, London, Bloomsbury Publishing.

Gray, E. K. and Watson, D. (2001) 'Emotions, mood and temperament: similarities, differences, and a synthesis' in Payne, R. and Cooper, C. (eds) *Emotions at Work: Theory, Research and Applications for Management*, Chichester, John Wiley and Sons, pp. 21–43.

Greenberg, J. (1993) 'The social side of fairness: Interpersonal and informational classes of organizational justice' in Cropanzano, R. (ed.) *Justice in the Workplace*, Hillsdale, NJ, Lawrence Erlbaum Associates, pp. 79–103.

Harlos, K. P. and Pinder, C. C. (2000) 'Emotion and injustice in the workplace' in Fineman, S. (ed.) *Emotions in Organisations*, Vol. 2, London, Sage Publications, pp. 1–24.

Homans, G. C. (1961) *Social Behavior: Its Elementary Forms*, New York, Harcourt, Brace and World.

Huy, Q. N. (1999) 'Emotional capability, emotional intelligence and radical change', *Academy of Management Review*, vol. 24, no. 2, pp. 325–45.

Huy, Q. N. (2001) 'Time, temporal capability and planned change', *Academy of Management Review*, vol. 26, no. 4, pp. 601–23.

Isabella, L. A. (1990) 'Evolving interpretations as a change unfolds: How managers construe key organizational events', *Academy of Management Journal*, vol. 33, no. 1, pp. 7–41.

Izard, C. E. (1992) 'Basic emotions, relations among emotions, and emotion-cognition relations', *Psychological Review*, vol. 99, pp. 561–65.

Jimmieson, N. L. et al. (2004) 'A longitudinal study of employee adaptation to organizational change: The role of change-related information and change-related self-efficacy', *Journal of Occupational Health Psychology*, vol. 9, no. 1, pp. 11–27.

Jordan, P. J. et al. (2002) 'Emotional intelligence as moderator of emotional and behavioural reactions to job insecurity', *Academy of Management Review*, vol. 27, no. 3, pp. 361–72.

Judge, T. A. et al. (1999) 'Managerial coping with organizational change: A dispositional perspective', *Journal of Applied Psychology*, vol. 84, no. 1, pp. 107–22.

Kabanoff, B. et al. (1995) 'Espoused values and organizational change themes', *Academy of Management Journal*, vol. 38, no. 4, pp. 1075–104.

Kickul, J. et al. (2002) 'Promise breaking during radical organizational change: Do justice interventions make a difference?' *Journal of Organizational Behaviour*, vol. 23, pp. 469–88.

Kiefer, T. (2002) 'Understanding the emotional experience of organizational change: Evidence from a merger', *Advances in Developing Human Resources*, vol. 4, no. 1, pp, 39–61.

Kiefer, T. (2004) 'Towards an integrated model for understanding antecedents and consequences of negative emotions in ongoing change', paper presented at 4th International Conference on Emotions in Organizational Life, London.

Kotter, J. A. and Schlesinger, L. A. (1979) 'Choosing strategies for change', *Harvard Business Review*, vol. 57, no. 2, pp. 106–14.

La Nuez, D. and Jermier, J. M. (1994) 'Sabotage by managers and technocrats: neglected patterns of resistance at work' in Jermier, J. M. (1994) *Resistance and Power in Organizations*, London, Routledge.

Lazarus, R. S. (1991) 'Cognition and motivation in emotion', *American Psychologist*, vol. 46, no. 4, pp. 352–67.

Lazarus, R. S. (1999) *Stress and Motivation: A New Synthesis*, New York, Springer Publishing Company.

Leventhal, G. S. (1980) 'What should be done with equity theory?' in Gergen, K. J. et al. (eds) *Social Exchange: Advances in Theory and Research*, New York, Plenum, pp. 27–55.

Lind, E. A. (2001) 'Fairness heuristic theory: Justice judgments as pivotal cognitions in organizational relations' in Greenberg, J. and Cropanzano, R. (eds) *Advances in Organizational Justice*, Stanford, CA, Stanford University Press, pp. 57–88.

Matheny, J. A. and Smollan, R. K. (2005) 'Taking change to heart: Exploring emotions experienced through change events' in Ashkanasy, N. M. et al. (eds) *The Effect of Affect in Organizational Settings*, Oxford, Elsevier.

Mayer, J. D. and Salovey, P. (1997) 'What is emotional intelligence' in Salovey, P. and Sluyter, D. J. (1997) *Emotional Development and Emotional Intelligence: Educational Implications*, New York, Basic Books, pp. 3–31.

Mikula, G. et al. (1998) 'The role of injustice in the elicitation of differential emotional reactions', *Personality and Social Psychology Bulletin*, vol. 24, pp. 769–83.

Mishra, A. K. and Spreitzer, G. M. (1998) 'Explaining how survivors respond to downsizing: The role of trust, empowerment, justice, and work redesign', *Academy of Management Review*, vol. 23, no. 3, pp. 567–89.

Mossholder, K. W. et al. (2000) 'Emotion during organizational transformation', *Group and Organization Management*, vol. 25, no. 3, pp. 220–43.

Neuman, J. H. and Baron, R. A. (1998) 'Workplace violence and workplace aggression: Evidence concerning specific forms, potential causes and preferred targets', *Journal of Management*, vol. 24, no. 3, pp. 391–419.

O'Neill, H. M. and Lenn, D. J. (1995) 'Voices of survivors: wards that downsizing CEOs should hear', *Academy of Management Executive*, vol. 9, no. 4, pp. 23–34.

Oreg, S. (2003) 'Resistance to change: Developing an individual differences measure', *Journal of Applied Psychology*, vol. 88, no. 4, pp. 680–93.

Organ, D. W. (1988) *Organizational Citizenship Behavior: The Good Soldier Syndrome*, Lexington, MA, Lexington Books).

Parry, K. W. and Proctor-Thomson, S. B. (2002) 'Perceived integrity of transformational leaders in organisational settings', *Journal of Business Ethics*, vol. 35, pp. 75–96.

Paterson, J. A. and Cary, J. (2002) 'Organizational justice, change anxiety and acceptance of downsizing: Preliminary tests of an AET-based model', *Motivation and Emotion*, vol. 26, no. 1, pp. 83–103.

Paterson, J. A. and Hartel, C. E. J. (2002) 'An integrated affective and cognitive model to explain employees' responses to downsizing' in Ashkanasy, N. M. et al. (eds) *Managing Emotions in the Workplace*, Armonk, NY, M. E. Sharpe, pp. 25–44.

Piderit, S. K. (2000) 'Rethinking resistance and recognizing ambivalence: A multi-dimensional view of attitudes towards organizational change', *Academy of Management Review*, vol. 25, pp. 783–94.

Porras, J. I. and Robertson, P. J. (1992) 'Organisational development: Theory, practice and research' in Dunette, M. D. et al. (1992) *Handbook of Organizational Psychology* (2nd edn), Palo Alto, Consulting Psychologist Press, pp. 719–822.

Rahe, R. H. et al. (2000) 'The stress and coping inventory: An educational and research instrument', *Stress Medicine*, vol. 16, pp. 199–208.

Robinson, S. and Rousseau, D. (1994) 'Violating the psychological contract, not the exception but the norm', *Journal of Organizational Behavior*, vol. 15, no. 3, pp. 245–59.

Rousseau, D. M. (1989) 'Psychological and implied contracts in organization', *Employee Rights and Responsibilities Journal*, vol. 2, pp. 121–39.

Russell, J. A. and Carroll, J. M. (1999) 'On the bipolarity of positive and negative affect', *Psychological Bulletin*, vol. 125, no. 1, pp. 3–30.

Salovey, P. and Mayer, J. D. (1990) 'Emotional intelligence', *Imagination, Cognition and Personality*, vol. 9, no. 3, pp. 185–211.

Sastry, M. A. (1997) 'Problems and paradoxes in a model of punctuated organizational change', *Administrative Science Quarterly*, vol. 42, no. 2, pp. 237–75.

Scherer, K. (1999) 'Appraisal theory' in Dalgleish, T. and Power, M. (eds) *Handbook of Emotion and Cognition*, New York, Wiley, pp. 637–65.

Shapiro, D. L. et al. (1995) 'When do employees choose deceptive tactics to stop unwanted change: A relational perspective', *Research in Organizations*, 5, Greenwich, CT, JAI Press, pp. 155–84.

Skarlicki, D. P. et al. (1999) 'Personality as a moderator in the relationship between fairness and retaliation', *Academy of Management Journal*, vol. 42, no. 1, pp. 100–08.

Sheppard, B. H. et al. (1992) *Organizational Justice: The Search for Fairness in the Workplace*, New York, Lexington Books.

Spector, P. E. and Fox, S. (2002) 'An emotion-centered model of voluntary work behaviour: Some parallels between counter-productive work behaviour and organizational citizenship behaviour', *Human Resource Management Review*, vol. 12, pp. 269–92.

Spreitzer, G. M. and Quinn, R. E. (1996) 'Empowering middle managers to be transformational leaders', *Journal of Applied Behavioral Science*, vol. 32, no. 3, pp. 237–61.

Tellegen, A. (1999) 'On the dimensional and hierarchical structure of affect', *Psychological Science*, vol. 10, no. 4, pp. 297–303.

Thibaut, J. and Walker, L. (1975) *A Theory of Procedure: A Psychological Analysis*, Hillsdale, NJ, Lawrence Eribaum Associates.

Turnbull, S. (2002) 'The planned and unintended emotions generated by a corporate change program', *Advances in Developing Human Resources*, vol. 4, no. 1, pp. 22–38.

Turnley, W. H. and Feldman, D. C. (1999) 'The impact of psychological contract violations on exit, voice, loyalty and neglect', *Human Relations*, vol. 52, no. 7, pp. 895–922.

Tyler, T. R. and Lind, E. A. (1992) 'A relational model of authority in groups', *Advances in Experimental Social Psychology*, vol. 25, pp. 115–91.

Wanous, J. P. et al. (2000) 'Cynicism about organizational change', *Group and Organization Management*, vol. 25, no. 2, pp. 132–53.

Wanberg, C. R. and Banas, J. T. (2000) 'Predictors and outcomes of openness to changes in a reorganizing work-place', *Journal of Applied Psychology*, vol. 85, no. 1, pp. 132–42.

Watson, D. A. and Clark, L. A. (1997) 'Measurement and mismeasurement of mood: Recurrent and emergent themes', *Journal of Personality Assessment*, vol. 68, no. 2, pp. 267–96.

Weber, M. (1946) *From Max Weber: Essays in Sociology*, New York, Oxford University Press.

Weiss, H. M. and Cropanzano, R. (1996) 'Affective events theory: A theoretical discussion on the structure, causes and consequences of affective experiences at work', *Research in Organizational Behavior*, vol. 18, pp. 1–74.

Weiss, H. M. et al. (1999) 'Effects of justice conditions on discrete emotions', *Journal of Applied Psychology*, vol. 84, no. 5, pp. 786–94.

Yukl, G. (1999) 'An evaluative essay on current conceptions of effective leadership', *European Journal of Work and Organizational Psychology*, vol. 8, no. 1, pp. 33–48.

Zajonc, R. B. (1980) 'Feeling and thinking: preferences need no inferences', *American Psychologist*, vol. 35, no. 2, pp. 151–75.

Part V
Leading Change

Introduction

In Part IV we looked at the issue of resistance and the strategies available to those leading or managing the change, to overcome that resistance. We now build on that wider issue of leading and managing change. We start by considering Mike Doyle's 2002 paper entitled 'Selecting managers for transformational change'. As we have seen previously, transformational change is characterised as complex to manage. It is radical, disruptive and affects a wide range of stakeholders. Using data from an empirical study Doyle makes two points. First that the multidimensional nature of transformational change mitigates against have a single change champion. Second he notes that where such a change champion is selected, the process of selection is flawed. Rather than aligning the selection criteria to specific change competences, the processes are generic, subjective and arbitrary.

In the second article 'Change management or change leadership', Roger Gill builds on the idea that the complexity of change requires multiple skill sets. He argues that change cannot be 'just' managed or 'just' lead, rather that successful change requires an integrative model which draws on the strengths of each. Effective management he contests is essential. An understanding of policies, processes and resources is key to designing a feasible plan for change. However, management per-se is not enough. Management doesn't attend sufficiently to the hearts and minds of those affected. Leadership of change needs to run in parallel.

In the third paper in this part we take a different perspective of change leadership, that of Debra Meyerson's notion of Tempered Radicalism. The previous two papers, as with much of the existing literature, assume that the leadership of change needs to come from those in senior positions within the organisation. What Meyerson and Sculley argue is that within the main body of organisations there are people who are deeply committed to the organisation that they work for; people who are also deeply committed to making things better or making things different by pursuing a cause or a new philosophy. As such, these people push for change from the inside. They try to make a difference by starting at a local level and then working outwards towards the wider organisation. They might not be in positions of authority but these people inspire, influence and motivate those around them to see things differently or to work differently. They do not fit easily with the culture of the organisation, yet despite this they are respected as innovators, as people with new ideas. Meyerson and Sculley conclude that these people should be one of the organisations most valued resources. These people provide the organisation with 'a unique source of vitality, learning and transformation' (1995, p. 598).

Selecting Managers for Transformational Change

13

Mike Doyle

Organisations, it is claimed, are now experiencing major environmental upheavals. These are triggering a complex multiplicity of overlapping, concurrent initiatives which in turn are radically altering existing structures, cultures and technologies (Tichy and Devanna, 1986; Eisenhardt and Bourgeois, 1988; Hambrick et al., 1998). The findings from recent research to be discussed in this article appear to confirm that, as a response to these 'high velocity', transformational change contexts, organisations have sought to introduce new working practices such as total quality management (TQM), business process re-engineering (BPR), continuous improvement, teamworking and culture change (Buchanan et al., 1999; Doyle et al., 2000).

These new working practices all have a common philosophical theme – to empower managers and employees by giving them the freedom to innovate, become involved in and manage aspects of the change process in their area of responsibility. For instance, managers at all levels are now expected to become innovative and flexible in their behaviour and to lead change in their designated areas of responsibility, with the aim of improving efficiency and adding value to organisation goals and purpose (Stewart, 1997; Rosenfeld and Wilson, 1999).

Non-managerial employees are also finding themselves 'invited', as part of a structural or cultural reorientation in the organisation, to share responsibility and participate in change. Through a range of HR and other performance management processes, employees are being persuaded to become team players and to take on extra responsibilities. Like their managerial colleagues, they are being encouraged to innovate and improve current systems and processes in the name of quality and customer service (Eccles, 1994).

Doyle, M. (2002) 'Selecting managers for transformational change', *Human Resource Management Journal*, vol. 12, no. 1, pp. 3–16.

One of the effects of this greater empowerment has been to challenge traditional notions of the singular, mandated change agent – usually an internal or external consultant or project manager employed as a professional or expert to manage change. This responsibility for change – 'change agency' – is now being extended to incorporate more diverse, multifarious groups of individuals drawn from a variety of functional and professional backgrounds. The strategic aim is to empower this 'cast of characters' to take a responsibility for managing organisational change (Hutton, 1994). This may involve them performing a variety of change roles, on both a full or part-time basis, for extended or relatively short periods of time (Buchanan and Storey, 1997; Doyle et al., 2000).

For instance, this diversity is apparent in Katzenbach et al. (1997). They identify what they term 'Real change leaders' (RCLs) who 'do not fit into a neat set of job categories or organisational levels – some are line managers, some are staff department heads, some are special-assignment team leaders and some are mavericks and champions' (1997, p. 9). In a similar fashion, Frohman (1997) identifies the emergence of change 'initiators' as those individuals driven by the need to 'make a difference' and from a 'fear of failure'. Sharing this generic, all-embracing perspective, La Marsh (1995) identifies change agents as:

> ...people who plan and support change. They are the project leaders, implementation teams, first-line supervisor, union steward and forklift truck driver on the third shift. Anyone and everyone who takes a responsibility for figuring out how to make the changes happen and how to support the targets are change agents'. (La Marsh, 1995, p. 91)

Ottaway (1979) employs an even more sweeping definition in which change agents are 'those people, either inside or outside the organisation, who are providing technical, specialised or consulting assistance in the management of a change effort' (1979, p. x). Finally, Rosenfeld and Wilson (1999) succinctly state: 'Change agents are the individuals or groups of individuals whose task is to effect change' (1999, p. 294).

What these and other commentators appear to be suggesting is that a responsibility for managing change is no longer confined to visionary leaders or organisational consultants. Responsibility is now being dispersed across the organisation. The assumption appears to be that everybody is, or can be, a change agent.

However, while this dispersal of change agency beyond the more traditional change agent boundaries may be welcomed as evidence of the efficacy of empowering work practices, it introduces potential risk into the change process. One area in particular is revealed by recent research as a cause for some concern: the processes by which change agents are currently being selected. This concern is heightened by a realisation that change agency is possibly being dispersed to individuals who may have had no previous experience of change management responsibilities. While they may be effective in their current roles, they may struggle to cope and adapt when they find themselves selected for a change role.

The aim of this article, therefore, is to examine the processes and mechanisms that are being used to select individuals for a change role in high velocity, transformational change contexts. It will argue that current processes are *ad hoc* and highly subjective, with evidence that poorly suited and ill-equipped individuals are being selected to manage change, presenting a consequent risk to the overall strategic change process and the potential to damage the individual's career and esteem. Furthermore, it will be argued that there is a need for a more structured and systematic process of selection which recognises and acknowledges the substantive and qualitative pressures and challenges that a change management responsibility may bring to operational and professional roles. With this in mind, it will be argued that organisations must be prepared to ensure that individuals are explicitly selected on the basis of their existing or potential change capabilities and not just on the basis of their performance in a current role or their desire to pursue a political or self-serving agenda.

Method

Research involved the membership of an organisation development and change forum which first met in Leicester in 1997 and was attended by managers representing 27 public and private sector organisations. The forum focused on major change issues currently facing participants and their organisations.

Surveys

Data were drawn from two substantial postal questionnaires involving a population of managers and professionals from the forum who had change responsibilities as a significant part of their operational or technical role. Questions were designed to explore the experience of managing high velocity, transformational change. The first survey was conducted in April 1997; 370 self-complete questionnaires were sent, of which 90 usable replies were received (for full details see Buchanan et al., 1999). The second survey was carried out in June 1998. A different set of questions was framed to explore in more detail some of the key issues identified in the first survey and the debates that took place in subsequent forum feedback workshops. The second survey was administered in a similar fashion to the first. This time, 415 questionnaires were distributed and 92 usable replies were received (for full details see Doyle et al., 2000).

Interviews

Both sets of survey findings gave important insights into the complex nature of change agency. They identified how change was being managed in contemporary organisations but, more importantly, highlighted some of the apparent ambiguity and lack of understanding surrounding the change agent role. To investigate this in more detail, the surveys were supplemented with a programme of semi-structured interviews with managers and professionals from two large organisations – one private, one public – which were represented in both surveys:

- **A privatised water utility** Since privatisation in 1989, this organisation has experienced continual change and restructuring as it had sought to shed overheads, increase efficiencies, improve customer service and water quality and meet shareholder and Ofwat expectations;
- **A large regional NHS teaching hospital** Since the earlier 1990s, this hospital had sought to re-engineer many of its key medical and administrative processes, with the aims of improving patient care and better utilising scarce resources. The trust had now embarked on a major amalgamation programme involving a number of hospitals in its locality.

Interview respondents were selected through a process of joint discussion with the organisations concerned. A total of 38 interviews were conducted during 1999 and 2000; these were tape-recorded and transcribed, and each lasted an average of 1.5 hours.

Secondary Data

To supplement the data gathered from surveys and interviews, organisational literature, records and archives were analysed. These data were further supplemented by information drawn from observations and notes taken during workshops and focus groups during which case study and survey organisations participated.

Selection for Change Agency

The survey findings lend support to the popular management rhetoric that everybody should now consider themselves to be an 'agent for change'. For example, in the first survey the findings reveal that 61 per cent of respondents agreed that change had meant an 'increase in empowerment for many people in my organisation', 87 per cent indicated that they 'combined change management responsibilities with their normal role' and 79 per cent disagreed that 'change management was a specialised area of expertise that should be left to full-time professionals' (Buchanan et al., 1999).

But if, as the findings suggest, change agency is being dispersed, how are individuals being selected for such roles and what are the risks if organisations are selecting the wrong people? Analysis of the qualitative research data reveals a complex and at times ambiguous and contradictory pattern of motives and pathways by which individuals are given or choose to acquire change agency.

Pathways into Change Agency

'You're just the person for the job' On the basis of the qualitative findings, this appeared to be the most common pathway into a change role. When individuals were asked to explain how they became involved, they indicated that selection was almost exclusively based on a subjective assessment of current performance, attitude and personal behaviour in an existing technical, professional or managerial role. This is typified in the following responses from the two case organisations:

> As a result of winning an award, it sort of raised my profile with somebody else in the company, one of the directors who then appointed me to the post of project manager. (Water company respondent)

> I was just approached to see if I would be interested in doing it. (NHS trust employee)

One explanation for resorting to this type of selection process is the perceived need for bosses and senior managers to 'play safe'. By using their subjective interpretations of superior performance and possession of what they perceive to be the 'right' cultural orientation, they can guard against a possible strategic risk to the change process of selecting an unsuitable individual for a specific change role. They also appeared to assume that the capabilities to manage change were the same as those required to perform in an operational or professional capacity. Paradoxically, however, by adopting this highly subjective approach and not challenging their assumptions about the required capabilities, they may have inadvertently introduced risk into the change process – the very thing they were trying to avoid. As one respondent remarked:

> We tried to pick senior and credible people in the organisation ... sometimes they were good and sometimes they weren't. Because it's a different sort of 'good' to be a change agent in the sense that somebody who is really excellent in a task-oriented line management role doesn't necessarily have the right skills for change. (NHS trust employee)

'I want to be part of this change project' Evidence emerged to suggest that individuals might be engaging in proactive strategies of impression management and manipulation with the aim of ensuring that the organisation judged them to be the 'right' person to lead change. In other words, they seized an opportunity to self-select themselves into the change process by influencing those who made decisions in respect of change agency dispersal. What were their motives? One respondent described their selection as being linked to their desire to make a difference:

> I had lots of ideas of my own. I was frustrated about what we were doing and the way we were doing it ... the opportunity to look at doing things differently appealed to me. (NHS trust employee)

Others suggested that selection was linked to personal ambition:

> My ego was such that I wanted to be involved in what I was sure was going to be a big success. (NHS trust employee)

'That's a good idea. You do it' One of the concomitant risks of an empowering culture is that those who innovate and create change may end up owning the change and are assumed to be the best people to manage it. But this may be an unsafe assumption to make in the sense that there can be no guarantee that individuals will possess the required skills and attributes to successfully implement change. This unease is highlighted by one respondent in the water company:

> One of the tests of somebody's commitment to an idea is to say: 'Okay, you manage it, you do it.' Which is fine at one level but at another level that person probably does not have the attributes that you need to make it happen. You may have the creativity and vision, but what makes us think you have the abilities to see it through?

'I'm free!' Faced with finite resources and constraints in terms of manpower, organisations may be tempted to transfer change agency to those who they feel they can spare at any given moment. These pressures and constraints may override any objective assessment of an individual's suitability for a change role. For instance, in the second survey the findings indicated that 38 per cent agreed and 15 per cent were neutral in their response to the statement that 'we select managers to handle change initiatives on the basis of "who's free" rather than on track record and change expertise' (Doyle et al., 2000). One water company respondent with a responsibility for organising and staffing change projects described being pressured by senior managers to make selection decisions on the basis of an individual's availability rather than any objective assessment of their suitability for the role.

'What are we going to do with you?' Similarly, there were suggestions that, in certain circumstances, organisations may be forced to second people to change

initiatives to overcome manpower problems following restructuring, and thus avoid the problems of demotion, dislocation or redundancy. Seconding people to manage or become involved in change projects may be 'a convenient way of dealing with the "victims" of restructuring' (water company employee). But it may only forestall career development problems until change management responsibilities are eventually relinquished and the problem re-emerges, or hopefully – from the organisation's viewpoint – the individual's inadequacies are exposed and they decide to leave the organisation.

However, on a more positive note, the dynamics of the change process may also produce a pool of expertise. In the NHS trust there was an opportunity to build up a cadre of change experts who then became a valuable resource for managing future change projects.

'It's your last chance' Linked to the last point, but on a much less positive note, suspicions were raised among some respondents that certain individuals were being selected for change responsibilities on the basis of their perceived under-performance. By seconding them or allocating additional change responsibilities to them, there was an opportunity for them to redeem themselves or to provide the evidence of under-performance required to initiate disciplinary action and the possible demise of their career.

'Let's see what you're made of' Giving agency to some individuals may also be a way of 'testing their mettle' and their suitability for career progression. In some cases it may provide opportunities for individuals to test themselves by facing new challenges and thereby enable them to develop generalist skills and personal qualities that improve their promotion potential. However, this may backfire if individuals are elevated to important change positions without any clear view of what they are supposed to achieve. A respondent from the HR department in the water company described how a line manager promoted to the role of business change manager told an assembled audience that he did not know what he was supposed to do. 'He has since left the company'.

'You haven't got any choice' There was some evidence of individuals feeling coerced to participate in change management. One middle manager described his anger and resentment at being forced to initiate changes in his department as a consequence of larger scale re-engineering in the NHS trust. The changes had a major impact on his area of responsibility (job losses and restructuring). Rejecting his protests, senior managers told him to implement the changes or face 'the adverse consequences for his career'. Another NHS trust respondent with a clinical background expressed her continuing anger and bitterness – even though her career benefited – at being coerced into participating in the change programme. Again, it was made clear that her career would suffer if she did not involve herself in the change project:

> I was given three options: I could leave, I could be made redundant or I could become involved in change.

'Come and join us' In both the NHS trust and the water company there were examples of people being drawn into change activities by the actions of others. For instance, in the water company a change project was initiated in one department to re-engineer its processes and save £4 million. At any one time it involved and affected 70 people directly and 50 people indirectly. In a similar fashion, the NHS trust had a continuous turnover of individuals who were appropriated for their perceived skills and qualities on an 'asrequired' basis to join the re-engineering project teams. According to one respondent:

> We identified project leaders and those project leaders weren't managers, they were people on the ground who we gave responsibilities to.

However, in both organisations reservations were expressed about the impact on operational quality and service provision as people were sucked into change and resources were stretched to the limit. This was more acute in the NHS trust, where a number of respondents voiced their concerns that selection into a change role on a full or part-time basis was having an adverse impact on their ability to meet the demands of patient care provision. Table 13.1 compares an idealised, systematic process of selection for change management with the reality of the selection process suggested by the findings.

Table 13.1   Comparison between idealised and actual model of the change agency selection process

Idealised approach to selection	Actual approaches adopted
Process is viewed as objective and systematic. Assumption is that change management is different from mainstream operational role requiring special consideration.	Process is subjective and *ad hoc*. Assumption is that change management is an extension of an operational or professional role requiring no special consideration.
Change management knowledge, skills and personal qualities are clearly defined and used as the basis for selection in the context of the organisational change process.	Skills and qualities are assumed to be synonymous with operational role. Little reference to discrete change skills or the need to take account of whether individuals have the expertise to deploy skills in a variety of contexts.
Range of pseudo-scientific techniques and approaches are used to add objectivity to the assessment of aptitude and suitability for performance in a future change role.	Little evidence of a systematic process. Reliance on a subjective and personalised judgement of the individual's performance is the main technique for selection. Individuals may select themselves into the change process.
Once selected, the individual receives comprehensive development and support, with a regular assessment of their suitability for change management responsibilities.	Individual is assumed to already possess the necessary knowledge and skills to manage change. Subsequent exposure to change pressures may highlight incompetence and lead to stress and risk for the individual and the organisation.

Discussion

The HRM/change literature highlights the importance of identifying and nurturing change competency in managers and employees when faced with conditions of complex and radical change (Buchanan and Boddy, 1992; Cockerill, 1994; Hartley et al., 1997; Paton and McCalman, 2000). It also emphasises the need for organisations to select individuals who possess the attributes to become agents of change (Flude, 1992; Cripe, 1993; Bott and Hill, 1994; Thornhill et al., 2000).

Flude (1992) identifies the importance of organisations fitting people to the role of 'ambassadors for change'. Here the primary concern is less with identifying suitability for change management and more about ensuring that 'high performing people' are selected for their skills and qualities to manage in those operational roles critical to the change process. The implication is that managing change is an integral part of the operational role and what matters is having the right people in those roles. In other words, according to Flude, there must be a careful and systematic assessment of suitability in the operational role using competency models, assessment centres and psychometric testing to minimise potential risk when change responsibilities are assumed.

In their case study of BICC Cables Bott and Hill (1994) demonstrate the practicalities of how this might be achieved. They argue that the selection process must contain specific mechanisms designed to identify a suitability and capability to manage change, as well as the ability to perform to required standards in an operational, supervisory role. In BICC Cables the focus for assessing capabilities for change was on the first-line managers who were seen by senior managers to be occupying a pivotal role in managing a major restructuring of the organisation. Carefully designed structured interviewing techniques were employed to identify 'change-creating behaviours'. Rather than looking for attributes and qualities that were 'externally imposed' (say, through training), the interviews explored inherent qualities and a predisposition towards culture change and the social processes required to effect change.

Cripe (1993) highlights the importance of selecting for change rather than operational management qualities and capabilities. In his estimation, 40 per cent of change agents are not meeting initial expectations some six months after appointment to the role, and he cites flaws in the selection process as being a contributory factor (1993, p. 52). What he advocates is a careful assessment of the 'degree of competency required for superior performance' (1993, p. 53). However, he also argues that any search for competency has to be underpinned by an explicit acknowledgement that managing change is different from an operational role. It follows, therefore, that expectations, objectives and performance measures must be defined and communicated to ensure that they fit the unique change context. Like Flude, Cripe argues that, while the selection process may employ many of the conventional techniques (assessment centres, personality testing etc.), there has to be a clear focus on measuring change management behaviour and testing that people can do what they claim they can do. However, this does not mean that organisations have to necessarily embark on a search for 'Mr or Ms Perfect Change Agent' from the outset. Instead, they should be prepared to look for a best fit between what is required and the attributes of the individual. The aim is then to provide the resources and support to develop that individual into a change management role.

According to Cockerill, 'very little work had been undertaken to prepare managers for dynamic environments' (1989, p. 54). Based on his work at NatWest, Cockerill argues that high performance in rapidly changing organisational environments is closely linked to managers developing self-awareness and insights into personal strengths, weaknesses, adequacies and limitations. Such insights can be aided by conventional selection and assessment techniques such as self-reports, guided interviews, group discussions and assessment centres. Once identified, these change attributes and competences become the basis for selection and development for change management roles.

So why, when there is an apparent recognition of the need to select individuals and teams specifically for a change role in the literature, does there appear to be a seeming *ad hoc*-ery and subjectivity in the practical implementation of selection suggested by the research findings, and how might this be explained? Some speculative possibilities are now discussed.

Everybody is now a change agent One possible explanation might lie in the organic, emergent nature of organisational change. Efforts to impose an orthodox model of selection might be rendered a waste of time and effort by the inherent complexity induced by diverse motives and pathways suggested by the findings. In high velocity change contexts, the change process emerges as a series of multiple and overlapping events, projects and initiatives that involve and implicate most, if not all, members of the organisation in a change role (Buchanan et al., 1999; Doyle et al., 2000). As the previous section suggested, there may be occasions and circumstances where choice about whether to become involved is not an option for most individuals, irrespective of their suitability for that role. Selection into the change process therefore becomes an almost 'automatic' by-product of change itself and thereby may defeat efforts to impose any form of rational process to identify suitability.

Opportunities are presented for individuals to self-select themselves into change agency roles As the previous section suggested, there appear to be multiple motives and pathways into change management. In some instances, selection may be determined by unilateral action on the part of the employee, facilitated by cultural efforts to empower managers and employees, and not by formalised selection processes.

However, as the findings have also suggested, there is an ever-present risk that individuals – who at first glance appear to be innovative, enthusiastic and committed to the goals of the organisations – are allowed to acquire change agency but then lack the capacities to exercise it effectively. For instance, even with the presence of formal selection processes, individuals with incompatible personalities and/or a lack of technical competence can still self-select themselves and acquire change agency. Consequently, their perceived 'incompetence' may place the whole change process at risk. The problem is further compounded when individuals self-select themselves without the knowledge or approval of the organisation, thus excluding themselves from any formalised arrangements for developing requisite change expertise or organisational arrangements designed to provide emotional and psychological support (Stuart, 1995).

Additionally, organisations may be at risk of being overwhelmed by too many change initiatives if the efforts of self-selecting individuals – whose legitimate desire is to innovate – place demands on the organisation that it cannot fulfil. The outcomes are unrealistic expectations – priorities and budgets that become distorted and resources that are spread too thinly across the organisation. Those responsible for selection therefore face a 'paradox of control'. They have to reconcile the creation of opportunities for people to select themselves into the change process, through innovative changes that they wish to see introduced, with a need to exert strategic control over the change process to avoid any threat to organisational goals (Kanter, 1983).

Strategic risk may also be exacerbated when self-selection is promoted through empowering cultures and organisations find themselves unwittingly permitting individuals to select themselves for motives that are self-serving and political. The outcome may be a weakening or even subversion of the strategic change process (Buchanan and Badham, 1999). The risk may be compounded when individuals, in their desire to manipulate change for their own ends, use impression management techniques designed to distort or deflect efforts to introduce objectivity into the selection process.

Change agency requires no special consideration for selection There is a third, and perhaps less complicated, explanation. Change management has now become such an integral part of organisational life that the process of selection requires no special consideration. For instance, in the second survey 91 per cent of respondents agreed that 'change management knowledge and skills are relevant to all levels in the organisation', and 92 per cent agreed that 'all managers require a good understanding of change management principles and practice' (Doyle et al., 2000). Could it be that the skills and qualities to manage change are seen to be little different from other technical, professional or managerial skills? Any special consideration in respect of change competence and expertise is therefore unnecessary when individuals are self-evidently seen to be performing competently in their existing role and are *de facto* seen to possess all the requisite skills and qualities to manage change.

This perception that change management may be little different from performing in a technical, professional or managerial role is clearly evident in the change literature where the knowledge, skills and personal attributes to manage change are well researched and documented in range of competency models, blueprints and checklists (see, for example, Buchanan and Boddy, 1992; Bott and Hill, 1994; McCrimmon, 1997; La Marsh, 1995; Hartley et al., 1997; Broussine et al., 1998). For example, Buchanan and Boddy (1992), researching the roles of those managers who find themselves in a project management role, have identified a range of 15 competences that they argue are required for effective change management (Table 13.2).

Table 13.2 Competences for effective change management

The change agent introducing large-scale technical and organisational change requires the following 15 skills and competences:

Goals

1. Sensitivity to change in key personnel, top management perceptions and market conditions, and to the way in which these have an impact on the goals of the project;
2. Clarity in specifying goals, in defining the achievable;
3. Flexibility in responding to changes outwith the control of the project manager – perhaps requiring major shifts in the project goals and management style – and risk-taking.

Roles

4. Team-building abilities to bring together key stakeholders and establish effective working groups, and clearly to define and delegate respective responsibilitis;
5. Networking skills in establishing and maintaining appropriate contacts within and outside the organisation;
6. Tolerance of ambiguity To be able to function comfortably, patiently and effectively in an uncertain environment.

Communication

7. Communication skills to transmit effectively to colleagues and subordinates the need for changes in project goals and in individual tasks and responsibilities;
8. Interpersonal skills across the range, including selection, listening, collecting appropriate information, identifying the concerns of individuals and managing meetings;
9. Personal enthusiasm in expressing plans and ideas;
10. Stimulating motivation and commitment in those involved.

Negotiation

11. Selling plans and ideas to others, by creating a desirable vision of the future;
12. Negotiating with key players for resources or for changes in procedures, and resolving conflict.

Managing up

13. Political awareness in identifying potential coalitions and in balancing conflicting goals and perceptions;
14. Influencing skills Gaining commitment to project plans and ideas from potential sceptics;
15. Helicopter perspective Ability to stand back from the immediate project and take a broader view of priorities.

Source: Adapted from Buchanan and Boddy (1992).

However, from studying these competences it could be argued that they map across and overlap closely those skills to perform in a technical, professional or managerial role, e.g. communication, teambuilding, networking, negotiating etc., as defined in mainstream management texts (Hales, 1993; Stewart, 1994; Salaman, 1995). In a similar manner, Cripe (1993), in a study of the skills and attributes required for change management, cites the McBer competence model as a possible blueprint for selecting change agents. Again, it is clear that there is little variation between its competences and what might be considered essential core management skills for a line or operational role, such as those found in the UK's Management Charter Initiative standards (Woodall and Winstanley, 1998). Does this explain – and is it to some extent used to justify – the use of current performance criteria as the basis for perceived suitability to manage change?

A challenge to the assumption that current operational or professional capabilities are sufficient qualifications for a change role is made by Buchanan and Boddy (1992). They argue that competency in an existing role is not by itself a sufficient basis for effective change management. Those who assume a responsibility for change management must be able to deal with the limitations and constraints imposed by unique organisational change contexts. They must be able to couple their possession of change competence to managerial judgement or 'expertise'. In other words, 'the effective change agent is able to deploy those core competences appropriately in context, and is not merely able to display those competences separately' (Buchanan and Boddy, 1992, p. 115).

The notion of 'expertise' is a critical feature of the change agent role – the capability to diagnose and make sense of change contexts as a precursor to the deployment of knowledge and skills in the most effective way. It therefore follows that, if change agency was seen to be a qualitatively different experience from a line or technical role both in its scope and in its intensity, then for some individuals existing levels of change expertise may not be enough – they are, in effect, change 'novices'. With this in mind, selection should logically hinge on their existing or future potential to perform as change 'experts'.

This need to perform as a change expert is captured by Stacey (1996). Faced with high velocity change scenarios that are 'far from certain' and where conflicting and confusing interpretations can be placed on events or situations, he argues that change agents will have to shift from 'ordinary' to 'extraordinary' forms of management action and behaviour. This may involve them challenging and even undermining current, orthodox and rational forms of management thinking and practice, coupled to a capacity to operate politically within the organisation's 'shadow system'. This ability to deploy 'extraordinary management' as a requirement for effective change management was a recurring theme in the survey and qualitative data obtained from the research.

Conclusions

The evidence presented in this article suggests that the introduction of new working practices has led to the dispersal of change agency across organisations, and this has involved and implicated managers and employees alike in the change process. As a consequence, traditional conceptions of the change agent role are now open to review and reinterpretation. One implication of this is the need to focus more closely on the processes by which individuals are being selected for change responsibilities. It would appear from the evidence presented here that, while the need for change competence is recognised, current processes do not appear to be measuring it or using it as the basis for selection into such a role. The process is *ad hoc* and subjective and may pose a degree of risk – not only to the overall change process but to the individual involved.

This risk was evident in the NHS trust when it became clear to senior managers that a number of individuals who had been seconded to the business process re-engineering teams on the basis of their effectiveness as professionals were out of their depth. Despite their undoubted professional capabilities as nurses, technicians etc., change agency had exposed them to wider pressures and challenges to which they were unable to respond. Although hard to gauge accurately, the qualitative evidence suggests a consequent effect on the overall change process due to individual under-performance and demotivation. It is interesting to note that individual inadequacies did not seem to centre on a lack of 'hard' technical skills but a lack of 'soft', behaviourial and political expertise. Eventually, a number of individuals had to be removed from the project and returned to their operational duties.

In the water company the level of strategic risk was even more pronounced but for different reasons. It came, paradoxically, from the enthusiasm to participate and become involved in change following major efforts by the organisation to imbue individuals with an empowering culture. The result was that a number of individuals were self-selecting themselves into a whole raft of change initiatives that eventually stretched far beyond any formalised mechanisms of control. The sheer volume of initiatives – some of which senior managers were unaware of – became unsustainable, and this has subsequently demanded a severe and draconian curtailment and much tighter control of the change process. The company has been forced to divert resources and establish a corporate change division to supervise and control the whole change process and thereby reduce risk.

While it is much harder to detect, there is also a suggestion from the findings that in both organisations an element of strategic risk may have been introduced by individuals who selected themselves for motives that were not fully congruent with the aims or goals of the organisation. In other words, their involvement in change management was a means to an individual end, whether that was to further ambition or to merely survive. It is possible that their concern to pursue this end may have deflected them from operational duties and activities, with a detrimental effect on organisational functioning as a whole.

So what should organisations do to improve selection processes? It could be argued that current selection techniques are adequate if they can adapted to give explicit consideration to assessing change capabilities (Cripe, 1993; Bott and Hill, 1994). But this may mean some acknowledgement on the part of the organisation that managing change is experienced as being substantively and qualitatively different from performing in an operational role. On the basis of the evidence presented in this article, this does not appear to be happening. Selection for change agency roles relies heavily on subjective interpretations of current levels of operational competency and expertise. This suggests that selection techniques and processes may have to be adapted, not only to identify the possession of change competency through the use of more objective selection methods, but also to identify those individuals who appear to have the potential to broaden and deepen their existing levels of competence and expertise, e.g. the ability to deploy conceptual and intellectual reasoning to cope with complex and dynamic change scenarios (Buchanan and Boddy, 1992; Cockerill, 1994).

Following Stacey (1996), organisations must identify those who have the ability to assimilate and deploy with confidence 'extraordinary management' skills and behaviour to suit contingent change circumstances and perform as change experts. This includes the psycho-emotional capability to absorb and withstand the challenges and stresses that change management brings to anyone involved in leading or participating in significant change in organisations, and added emphasis should be given to identifying capabilities in these areas. In this sense, it may be appropriate to involve experienced change agents in the selection process, for example as assessors and interviewers.

However, it also becomes clear from the evidence presented here that HR strategies for assessing and selecting change agents are limited and constrained in the sense that new organisational structures and cultures have presented individuals with the opportunity to assume change responsibilities through informal self-selection. Selection decisions may therefore have to be *post hoc*. Suitability is measured after the event through performance management systems and concomitant action taken.

Finally, the findings suggest that those who are responsible for selection may have to develop an ethical as well as a strategic awareness. It is apparent from the findings that organisations may have been exposed to strategic risk through a failure to give adequate consideration to selection processes aimed at assessing suitability for a change role. But this lack of consideration may also have resulted not only in damaged credibility and career prospects but also in added levels of stress, with concomitant 'damage' to individual physical and mental wellbeing. Paradoxically, those individuals who may have been damaged are likely to be the very individuals who were selected because they were perceived to be – as a number of NHS trust respondents commented – the 'brightest and best' in their operational or professional roles. Change agency, with its new opportunities, may have now presented them with the prospect of a truncated career or having to exit the organisation, with a longer term damaging effect for the overall management skills base of the organisation and, ultimately, the change process itself.

_____ *References* _____

Bott, K. and Hill, J. (1994) 'Change agents lead the way', *Personnel Management,* August, vol. 26, no. 8, pp. 24–27.

Broussine, M., Gray, M., Kirk, P., Paumier, K., Tichelar, M. and Young, S. (1998) 'The best and worst time for management development', *Journal of Management Development,* vol. 17, no. 1, pp. 56–67.

Buchanan, D. and Badham, R. (1999) *Power, Politics and Organisational Change: Winning the Turf Game,* London, Sage Publications.

Buchanan, D. and Boddy, D. (1992) *The Expertise of the Change Agent: Public Performance and Backstage Activity,* Hemel Hempstead, Prentice-Hall.

Buchanan, D. and Storey, J. (1997) 'Role taking and role switching in organisational change: the four pluralities' in McLoughlin, I. and Harris, M. (eds) *Innovation, Organisational Change and Technology,* London, International Thomson Business Press.

Buchanan, D., Claydon, T. and Doyle, M. (1999) 'Organisation development and change: the legacy of the nineties', *Human Resource Management Journal,* vol. 9, no. 2, pp. 20–37.

Cockerill, T. (1989) 'The kind of competence for rapid change', *People Management,* September, 52–56. (Reproduced in Mabey, C. and Iles, P. (eds) (1994) *Managing Learning,* London, Open University/Routledge.)

Cripe, E. (1993) 'How to get top-notch change agents', *Training and Development USA,* December, vol. 47, no. 12, pp. 52–59.

Doyle, M., Claydon, T. and Buchanan, D. (2000) 'Mixed results, lousy process: contrast and contradictions in the management experience of change', *British Journal of Management,* vol. 11, special issue, pp. 59–80.

Eccles, T. (1994) *Succeeding With Change: Implementing Action-Driven Strategies,* London, McGraw-Hill.

Eisenhardt, K. M. and Bourgeois, L. J. (1988) 'Politics of strategic decision making in high velocity environments: towards a mid-range theory', *Academy of Management Journal,* vol. 31, no. 4, pp. 737–70.

Flude, R. (1992) 'Selecting the ambassadors for change', *Recruitment, Selection and Retention,* vol. 1, no. 2, pp. 6–12.

Frohman, A. (1997) 'Igniting organisational change from below: the power of personal initiative', *Organisational Dynamics,* vol. 25, no. 3, pp. 39–53.

Hales, C. (1993) *Managing Through Organisation* (2nd edn), London, Routledge.

Hambrick, D., Nadler, D. and Tushman, M. (1998) *Navigating Change: How CEOs, Top Teams and Boards Steer Transformation,* Boston, MA, Harvard Business School Press.

Hartley, J., Benington, J. and Binns, P. (1997) 'Researching the role of internal change agents in the management of change', *British Journal of Management,* vol. 8, no. 1, pp. 61–73.

Hutton, D. (1994) *The Change Agent's Handbook: A Survival Guide for Quality Improvement,* Milwaukee, WI, ASQC Quality Press Publications.

Kanter, R-M. (1983) *The Changemasters: Corporate Entrepreneurs at Work,* London, George Allen and Unwin.

Katzenbach, J., Beckett, S., Dichter, S., Viegen, M., Gagnon, C., Hope, Q. and Ling, T. (1997) *Real Change Leaders,* London, Nicholas Brealey Publishing Ltd.

La Marsh, J. (1995) *Changing the Way we Change: Gaining Control of Major Operational Change,* Reading, MA, Addison-Wesley Publishing Co.

McCrimmon, M. (1997) *The Change Masters: Managing and Adapting to Organisational Change,* London, Institute of Management/Pitman Publishing.

Ottaway, R. (1979) *Change Agents at Work,* London, Associated Business Press.

Paton, R. and McCalman, J. (2000) *Change Management: A Guide to Effective Implementation* (2nd edn), London, Paul Chapman Publishing.

Rosenfeld, R. and Wilson, D. (1999) *Managing Organisations: Texts, Readings and Cases* (2nd edn), London, McGraw-Hill.

Salaman, G. (1995) *Managing,* Buckingham, Open University Press.

Stacey, R. (1996) *Strategic Management and Organisational Dynamics* (2nd edn), London, Pitman Publishing.

Stewart, R. (1994) *Managing Today and Tomorrow,* Basingstoke, Macmillan.

Stewart, R. (1997) *The Reality of Management* (3rd edn), Oxford, Butterworth-Heinemann.

Stuart, R. (1995) 'Experiencing organisational change: triggers, processes and outcomes of change journeys', *Personnel Review,* vol. 24, no. 2, pp. 5–53.

Thornhill, A., Lewis, P., Millmore, M. and Saunders, M. (2000) *Managing Change: A Human Resource Strategy Approach*, London, Financial Times/Prentice-Hall.

Tichy, N. and Devanna, M. (1986) *The Transformational Leader,* New York, Wiley and Sons.

Woodall, J. and Winstanley, D. (1998) *Management Development: Strategy and Practice,* Oxford, Blackwell Business.

Change Management or Change Leadership?

Roger Gill

> ...there is no more delicate matter to take in hand, nor more dangerous to conduct, nor more doubtful in its success, than to set up as a leader in the introduction of changes. For he who innovates will have for his enemies all those who are well off under the existing order of things, and only lukewarm supporters in those who might be better off under the new. (Machiavelli, 1469–1527)

In the early sixteenth century, Niccolò Machiavelli clearly understood the problem of change. In *The Prince*, he points out the difficulty and risk involved in implementing change, in particular resistance to change and, at best, lack of commitment to it.[1] Some 500 years later, this is still a familiar problem. As Andrew Mayo says, 'Our organisations are littered with the debris...of yesterday's [change] initiatives' (Mayo, 2002). The reason for this, this paper contends, is not necessarily poor management of change but more likely a lack of effective leadership.

While change must be well managed – it must be planned, organised, directed and controlled – it also requires effective leadership to introduce change successfully: it is leadership that makes the difference. This paper proposes a new model of leadership which is the result of a three-year study of the burgeoning literature on the subject and which has been successfully applied in several organisations in a variety of sectors planning and implementing strategic change. The model proposes that the leadership of successful change requires vision, strategy, the development of a culture of sustainable shared values that support the vision and strategy for change, and empowering, motivating and inspiring those who are involved or affected. This behaviour reflects

Gill, R. (2003) 'Change management or change leadership', *Journal of Change Management*, vol. 3, no. 4.

the underlying dimensions and requirements of leadership: the cognitive, the spiritual, the emotional and the behavioural.

Why 'Management' is Necessary but Not Sufficient

Change programmes often fail because of poor management: poor planning, monitoring and control, lack of resources and know-how, and incompatible corporate policies and practices. Good management of change is a *sine qua non*.

How change may be mismanaged is well known. Change efforts may fail because of poor planning, monitoring and control, focusing more on the objective than on the steps and process involved, a lack of milestones along the way, and failing to monitor progress and take corrective action. Change efforts often lack the necessary resources, e.g. budget, systems, time and information, and the necessary expertise – knowledge and skills. Corporate policies and practices sometimes remain the same and become inconsistent with the aims and strategies for change. For example, the performance criteria used in appraisal and reward policies may not support and reinforce a desired performance-driven, teamwork-oriented culture, resulting in a disincentive or lack of incentive to change behaviour. A large European study found that the most successful organisations make mutually supportive changes in terms of changes in roles, governance structures and strategies (Whittington et al., 1999).

Change is all too often regarded as a 'quick fix'. This fails to address the implications of the change for the organisation as a whole and therefore causes unforeseen and unacceptable disruption. Change initiatives are often the result of the naïve adoption of management fads. Such fads frequently deal with only one aspect of an organisation's functioning without regard to their implications for other aspects. Lack of communication or inconsistent messages and the resulting misunderstanding of the aims and process of change lead to rumours that demoralise people and to a lack of commitment to change.

A lack of commitment to change may be due to a lack of compelling evidence for the benefits of change. It shows itself in objections, unwillingness to consider options or look at process issues, and the use of 'hidden agendas' or delaying tactics. Top management itself may display a lack of commitment to change. Their commitment is evident in several ways: their unequivocal acceptance of ownership and responsibility for success of the change initiative, eagerness to be involved, willingness to invest resources, willingness to take tough decisions when required, awareness of the impact of their own behaviour, a consistent message, and the holding of regular reviews of progress.

Change efforts that are purely 'managerial' in nature, especially those that are mismanaged, result in a lack of dedicated effort, conflict between functional areas and resistance to change. Resistance to change is a common phenomenon. Kubr (1996) provides a good account of why people resist change. A cognitive and behavioural reason is lack of know-how. A lack of conviction that change is needed – questioning the meaning and value of the change for individuals – inevitably leads to a lack of motivation to change. Perhaps the most powerful forces of resistance to change, however, are emotional:

- dislike of imposed change
- dislike of surprises
- lack of self-confidence and confidence in others: fear of the unknown and of inadequacy and failure and the adverse consequences, such as share price decline and blame
- reluctance of management to deal with difficult issues (especially in the case of managers approaching retirement)
- disturbed practices, habits and relationships: 'We've always done it this way'. Moving people from their 'comfort zone' means moving from the familiar, secure and controllable to the unfamiliar, insecure and uncertainly controllable
- self-interest and shifts in power and influence such as loss or change of role in the organisation
- lack of respect and trust in the person or people promoting change and scepticism as a result of the failure of previous change initiatives.

The human and political aspects of change are often not well thought through in change management initiatives. Mulligan and Barber (1998) speak of the yin and yang of change: respectively the social and emotional considerations (leadership) and the technical aspects (management). McLagan (2002) points out that taking a purely rational and technical approach to change, 'making sure it's technically sound and offers economic advantage to the organisation', tends to lead to the false assumption that the organisation will naturally absorb it. Kotter (1995a) says:

> In failed transformations, you often find plenty of plans and directives and programs ... [with] procedures, goals, methods, and deadlines. But nowhere was there a clear and compelling statement [a vision] of where all this was leading. Not surprisingly, most of the employees with whom I talked were either confused or alienated. [The 'managerial' approach] did not rally them together or inspire change. In fact, [it] probably had just the opposite effect.

In his classic statements on management and leadership, Kotter (1990a, 1990b) says that management produces orderly results which keep something working efficiently, whereas leadership creates useful change; neither is necessarily better or a replacement for the other. Both are needed if organisations and nations are to prosper. He also says, however:

> Management's mandate is to minimise risk and to keep the current system operating. Change, by definition, requires creating a new system, which in turn always demands leadership. (Kotter, 1995a)

Sadler (1997) concurs:

> we have observed dramatic transformations in British industry in recent times which appear to be due more to inspirational leadership than to good management as traditionally conceived. British Airways under Colin Marshall, and ICI under John Harvey-Jones are oft-quoted examples.

Change, therefore, is primarily about leadership.

The Leadership of Change

The keys to successful change, according to an American Management Association survey (American Management Association, 1994), are first and foremost leadership, followed closely by corporate values and communication (Table 14.1).

If change is a process of taking an organisation (or a nation) on a journey from its current state to a desired future state and dealing with all the problems that arise along the journey, then change is about leadership as well as management. Leadership, in The Leadership Trust's view, is about showing the way: using personal power to win the hearts and minds of people to work together towards a common goal (Gill, 2001). The leadership of change, for the chief executive, Hooper and Potter (2000) say, means 'developing a vision of the

Table 14.1 Keys to successful change: Survey of 259 senior executives in Fortune 500 companies in the USA

	% mentioning this as important
Leadership	92
Corporate values	84
Communication	75
Teambuilding	69
Education and training	64

future, crafting strategies to bring that vision into reality [and ensuring] that everybody in the organisation is mobilising their energies towards the same goals... the process we call "emotional alignment" '. It can be argued that the most difficult challenges facing leaders today are making sure that people in the organisation can adapt to change and that leaders can envisage where the organisation is currently placed in the market and where it should be in the future (Heifetz and Laurie, 1997).

The case for alignment is made in a report by World Economic Forum (2000) in partnership with management consultants Booz Allen and Hamilton and the Center for Effective Organisations at the University of Southern California:

> Alignment... galvanizes people around the aspirations and objectives of the company. People know what is to be done, and understand how they as individuals contribute to the whole. Adaptability enables the organisation to change rapidly and effectively in response to external threats or opportunities.

Alignment is displayed by a shared understanding, common orientation, common values and shared priorities. Adaptability is displayed by environmental sensitivity, tolerance for contrary views, a willingness to experiment, tolerate failure and learn from it, and the ability to respond quickly to change – organisational agility. Both alignment and adaptability are needed (World Economic Forum, 2000):

> Alignment without adaptability results in bureaucratic, sclerotic organisations that 'can't get out of their own way'... Adaptability without alignment results in chaos and resources wasted on duplicate and conflicting efforts.

The former chairman of ICI, Sir John Harvey-Jones (1988), takes a radical view of alignment:

> In the future the organisation will have to adapt to the needs of the individual, rather than expecting the individual to adapt to the needs of the organisation.

Nixon (2002) identifies 'big issues' concerning global business leaders: creating successful and sustainable workplaces, the need to be good corporate citizens and at the same time profitable, the gap between strategy makers and those not involved, products that damage the quality of life, and a yearning for meaning and balance in life, 'uniting body, mind, heart and spirit'. Dubrin (2001) says that 'The transformational leader... [helps] group members understand the need for change both emotionally and intellectually.' How to meet the challenge of change can be understood more broadly using a new model of transformational leadership. This model attempts to integrate the multiple dimensions and requirements of leadership – the cognitive, spiritual, emotional and behavioural.[2]

The Dimensions and Requirements of Leadership

Leadership theory has developed along separate tracks that have never fully or usefully converged. Nevertheless, each track provides a distinct dimension and set of requirements for effective leadership. These tracks are the study of cognitive or rational processes (cognitive intelligence), the need for meaning and worth in people's work and lives (spiritual intelligence), emotions or feelings (emotional intelligence) and volitional action or behaviour (behavioural skills) in leadership (Gill, 2002).

The Intellectual/Cognitive Dimension and Requirements of Leadership – 'Thinking'

Strategic failure, especially in times of rapid change, is often the result of the inability to see a novel reality emerging: the corporate mind is wedded to obsolete assumptions that blind it to the perception of change. Effective leadership requires the intellectual or cognitive abilities to perceive and understand information, reason with it, imagine possibilities, use intuition, make judgments, solve problems and make decisions. These abilities produce vision, mission (purpose), shared values and strategies for pursuing the vision and mission that 'win' people's minds.

The Spiritual Dimension and Requirements of Leadership – 'Meaning'

'Spirit', according to *Webster's Dictionary* and the *Oxford English Dictionary*, is a person's animating principle. The spiritual dimension of leadership concerns the yearning for meaning and a sense of worth that animate people in what they seek and do. Meaning and this sense of worth depend on the vision and shared values to which one is party. William W. George, chairman and CEO of Medtronic, Inc. – one of the world's leading medical technology companies, based in Minneapolis – and the Academy of Management's 2001 'Executive of the Year', argues that people at work today seek meaning and purpose in their work. When they find it, '[they] will buy into the company's mission and make the commitment to fulfilling it' (George, 2001). Dess and Picken (2000) quote

Xerox PARC guru John Seely Brown as saying: 'The job of leadership today is not just to make money: it's to make meaning.' Effective leadership 'wins people's souls'.

The Emotional Dimension and Requirements of Leadership – 'Feeling'

Effective leadership also requires well-developed emotional intelligence – the ability to understand oneself and other people, display self-control and self-confidence, and to respond to others in appropriate ways. Emotionally intelligent leaders use personal power rather than positional power or authority. Emotional intelligence, in addition to cognitive and spiritual intelligence, is key to identifying and promoting the shared values that support the pursuit of vision, mission and strategies and to empowering and inspiring people. Emotionally intelligent leaders 'win people's hearts'.

The Behavioural Dimension and Requirements of Leadership – 'Doing'

While the necessary behavioural skills of leadership include both using and responding to emotion, for example through 'body language', they also comprise communicating in other ways through writing, speaking and listening – using personal power – and through physical behaviour, for example MBWA ('managing by walking around'). Communication is the 'life blood' of the organisation and the 'oxygen' of change within it.

A New Model of Leadership for Change

Effective leadership of change reflects all of these dimensions of leadership. An integrative model of leadership for successful change needs to explain the following elements of effective leadership practice: vision, values, strategy, empowerment and motivation and inspiration. Effective emotional and behavioural leadership without valid vision and strategic thinking can be misguided, even dangerous. The converse is impotent.

Vision

'Without vision, a people perish', one is told in the Bible,[3] and so does an organisation. The foundation of effective leadership is defining and communicating an appealing vision of the future. One of the best definitions of a vision comes from the *Oxford English Dictionary:* 'something seen vividly in the imagination, involving insight, foresight and wisdom'. A vision is a desired future state: this is the basis for directing the change effort.

Kotter (1995a) suggests that the starting point in a successful change process is attaching a sense of urgency and importance to change. Kotter says it is necessary to create dissatisfaction with the status quo and an understanding of the need to change. He quotes a former CEO of a large European company as saying that successful change begins by '[making] the status quo seem more dangerous than launching into the unknown'. This is the basis for developing a vision for change.

Sylvie Jackson of Cranfield University's Royal Military College of Science starkly illustrates how little vision figures in communication in organisations:

> Total amount of communication going on to an employee in three months = 2,300,000 words or numbers. Typical communication of a change vision over a period of three months = 13,400 words or numbers. 13,400/2,300,000 = 0.0058. The change vision captures only 0.58% of the communication 'market share'. (Jackson, 2001)

The British government has identified leadership as key to meeting the challenges of change in public services (Performance Improvement Unit, 2001). Change starts with a vision: 'The Government has to present a clear picture... of the kind of society it [wants] from its reforms and stop being seen as a "value-free zone"', says health secretary Alan Milburn. Prime minister Tony Blair responds: '[New Labour] needs to rediscover its political vision... building a Britain of opportunity for all' (Waugh and Morris, 2002).

Vision needs to be meaningful, ethical and inspiring. Effective visions are imaginable, desirable, feasible, focused, flexible and communicable (Kotter, 1995b). They are memorable and quotable. Senge (1990) sees vision as a driving force, while Covey (1992) describes vision as 'true north', providing a 'compass'. Vision helps to create commitment, inspiration and motivation by connecting and aligning people intellectually and emotionally to the organisation; and it is associated with organisational growth and success (Baum et al., 1998).

A shared vision is key to successful change. Kakabadse (2002) reports the finding from a survey at Cranfield School of Management of over 12,000 organisations that more than one-third of directors have a vision of the future of their organisation that is different from those of their colleagues. Without a shared vision, there is no alignment. Senge (1990) puts it this way:

> In a corporation, a shared vision changes people's relationship with the company. It is no longer 'their company'; it becomes 'our company'. A shared

vision is the first step in allowing people who mistrusted each other to begin to work together. It creates a common identity.

Kotter (1997) makes the point that, for organisational change, only an approach based on vision works in the long term. He says a shared vision:

- clarifies the direction of change and ensures that everything that is done (new product development, acquisitions, recruitment campaigns) is in line with it
- motivates people to take action in the right direction, even though the initial steps in the change process may be painful to some individuals
- helps to align individuals and coordinate their actions efficiently.

Values and Culture

A Nepalese Buddhist mantra says: 'Open your arms to change, but don't let go of your values'. Values are principles held dear in people's hearts by which they live (and sometimes die). Covey (1992) makes the distinction between personal values, which are intrinsic, and corporate values, which he regards as extrinsic guiding principles for behaviour throughout the organisation.

The challenge of change has stimulated an emphasis on values-based leadership. O'Toole (1995) says that there is a widespread belief among corporate executives in the need to create strong, shared values to unite people in a fragmented world. The fear, though, is the danger of 'groupthink'. Yet, if there is one organisational characteristic that provides the 'glue' in uniting people, it is trust. As O'Toole suggests, trust 'emanates from leadership based on shared purpose, shared vision, and, especially, shared values' (O'Toole, 1995).

Bennis and Goldsmith (1997) point out that 'Leaders walk their talk; in true leaders, there is no gap between the theories they espouse and their practice'. Effective leaders are role models for corporate values: they set an example. Collins and Porras (1998) contend that corporate values are 'not to be compromised for financial gain or short-term expediency'.

Effective leadership entails identifying and promoting shared values. Shared values are a key feature of a strong organisational culture (that includes beliefs, attitudes and patterns of habitual behaviour) that supports a common purpose and engenders commitment to it. Values that are not shared can be dysfunctional (Drucker, 1999). Shared values create a sense of belonging and may contribute positively to competitive advantage (Deetz et al., 2000). Indeed, a change orientation is one of the common values among the most admired companies in the USA (Kets de Vries, 2000), and firms have become more customer and stakeholder focused, more time-competitive and more value-added and quality focused (Cannon, 2000).

Networks of power and influence and 'horizontal' relationships will replace the formal hierarchies found in bureaucratic organisations (Gill et al., 1998).

New organisational cultures will supplant bureaucratic cultures that are characterised by hierarchy, boundaries, internal orientation, control and the need to avoid mistakes (Hastings, 1993). Bureaucracy is a well-documented hindrance to developing a learning culture.

One of the problems of change during mergers and acquisitions is that change is exciting for those who do it and threatening for those to whom it is done. The solution that worked for one company was to get people to participate in it. When ScottishPower acquired Manweb and Southern Water in the 1990s, it created 'transition teams' with managers from the acquired company to create shared values and human resource policies and practices.

Culture change programmes are about 'changing hearts, minds and souls' of employees (Rajan, 2000). This takes a long time, and it requires some luck: Amin Rajan says, 'The "big bang" approach has the potential to inflict ... collateral damage', although sometimes it may be necessary. Bill Cockburn, managing director of British Telecoms' UK operations, believes that in his business, incrementalism does not work: 'radical reinvention' is required (Monks, 2000). But, to be more effective, culture change requires leaders to plan and implement sequential, but incremental, changes.

An example of a culture change programme aimed at changing feelings of involvement, consultation and values is that experienced at Marks and Spencer. Marks and Spencer fell from grace at the end of 1998, with a drastic fall in shareholder value. Under a new chairman, Luc Vandervelde, in early 2000, a major initiative was introduced to revolutionise the corporate culture as part of the recovery strategy. This entailed improving consultation – on key business issues rather than 'tea and toilets' – among managers and employees through Business Involvement Groups (BIGs) and training in consultation processes. The outcome, by May 2002, according to Marks and Spencer's Helen Eaton, was 'a greater mutuality of interest at meetings, with managers and staff beginning to work together on key business issues ... [and] ... more openness, honesty, trust and professionalism' as well as a clearer sense of direction (Law, 2002).

Wendy Sullivan and her colleagues describe how aligning the values of the people in the organisation – and those of the organisation itself – can help to bring about rapid change, citing the case of Sellotape (Sullivan et al., 2002). The company significantly improved business performance, with profitability increasing from 3 per cent to 10 per cent over two and a half years, and significant improvements in individual job satisfaction and fulfilment and in morale and teamwork.

Strategy

Without strategies for change, vision is a dream. Strategies are ways of pursuing the vision and mission; they are informed by vision, and mission and values. Strategic plans are 'road maps' of a changing terrain in which a compass (vision) is needed (Covey, 1992). Effective leadership entails developing, getting commitment to and implementing rational business strategies based on possible future scenarios for the organisation. A key issue with the effectiveness of strategies is where their ownership lies and commitment to them: effective strategy development taps the wisdom of people in the organisation (Eden, 1993).

William W. George of Medtronic says, 'Employees can adapt to major strategic shifts as long as the company's mission and values remain constant' (George, 2001). This is an important factor in maintaining trust in top management. Medtronic is 'completely reinvented' every five years in terms of its business strategies. For example, between 1989 and 1994, the company was transformed from a pacemaker company into a broader cardiovascular business, with revolutionary new therapies during the following five years, and with further innovations likely over the next five to ten years reflecting its 'Vision 2010'.

Meanwhile, mission and values have remained, and will remain, constant. Innovation and change require structural flexibility, but with the stability to deliver products and services on time. Peters (1993) calls this 'permanent flexibility'. It is well established in the management literature that structure must serve strategy, not the converse. An example of how structures have changed is the introduction of short-term, high-performance teams, superseding permanent functional or departmental teams and cross-functional teams. They come together for a specific purpose and, on achieving it, disband. The consequences are roles that frequently change and temporary and varied leadership roles.

An effective strategy for change entails creating a guiding coalition – putting together a group of people with enough power to lead the change – and getting it to work together as an effective team (Kotter, 1995a). Kotter also emphasises the need to use every method possible to communicate constantly and explain the new vision and strategy and ensure the guiding coalition models the behaviour expected of all employees.

Empowerment

Like so many aspects of leadership, empowerment is not a new idea. In the fifth century BC, Lao Tzu wrote:

> As for the best leaders, people do not notice their existence.
> The next best, the people honour and praise.
> The next, the people fear.
> And the next, the people hate.
> But when the best leader's work is done, the people say, 'We did it
>   ourselves.'[4]

Empowerment literally is giving people power. It is about making them *able to do* what needs to be done in the change process. In practice, empowerment is giving people the knowledge, skills, opportunity, freedom, self-confidence and resources to manage themselves and be accountable. Important aspects of empowerment are stimulating people's intellects and imagination, in particular their creativity in the change process, risk taking and trust. Empowering people for action in part entails getting rid of obstacles to change, removing or changing systems or structures that undermine the vision, and encouraging risk taking, new ideas and innovative activities (Kotter, 1995b).

Bennis (1999) suggests that a 'shrinking' world with increasing technological and political complexity offers fewer and fewer arenas for effective top-down leadership. The key to real change, he says, is empowered teams. The need for rapid response and innovation has created a culture of 'intrapreneurship' in many companies. Innovation has become the province of *all* employees, not just those in the product development department. Encouraging intrapreneurship is an example of empowerment.

General Electric successfully underwent extensive restructuring in the 1980s under chairman and CEO Jack Welch, to build a network of inter-related businesses with the aim of capturing top market-share positions in their respective industries. The change process included 'Work-Out', a way in which employees could participate in teams in the process, and 'Town Hall Meetings' with all employees to strengthen dialogue and understanding in respect of the change process and the new roles and work habits that were needed. Managers had previously been appraised solely on their ability to manage in a 'command-and-control' culture. Now, however, they were required to meet ownership, stewardship and entrepreneurial goals. Performance expectations and rewards were therefore realigned. As a result, GE strengthened its position in several global markets and greatly increased its market value.

Empowerment is also about involving people in the change process. People are much more inclined to support what they help to create (and they resist what is forced on them). Myers (1993) writes:

> Study after study finds that when workers have more control – when they can help define their own goals... and when they participate in decision making – their job satisfaction rises.

Tom Cannon describes how organisations have responded to the challenge of change (Cannon, 2000). They have created flatter structures with more empowered employees who are trusted more, expected to conform to shared values and encouraged to be more entrepreneurial and innovative. They have introduced flexible learning programmes to enhance competencies in initiating and achieving successful change.

Motivation and Inspiration

Effective leaders motivate and inspire people to want to do what needs to be done. In any change process, the change champions – leaders – must be credible. Credibility comes from perceptions of honesty and competence in leaders and from their ability to inspire, say Kouzes and Posner (2002). Motivation and inspiration arise from alignment of organisational goals with individuals' needs, wants, values, interests and aspirations and from the use of positive and appealing language.

Motivation also arises from short-term wins. Gaining short-term wins entails planning and creating visible improvements during the change process. It also entails visibly recognising and rewarding people who made the wins possible (Kotter, 1995a).

Positive and appealing language is characterised by framing the message and crafting one's rhetoric. Framing the message, Conger (1999) says, is 'connecting your message with the needs, interests and feelings of those whose commitment you need' and, thereby, Goodwin (1998) says, 'making people feel they have a stake in common problems'. Examples of framing language are:

- linking the message with the benefits for everybody involved
- reflecting their values and beliefs
- talking in their language
- matching body language with words
- moving from 'I' statements to 'we' statements
- making positive comparisons of their situation with that of others
- expressing confidence in people's ability to achieve.

Rhetorical crafting of language consists of giving examples, citing quotations, reciting slogans, varying one's speaking rhythm, using familiar images, metaphors and analogies to make the message vivid (Martin Luther King's allusion to 'the jangling discords of our nation' comes to mind), waxing lyrical and using repetition.

Applying the Leadership Model

This integrative model of leadership has been successfully applied in leadership development programmes in several organisations concerned with change: a manufacturing company, a private mental healthcare company, a public sector defence agency, the top management teams of two universities, a youth charity, and an insurance and emergency assistance company.

Former US president Harry S. Truman is on record as saying: 'Men make history and not the other way round. In periods where there is no leadership, society stands still. Progress occurs when courageous, skilful leaders seize the opportunity to change things for the better.'[5] Change requires good management, but above all it requires effective leadership.

Notes

1. Niccolò Machiavelli (1469–1527) *The Prince*, translated from the Italian by Hill Thompson, Collector's Edition, 1980, The Easton Press, Norwalk, CT, 55.
2. Roger Gill, *Defining Leadership*, Sage Publications, London, in preparation.
3. The Bible, Proverbs, 29: 18.
4. Lao Tzu (c. 500BC) *The Way of Lao Tzu*, Number 17.
5. Quoted by Dana Hield Whitson and Douglas K. Clark (2002) 'Management audits: Passé, or a useful quality improvement tool?' *Public Management*, vol. 84, no. 4, p. 6.

References

American Management Association (1994) *Survey on Change Management*, New York, AMA.

Baum, J. R., Locke, E. A. and Kirkpatrick, S. A. (1998) 'A longitudinal study of the relation of vision and vision communication to venture growth in entrepreneurial firms', *Journal of Applied Psychology*, vol. 83, no. 1, pp. 43–54.

Bennis, W. (1999) 'The end of leadership: Exemplary leadership is impossible without full inclusion, initiatives, and cooperation of followers', *Organizational Dynamics*, vol. 27, July, p. 71.

Bennis, W. and Goldsmith, J. (1997) *Learning to Lead*, London, Nicholas Brealey.

Cannon, T. (2000) 'Leadership in the new economy', paper presented at The National Leadership Conference, 'Leaders and Managers: Fit for the Future', The Royal Military Academy, Sandhurst, 24 May.

Collins, J. and Porras, J. (1998) *Built to Last*, London, Random House.

Conger, J. (1999) 'The New Age of Persuasion', *Leader to Leader*, Spring, pp. 37–44.

Covey, S. (1992) *Principle-Centered Leadership*, London, Simon and Schuster.

Deetz, S. A., Tracy, S. J. and Simpson, J. L. (2000) *Leading Organizations Through Transition*, Thousand Oaks, CA, Sage.

Dess, G. G. and Picken, J. C. (2000) 'Changing roles: Leadership in the 21st century', *Organizational Dynamics*, vol. 28, no. 3, pp. 18–34.

Drucker, P. F. (1999) 'Managing oneself', *Harvard Business Review*, March–April, pp. 65–74.

Dubrin, A. J. (2001) *Leadership: Research Findings, Practice, and Skills* (3rd edn), Boston, MA, Houghton Mifflin, p. 76.

Eden, C. (1993) 'Strategy development and implementation: Cognitive mapping for group support' in Hendry, J. Johnson, G. and Newton, J. (eds) *Strategic Thinking: Leadership and the Management of Change*, Chichester, John Wiley.

George, W. W. (2001) 'Keynote address, academy of management annual conference, Washington, D.C., August' in *Academy of Management Executive*, vol. 15, no. 4, pp. 39–47.

Gill, R. (2001) *Essays on Leadership*, Ross-on-Wye, The Leadership Trust Foundation.

Gill, R. (2002) 'Towards an integrative theory of leadership', paper presented at the Workshop on Leadership Research, European Institute for Advanced Studies in Management, Oxford, 16–17 December.

Gill, R., Levine, N. and Pitt, D. C. (1998) 'Leadership and organizations for the new millennium', *The Journal of Leadership Studies*, vol. 5, no. 4, pp. 46–59.

Goodwin, D. K. (1998) 'Lessons of presidential leadership', *Leader to Leader*, vol. 9, pp. 23–30.

Harvey-Jones, J. (1988) *Making It Happen*, London, HarperCollins.

Hastings, C. (1993) *The New Organization*, London, IBM/McGraw-Hill.

Heifetz, R. A. and Laurie, D. L. (1997) 'The work of leadership', *Harvard Business Review*, January–February, vol. 75, no. 1, pp. 124–34.

Hooper, A. and Potter, J. (2000) *Intelligent Leadership*, London, Random House.

Jackson, S. (2001) *Leadership and Change Management: Leading Change*, Shrivenham, Cranfield University Royal Military College of Science.

Kakabadse, A. (2002) 'Management teams need to pull together', *Professional Manager*, September, p. 37.

Kets de Vries, M. (2000) 'Beyond Sloan: Trust is at the core of corporate values', Mastering Management, *Financial Times*, 2 October.

Kotter, J. P. (1990a) 'What leaders really do', *Harvard Business Review*, May–June, pp. 156–67.

Kotter, J. P. (1990b) *A Force for Change: How Leadership Differs from Management*, New York, Free Press.

Kotter, J. P. (1995a) 'Leading change', *Harvard Business Review*, March–April.

Kotter, J. P. (1995b) *The New Rules: How to Succeed in Today's Post-Corporate World*, New York, Free Press.

Kotter, J. P. (1997) 'Leading by vision and strategy', *Executive Excellence*, October, pp. 15–16.

Kouzes, J. M. and Posner, B. Z. (2002) *The Leadership Challenge* (3rd edn), San Francisco, CA, Jossey-Bass.

Kubr, M. (1996) *Management Consulting: A Guide to the Profession* (3rd (revised) edn), Geneva, International Labour Office.

Law, S. (2002) 'Getting involved in culture change at M&S', *Professional Management*, May, pp. 24–25.

Mayo, A. (2002) 'Forever change', *Training Journal*, June, p. 40.

McLagan, P. (2002) 'Change leadership today', *Training & Development*, vol. 56, no. 11, pp. 26–31.

Monks, J. (2000) 'Engaging the workforce during change', paper presented at The National Leadership Conference, 'Leaders and managers: Fit for the future', Sandhurst, The Royal Military Academy, 24 May.

Mulligan, J. and Barber, P., quoted in Sadler, P. (1998) *Management Consultancy: A Handbook of Best Practice*, London, Kogan Page.

Myers, D. G. (1993) *The Pursuit of Happiness*, London, The Aquarian Press.

Nixon, B. (2002) 'Responding positively to the big issues', *Professional Consultancy*, vol. 4, April, pp. 24–26.

O'Toole, J. (1995) *Leading Change: Overcoming the Ideology of Comfort and the Tyranny of Custom*, San Francisco, CA, Jossey-Bass.

Performance Improvement Unit (2001) *Strengthening Leadership in the Public Sector*, Research Study by the PIY, Cabinet Office, UK Government, www.cabinet-office.gov.uk/innovation/leadershipreport.

Peters, T. (1993) *Liberation Management*, London, Macmillan.

Rajan, A. (2000) *How Can Leaders Achieve Successful Culture Change?*, Tonbridge, Kent, Centre for Research in Employment and Technology in Europe.

Sadler, P. (1997) *Leadership*, London, Kogan Page.

Senge, P. (1990) *The Fifth Discipline*, New York, Doubleday.

Sullivan, W., Sullivan, R. and Bufton, B. (2002) 'Aligning individual and organisational values to support change', *Journal of Change Management*, vol. 2, no. 3, pp. 247–54.

Waugh, P. and Morris, N. (2002) 'Ministers warn Blair that Labour lacks core values', The Independent, 9 March.

Whittington, R., Pettigrew, A., Peck, S., Fenton, E. and Conyon, M. (1999) 'Change and complementarities in the new competitive landscape: A European panel study, 1992–1996', *Organization Science*, vol. 10, no. 5.

World Economic Forum (2000) *Creating the Organizational Capacity for Renewal*, New York, Booz Allen and Hamilton/World Economic Forum.

Tempered Radicalism and the Politics of Ambivalence and Change

15

Debra E. Meyerson and Maureen A. Scully

A woman executive can identify with feminist language that is far from commonplace in corporate life and challenges the very foundations of the corporation in which she holds office. She can also be loyal to her corporation, earnestly engaged by many of its practices and issues, and committed to a career in a traditional, male-dominated organization or profession. A male business school professor can hold an identity as a radical humanist and embrace values directly in contest with capitalist corporations. He can also be committed to his job in the business school and teach practices that, in effect, enforce the tenets of capitalist organizations. An African-American architect can identify with her ethnic community and be committed to creating a more equitable and healthy urban environment. She can also identify with a professional elite and be committed to an organization that perpetuates the decay of urban neighborhoods. These individuals do not easily fit within the dominant cultures of their organizations or professions. However, despite their lack of fit, or perhaps because of it, they can behave as committed and productive members and act as vital sources of resistance, alternative ideas, and transformation within their organizations.

These individuals must struggle continuously to handle the tension between personal and professional identities at odds with one another. This struggle may be invisible, but it is by no means rare. Women and members of minorities have become disheartened by feelings of fraudulence and loss as they try to fit into the dominant culture. Some leave the mainstream. Others silence their complaints and surrender their identities.

Meyerson, D. and Scully, M. (1995) 'Tempered radicalism and the politics of ambivalence and change', *Organization Science,* vol. 6, no. 5, pp. 585–600.

However, separatism and surrender are not the only options. While frustration may be inevitable, individuals can effect change, even radical change, and still enjoy fulfilling, productive, authentic careers. We write this paper about and for the people who work within mainstream organizations and professions and want also to transform them. We call these individuals 'tempered radicals' and the process they enact 'tempered radicalism'.

We chose the name 'tempered radical' deliberately to describe our protagonist. These individuals can be called 'radicals' because they challenge the status quo, both through their intentional acts and also just by being who they are, people who do not fit perfectly. We chose the word 'tempered' because of its multiple meanings. These people are tempered in the sense that they seek moderation ('temper blame with praise', *Webster's New World Dictionary,* 1975). In the language of physics, they are tempered in that they have become tougher by being alternately heated up and cooled down. They are also tempered in the sense that they have a temper: they are angered by the incongruities between their own values and beliefs about social justice and the values and beliefs they see enacted in their organizations. Temper can mean both 'an outburst of rage' and 'equanimity, composure', seemingly incongruous traits required by tempered radicals.

Tempered radicals experience tensions between the status quo and alternatives, which can fuel organizational transformation. While a great deal of attention has been devoted to issues of organizational 'fit', change often comes from the margins of an organization, borne by those who do not fit well. Sources of change can give organizations welcomed vibrancy, but at the same time, the changes that the tempered radical encourages may threaten members who are vested in the status quo. Is this transformation 'good for' the organization? The answer may change as standards of judgment change, for example, when an organization shifts from a stockholder to a stakeholder model. Many people ask us 'what exactly' the tempered radical can change, and 'how much'. One dilemma for the tempered radical is that the nature and effectiveness of change actions is elusive, emergent, and difficult to gauge. The yardstick for change frequently changes metrics. In this paper, we will not focus on whether the tempered radical ultimately wins the battle for change, but rather on how she remains engaged in the dual project of working within the organization and working to change the organization. We focus on the individuals themselves, the perspectives they assume, the challenges they face, and the survival strategies they use. It is important to understand these individuals as central figures in the battle for change because if they leave the organization, burn out, or become coopted, then they cannot contribute fully to the process of change from inside.

Writing this paper is an example of tempered radicalism. We discuss our own and others' radical identities and implicitly critique professional and bureaucratic institutions. We draw from formal interviews and dozens of informal conversations with tempered radicals, first-person accounts from related literatures, and descriptions of tempered radicals in the popular press. We experiment with modes of scholarship as we attempt to weave personal narrative into our paper. The content of our stories illustrates substantive dilemmas of tempered radicalism; the form of the stories, which makes our subjectivity explicit, is an example of tempered radicalism insofar as it pushes traditional notions of social science writing and draws inspiration from feminist approaches to scholarship (e.g., Krieger, 1991; Reinharz, 1992).

The first section below paints a portrait of the tempered radical. The second and third sections discuss the advantages and the disadvantages of ambivalence as a cognitive and political stance. The last section describes some strategies used by tempered radicals to sustain their ambivalence and work for change.

Tempered Radicalism:
The Process and Practitioners

Tempered Radicalism

Individuals come to work with varied values, beliefs, and commitments based on multiple identities and affiliations that become more and less salient in different circumstances; they have situational identities (Demo, 1992; Gecas, 1982). The tempered radical represents a special case in which the values and beliefs associated with a professional or organizational identity violate values and beliefs associated with personal, extra-organizational, and political sources of identity. In the tempered radical, both the professional and personal identities are strong and salient; they do not appear alternately for special situations. In most situations, the pull of each identity only makes the opposite identity all the more apparent, threatened, and painful.

Threats to personal identity and beliefs can engender feelings of fraudulence, misalignment (Culbert and McDonough, 1980), and even passion and rage (hooks, 1984). These feelings can bring about change. For the tempered radical alignment and change are flip sides of the same coin. When tempered radicals bring about change, they reshape the context into one where it is a bit easier to sustain their radical identities. Untempered, this approach may alienate those in power and threaten the tempered radical's professional identity and status. The tempered radical may therefore cool-headedly play the game to get ahead, but does not want to get so caught up in the game that she violates or abandons her personal identity and beliefs. In this sense, tempered radicals must be simultaneously hot-and cool-headed. The heat fuels action and change; the coolness shapes the action and change into legitimate and viable forms.

Who are the Tempered Radicals?

This paper has been difficult and exciting for us to write because we view ourselves as tempered radicals, struggling to act in ways that are appropriate professionally and authentic personally and politically. Both of us are feminists and radical humanists; we strongly believe in eradicating gender, race, and class injustices. We are also both faculty members in business schools and members of a discipline known as 'management', although we teach about a variety of stakeholders other than managers. Both of us identify with our profession and want to advance within it. Yet we also believe that the business schools in which we work reproduce certain inequalities systematically, if unintentionally. We find ourselves in the awkward position of trying to master the norms of our profession in order to advance and maintain a foothold inside important institutions, but also trying to resist and change the profession's imperative and focus. Often people keep such feelings to themselves lest they undermine their credibility. Tempered radicalism can be lonely and silent. Nonetheless, we have learned to articulate this experience, first by talking with each other, and then by talking with, interviewing, and reading about others who have influenced us deeply. In the words of one of them:

> I've often felt that it's extremely difficult to be a critically oriented scholar within a business school and that I'd fit better someplace else on campus. Is it possible to talk about underlying values, assumptions, hopes and fears, and question the ultimate purposes of organizations when the dominant ethos is focused on the technical, the instrumentally rationale, and that defines values and purposes as outside the scope of 'the problem'...And finally, is it possible to be a feminist and live in a business school? Can I still be me and survive in this profession? I've asked myself these questions many times. (Smircich, 1986, p. 2)

Women of color in professional positions have articulated the tensions of tempered radicalism quite clearly, perhaps because their history is marked by their struggle with multiple injustices (e.g., Bell, 1990; Collins, 1986; Gilkes, 1982; Hooks, 1989). Bell (1990) found that Black women professionals face significant pressure to conform to professional standards and the dominant culture of the organization as well as to live up to expectations, values, and identities based in the Black community. They must also overcome stereotypes by passing extra tests of competence and loyalty at work. Sutton (1991) describes the tension she experiences each day as an African American architect:

> With part of our selves, we work to achieve power and authority within the traditions of the dominant culture. We hoist each other toward personal success through an invincible network of friendship, economic support,

mentoring, information exchange .... No matter how little we earn, we join the costly American Institute of Architects and make our presence felt in that organization.

With another part of our selves, we reject the competitive, elitist mentality of architectural design which differentiates professionals and clients, professors and practitioners, designers and builders, and builders and users. We reject this segmentation because it reflects the segmentation that exists in the larger society between men and women, rich and poor, young and old, colored and white. (Sutton, 1991, pp. 3–4)

For men of color who try to succeed within predominantly white institutions, the experience of tempered radicalism is 'substantively as much a part of the minority professional in this country as baseball and apple pie' (African American law student). This same student argued:

Struggling to get ahead in white dominated society – while struggling desperately to maintain what little we were 'allowed' to develop and espouse as a black identity – has been a mainstay of the very fabric of black culture for over a century.

Gay men and lesbians who work within traditional, heterosexual institutions also experience the tensions of tempered radicalism. They must game how much to disclose, how much to risk, how much to trust. Those who attempt to hide their sexual orientation from colleagues report feelings of fraudulence and shame, which get exacerbated when they are accused of selling out by their more 'out' gay and lesbian peers. Because gay and lesbian professionals can choose to hide their source of difference, however painfully, they face, perhaps more than any group, constant decisions about the politics of identity.

The conflicting identities faced by white heterosexual men may not be as visible, predictable, or stressful as those faced by women of all colors, men of color, or gay men and lesbians, but they certainly do exist. For example, a white man from the Boston area was coached by a colleague on how to lose his class-based accent, but was ambivalent about abandoning his working class origins precisely because he thought he could use his managerial position to lobby for working class employees during economic downturns. He also knew that adopting a higher class accent could help in that lobbying effort, and thus he experienced 'status inconsistency' (Lenski, 1954).

We speak in this paper about some of the shared experiences of tempered radicals. At the same time, we acknowledge that different groups experience different identity challenges. They undoubtedly respond with different strategies as well, using the distinctive types of insider knowledge they acquire. We hope that this paper encourages tempered radicals to share their experiences with one another and to add to the general strategies described here.

The Advantages of Ambivalence

The dual nature of the tempered radical's identity creates a state of enduring ambivalence. In this section we detail some of the advantages of ambivalence and challenge the predominant view that ambivalence is a temporary or pathological condition to resolve (e.g., Merton, 1976). Weigert and Franks (1989) summarize the sociological understanding of ambivalence:

> Insofar as ambivalence creates uncertainty and indecisiveness, it weakens that organized structure of understandings and emotional attachments through which we interpret and assimilate our environments (Marris, 1975).... Clearly experienced emotion is an important cue to the formation of coherent inner identity (Hochschild, 1983, p. 32). Without firm feelings of who we are, our actions are hesitant, halting, and incomplete. (Weigert and Franks, 1989, p. 205)

'Ambivalence' stems from the Latin *ambo* (both) and *valere* (to be strong) (Foy, 1985); it can be tapped as a source of strength and vitality, not just confusion and reluctance. We suggest that individuals can remain ambivalent *and* quite clear about their attachments and identities. In contrast to compromise, ambivalence involves pure expression of both sides of a dualism; compromise seeks a middle ground which may lose the flavor of both sides. Cooptation – eventually espousing only the voice of tradition – might be averted by clever compromises, but might be better fended off by the clear oppositional voices retained in a posture of ambivalence. Because both parts of a duality are represented, ambivalent responses can be more responsive to equivocal situations than compromises (Weick, 1979).

The tempered radical's ambivalence resembles the experiences of marginality and biculturalism, which others have described as a tenuous balance between two cultural worlds:

> A *marginal person* is one who lives on the boundary of two distinct cultures one being more powerful than the other, but who does not have the ancestry, *belief system,* or social skills to be fully a member of the dominant cultural group (Park, 1928; Stonequist, 1937). (Bell, 1990, p. 463)

Like marginal people, tempered radicals experience ambivalence in three interrelated forms, each of which has its own advantages. First, and most fundamentally, tempered radicals are 'outsiders within'. They can access the 'knowledge and insight of the insider with the critical attitude of the outsider' (Stonequist, 1937, p. 155). While insider status provides access to opportunities for change, outsider status provides the detachment to recognize that there even is an issue or problem to work on. Merton (1976) described a result of this dual cognitive posture as 'detached concern', where one is both objective and subjective. We suggest that the tempered radical may also experience 'passionate concern', which involves dual subjectivities. Memories of being outside of the center can become a source of creativity and transformation:

> Living as we did – on the edge – we developed a particular way of seeing reality. We looked both from the outside in and from the inside out. We focused our attention on the center as well as the margin. We understood both…. Our survival depended on an ongoing public awareness of the separation between margin and center and an ongoing private acknow-ledgment that we were a necessary, vital part of that whole. … This sense of wholeness, impressed upon our consciousness by the structure of our daily lives, provided us with an oppositional world view – a mode of seeing unknown to most of our oppressors, that sustained us. … These statements identify marginality as much more than a site of deprivation; in fact, I was saying just the opposite, that it is a site of radical possibility, a space of resistance…. It offers one the possibility of radical perspective from which to see and create, to imagine alternative new worlds. (Hooks, 1984)

Second, tempered radicals can act as critics of the status quo *and* as critics of untempered radical change. Stonequist (1937) praised marginals for being 'acute and able critics'. In Hasenfeld and Chesler (1989, p. 519), Chesler claims that his marginality (or the ambivalence inherent in his marginality) has allowed him to be critical of the status quo: to 'break away from dominant professional symbols and myths to question their validity, and to undertake innovative theory building and research. Being free of existing professional paradigms has enabled him to develop new bodies of knowledge now rec-ognized as important to the profession'. In interviews, others echoed the importance of remaining 'independent'. Tempered radicals may also critique a more radical approach to change. Tempered radicals have chosen to work for change from within organizations, although their career path may be as much a default, a playing out of the usual route through the education and career system, as an active political choice. In any case, because of their location, they may critique some forms of radical change for provoking fear, resistance, and backlash. Pamela Maraldo, president of Planned Parenthood, has stirred controversy among feminists by taking a tempered approach to the risks of being too radical:

> I don't believe in a strident, radical approach to things, because right away you lose many of your followers. … I think that 'feminist' plays differently in different circles. Many people in mainstream America have vague, radical associations with the term. I do not, so I apply it easily and comfortably to myself. But I think that to present myself as a feminist would be to lose the

attention early on of a lot of the important public…. Whatever we choose to call [feminism], the important thing is that it work. (quoted in Warner, 1993, p. 22)

Third, in addition to being critics of the status quo and critics of radical change, tempered radicals can also be advocates for both. Their situation is therefore more complex than that of change agents who act strictly as critics of the status quo. As advocates for the status quo, tempered radicals earn the rewards and resources that come with commitment and (tempered) complicity, and these become their tools for change. Sutton (1991) envisions this dual posture:

From this admittedly radicalized perspective. I imagine an alternative praxis of architecture that simultaneously embraces two seemingly contradictory missions. In this alternative approach we use our right hand to pry open the box so that more of us can get into it while using our left hand to get rid of the very box we are trying to get into. (Sutton, 1991, p. 3)

Tempered radicals can and will be criticized by both radical and conservative observers. Radicals may suspect that tempered radicals' agendas are futile or retrogressive. Audre Lorde wrote, in words now famous among feminists, 'The master's tools will never dismantle the master's house.' Defenders of the status quo find ways to exclude suspected deviants from full entry into the institution. Jackall (1988, p. 54) quoted two managers speaking candidly about invoking group conformity pressures to silence radical voices. One said, 'You can indict a person by saying he's not a team player', and the other noted, 'Someone who talks about team play is out to squash dissent.' Faced with pulls toward more radical and conservative stances, and with voices of uncertainty in their own heads, tempered radicals must deal with the disadvantages of ambivalence discussed in the next section.

The Challenges of Ambivalence

Despite the benefits of an ambivalent stance, a number of social and psychological forces work to persuade tempered radicals to forfeit one side of themselves or the other. Below we discuss pressures against an ambivalent stance. Most of these are forces of assimilation. We begin with a discussion of the painfulness of being seen as a hypocrite, of feeling isolated, and of being tempted to abandon the fight. We then tell a story of our own gradual cooptation from a feminist to a more mainstream research agenda. We identify from within this story several forces that can lead a tempered radical to resolve the inconsistency of her identities by trying to become an insider.

Perceptions of Hypocrisy

Tempered radicals speak to multiple constituencies, which poses the problem that they will be seen as too radical for one and as too conservative for another. An even more complex problem for a tempered radical is receiving mixed feedback from within a single constituency, particularly one she thought she understood and represented. The headline on a front page article in the *London Herald Tribune* – '[Jesse] Jackson is a Symbol to Some U.K. Blacks and Sellout to Others' – speaks to this difficulty.

> At the mention of the Reverend Jesse L. Jackson, they (a group of Black, working class 'Brits') began, grudgingly at first, to show interest. 'If he's gone that far', insisted one, 'it must be because he's White inside.' ... 'Listen, man' said a third (man), 'A Black man running for president of the United States. It's important.' In London's Black ghettos. Mr. Jackson is a curiosity, a symbol of success and to some, a sellout. It is the latter view, held by many of this generation of British-born Blacks, that is most worrying to those who believe, like Mr. Jackson, that the way to equality is to win power within the institution .... Yet few Black Britons seem to share Mr. Jackson's faith in the concept of pushing from within and some of these see him as a sellout. (De Young, 1988, p. 1)

That some Black, working class 'Brits' viewed Jackson as a 'sellout' while others viewed him as a sign of hope and change may, ironically, reflect his effectiveness as a tempered radical.

If the issue were only that some people see a tempered radical one way and others see her another way, then the tempered radical could simply manage these images separately and sequentially. Theories of managing multiple constituencies counsel letting each side see that which is most favorable to its interests (Goffman, 1959). However, some people can see both images simultaneously. In this situation, tempered radicals may be accused of being hypocritical, that is, of trying to act in a situation like they are different from or better than who they in fact really are. 'Liberals are particularly likely to be charged with [hypocrisy], because they are given to compromise' (Shklar, 1984, p. 48). Some observers may be confused about who the tempered radical is or what she 'really' stands for. Her activist friends may think she lets them take the heat from conservatives while she wins favor and the perquisites of being an insider. Her friends inside the organization may wonder if she is secretly more critical of them than she lets on.

The problem is that the tempered radical does not have a single identity that is 'true' and another that is 'staged'. The ambiguity of having two identities may cause others to believe the tempered radical is strategically managing impressions and trying to win approval from two audiences. Once impression management is suspected, observers give less credibility to the person who appears inconsistent (Goffman, 1969). Some of the tempered radicals we interviewed experienced significant stress from being labeled hypocritical or from worrying about such impressions. In the words of an anonymous tempered radical, 'The worst is feeling like people who I care about think I am being fickle. I've been called a hypocrite. It stinks.'

The social stigma of hypocrisy is painful. Combined with the psychological discomfort of dissonance (Bem, 1972; Festinger, 1964), it might drive a tempered radical to want to seek the relief of consistency and a more consonant identity. This adaptation would require forfeiting one side of her ambivalent stance or the other. We feel that most pressures point toward assimilation and surrendering the 'outside' identity and commitments.

Though forces of assimilation are powerful, one tempered radical pointed out to us that we overemphasized how 'easy' it was for a tempered radical to become coopted and end up fully an insider. She cautioned us that, for her and others, one of the main challenges of a professional career was to be accepted as an insider at all. The insiders were insistent on seeing her as different and on treating her as such in a variety of obvious and subtle ways. The number of help books that try to teach women how to fit in (e.g., Harrigan, 1977) attests to both the appeal of learning the rules of the game and the high hurdles to succeeding.

Isolation

Perhaps a tempered radical can never go home to one community and identity or another. Tempered radicals are often lonely. A tempered radical may fear that affiliating too strongly with an identifiable group, either outside or inside the organization, may push her too close to one side and jeopardize her credibility with the other side. One tempered radical described her fear:

> In my field (forestry), if you are seen with women you are viewed as unprofessional. Real professionals talk to men about forestry, not to women about recipes. So if you talk to other women you are seen as either a lesbian or not professional. [I am] terrified to be seen with a group of women.

Given this fear, some tempered radicals become vague about their identification with various coalitions in the hopes of not threatening their legitimacy and affiliation with insiders. The feeling of isolation may cause the tempered radical to look for acceptance and companionship in the organization. Some try to prove their loyalty by conforming, sometimes emphatically, to dominant patterns of behavior or by turning on members of their outside group (Kanter, 1977).

Feelings of isolation may intensify as the tempered radical advances within the organization. Ironically, just as a tempered radical approaches a higher position from which she hopes to effect change, she experiences more intensely the feelings of isolation that could pull her away from her change agenda into a position of comfortable belonging. One feminist executive reported to us that once she had become well established in a conservative organization, the few women who had been her peers along the way had dropped out, been dismissed, or been completely assimilated into the mainstream. As a relatively high-status insider (with strong ambivalence), she was structurally and institutionally closer to the center of her work organization and profession and therefore felt even more distance between her professional and personal identities. Among peers, her gender still kept her distant from male colleagues perceived as more promising candidates for further advancement. With respect to lower level employees, her high status created an awkward social and emotional distance. She hoped that junior employees with radial and idealistic beliefs would come talk to her, yet, because of her status, they did not assume she was like-minded or approachable. Because she did not advertise her outsider affinities, precisely so that she could be more effective, she experienced the pain of not being taken seriously by those whom she would have liked to reach.

Pressures of Cooptation

A number of pressures push the tempered radical away from the 'outsider' piece of her identity and more fully toward the 'insider' piece. The remainder of this section describes in detail the ways in which compromises can lead to cooptation. Since we experienced a variety of these coopting mechanisms over the course of this project, we tell our story as an illustration.

We began what we now call the 'tempered radical' project as graduate students with a concern about the problems of feminist executives and academics. We wondered where those with the radical voices heard in the 1960s and 1970s had gone to work in the 1980s and whether they had found ways to change institutions. We were warned by faculty members that asking questions about 'radical' or 'feminist' change within organizations was itself radical and risky, particularly for graduate students who had not established secure positions within the academic or business communities. In addition, our identification and emotional investment threatened our perceived legitimacy as 'objective' researchers. We were advised to conceive of this problem, not as a problem for feminists or radicals, but as a more general problem: effecting change from within a system. This approach would allow us to detach ourselves and, most important, avoid being labeled 'radicals' – or worse, 'feminists' – so early in our careers.

The advice to detach ourselves and cast the problem in the more abstract and conceptual terms of the field seemed like a reasonable compromise and like an intellectual exercise from which we might learn. We planned to come back to the feminist executive as a special case after we had developed theory about the general case. We hoped we could avoid the two painful pulls we were beginning to study: being dismissed as radicals or indefinitely deferring our true interests.

As we searched for comparable change agents inside organizations, we were presented with an opportunity to study corporate ethics officers, who were charged with implementing possibly controversial ethics programs within corporations. Corporate ethics officers, unlike feminist executives, were accessible and easy to study. Ethics programs had recently been mandated and the ethics officers were negotiating immediate change, so we seized the moment. The research involved extensive traveling, interviewing, and data analysis. We found that the topic interested academic and nonacademic audiences and could easily attract research funding. When we were asked about our research interests, it became easier for us to talk about corporate ethics programs in a vividly illustrated, theoretically compelling, and not too provocative way than to talk about the touchy subject of feminist executives. No one suggested that we try another topic or bundle this study into another research package.

Our language, audience, and ultimately our research problem gradually changed. Our study took on a life of its own and resulted in several papers about corporate ethics programs in the defense industry. This story illustrates how compromises in (1) language, (2) timing, and (3) emotional expression can lead to cooptation. We discuss each of these in detail below.

Diverse literatures dealing with change recommend using insider language to package, 'sell', or legitimate a change program (e.g., Alinsky, 1972; Dutton and Ashford, 1993). The use of insider language may be even more essential when proposed changes intervene at a deep level to challenge the assumptions and values of the organization (Frost and Egri, 1991). Catchy specifics in the language of the status quo can catalyze cooptation. For example, as our study progressed, we talked more about 'corporate ethics officers' in place of internal change agents and 'defense industry ethics programs' in place of organizational change efforts. Our language shifted, in a direction and with a speed, that suprised us. To reflect our insider knowledge of the world of ethics programs in the defense industry, we spoke of 'ethics hotlines', 'fraud, waste, and abuse', and the 'defense industry initiative'. Before we knew it, the 'feminist executive' had faded in our memories and was filed away for 'future research'.

The role of language in coopting participants has been vividly portrayed in Cohn's (1987) study of the world of defense intellectuals. In a world where men (almost exclusively) spend their days matter-of-factly strategizing about 'limited nuclear war', 'clean bombs', 'counterforce exchanges', and 'first strikes', Cohn assumed the role of participant observer to ask the question: 'How could they talk this way?' To gain legitimacy in the system, she learned to speak the language of insiders. As Cohn learned the language, she became less shocked by the cold-bloodedness of the talk, and eventually engaged by it:

> The words are fun to say; they are racy, sexy, snappy.... Part of the appeal was the power of entering the secret kingdom, being someone in the know. ... Few know, and those who do are powerful. ... When you speak it, you feel in control. (Cohn, 1987, p. 704)

The more proficient she became in the language, the easier it became to talk about nuclear war and the more difficult it became to speak as a critical outsider. As her language shifted to 'defense-speak', the referent shifted from people to weapons. Human death became 'collateral damage'.

> I found that the better I got at engaging in this (insider) discourse, the more impossible it became for me to express my own ideas, my own values. I could adapt the language and gain a wealth of new concepts and reasoning strategies – but at the same time the language gave me access to things I had been unable to speak about before, it radically excluded others. I could not use the language to express my concerns because it was physically impossible. This language does not allow certain questions to be asked or certain values to be expressed. (Cohn, 1987, p. 708)

Thus, the power of language was not in the ability to communicate technically, but rather in its capacity to rule out other forms of talk, thought, and identity.

The temptation to defer radical commitments adds another pressure toward cooptation, as we learned in our own experience. Our ethics officer study was intended as a short deferral, but we strayed from our original concern further and for longer than we planned. Early invitations to talk about this topic at conferences took us deeper into this line of research, which forced us to learn more, which led to more opportunities and papers, which generated more knowledge and questions to be researched. Such is the course of a 'research stream'. Compromise behaviors create environments that require more of the same behaviors (Weick, 1979).

Like other compromise solutions, the strategy of deferring radical commitments until a foothold is established seems reasonable. From the tempered radical's perspective, it might seem less risky to advance more threatening agendas from a position of power and security. She might be tempted to wait and collect what Hollander (1958) calls 'idiosyncrasy credits' by initially conforming to and exemplifying the organization's norms. Later, when she accumulates enough credibility, trust, and status, she would 'spend' these credits to reshape organizational norms. However, this deferred radicalism may stall the change effort in two ways. First, when 'later on' arrives, the tempered radical may have lost sight of her initial convictions. Second, it may become impossible to tell when 'the moment' has arrived to cash in credits. It is always tempting to wait until one has yet more formal power and security and can *really* effect change.

As individuals wait longer to disclose their identities and agendas and spend more time investing in their careers, it becomes more difficult to resist cooptation on material, psychological, and political grounds. Ferguson (1984) doubts that women can transform traditional bureaucracies from within them:

> They (liberal feminists) hold out the hope that once women have made their way to the top, they will then change the rules: 'When they get to be dealer – they can exercise their prerogative to change the rules of 'dealer's choice''.... . They see women as the hope for humanizing the work would and convincing men of the need for change. By their own analysis, this hope is absurd. After internalizing and acting on the rules of bureaucratic discourse for most of their adult lives, how many women (or men) will be able to change? After succeeding in the system by those rules, how many would be *willing* to change? (Ferguson, 1984, pp. 192–93)

In addition, it becomes difficult for the tempered radical to turn her back on, or even criticize, those who were part of her career success. Individuals confront extreme backlash and resentment when they suddenly speak out against injustice after years of quietly tolerating it. Anita Hill is a compelling recent example. Reactions are particularly severe if the people involved have succeeded in the system. They are asked: 'If the system is so sexist, why has it treated you so justly and well?' 'If you have been quiet in the past, what's the motive for your sudden fuss?' Fear of such accusations cause many to silence their frustrations indefinitely.

Deferral poses one source of cooptation. Tempted radicals can also be coopted by the process of tempering their emotions to appear rational and cool-headed, to be 'the reasonable feminist'. Hot-tempered emotion fuels a tempered radical's desire and impetus for change, but this hot side of the emotional balancing act may often lose out to the cool organizational persona, particularly because real, spontaneous emotional expression is far from the norm in most organizational contexts (Mumby and Putnam, 1992). Again, our project may be illustrative. We have tried to make this paper, in form and content, an expression of our own tempered radicalism. As such, we have struggled with the balance between making it legitimate for publication and making it true to the lived experience. As we read and re-read interview transcripts, we began to think of our allies and colleagues as 'data'. In our effort to get the paper published, part of the 'balance', we consistently have 'overtempered'. Our tempered radical began to appear as a highly rational strategist who at every turn attempts to reach a balance, appeal to multiple constituencies, and optimize impressions.

Many of our tempered radical colleagues complained that our description missed the essence of the experience: the heat, passion, torment, and temper that characterize the experience of being a tempered radical. Some argued that in our effort to construct a theory about tempered radicals, we overcategorized and overrationalized the phenomenon and, in doing so, unwittingly made our protagonist and paper complicit in maintaining traditional constraints. Other reviewers, however, complained that the paper lacked a coherent theoretical strategy, was not sufficiently grounded in a single literature, and was too inconsistent in its style. The interweaving of self-reflective narrative and theory in this paper represents our ambivalent and somewhat unsatisfying response to this problem. As we tried to satisfy some readers, we inevitably lost others. This very experience heated up the frustration of tempered radicalism for us.

Emotional Burdens

As sociologists and psychologists remind us, ambivalence generates anger plus a variety of powerful, unpleasant emotions, which also contribute to the difficulty of sustaining this posture. Among others feelings, a tempered radical's ambivalence may result in guilt and self doubt (Weigert and Franks, 1989), which arise when people cannot live up to their own ideals (Goffman, 1963). An assistant to the Chancellor of a major university revealed to us her continuing anguish:

> There are qualified people who get turned down (for tenure) just because they are women. And my job is to make sure that doesn't happen. Sometimes I feel like I have hit a grandslam, but my team was already behind by seven and so ... there's no victory for me and there's no victory for her. There's only the lingering feeling in both of our minds that I didn't do it good enough. If I had just done a little more or done it a little better, done a little differently, played my cards a little better or viewed it from a slightly different angle or made a slightly different argument .... I find that it is impossible for me to suffer enough to absolve myself when we get done. It's extremely difficult for someone to deal with that because my energy has nowhere to go. And so I find myself flagellating myself in most extraordinary and creative ways when the problems are institutional and it didn't matter what I did .... The pressure I feel because I know the pain that they are in. I don't sleep.

For those with a history of being outsiders, the self-doubt arising from ambivalence can be particularly debilitating, as illustrated in this depiction of Black students' experiences:

> Students who strive to assimilate while covertly trying to remain engaged with Black experience suffer extreme frustration and psychological

distress...Maintaining this separation is difficult, especially when these two contradictory longings converge and clash...On the surface, it may appear that he has coped with this situation, that he is fine, yet his psychological burden has intensified, the pain, confusion, and sense of betrayal a breeding ground for serious mental disturbance. (Hooks, 1989, pp. 67–68)

One tempered radical says, 'It is corrosive to constantly feel disrespected by the system...It has been a struggle for me to feel good about myself in the face of collegial disapproval and disrespect'. Another interviewee admitted that she continually worked in an environment in which 'people act as if I am not here'. If sustenance for tempered radicals comes from artfully working the system to make changes, this feeling of being devalued can make them wonder whether they are effective and whether it is worth carrying on. Many choose not to and leave, including those who might be important contributors to the organization (Kolb and Williams, 1993).

Several features of tempered radicalism can produce stress. Tempered radicals frequently experience role conflict and role ambiguity, which can lead to stress and strain (e.g., Kahn et al., 1964). The tedious rate at which change occurs further frustrates tempered radicals, many of whom report periodic battles with burnout. Because tempered radicals must learn to suppress or temper emotions at times or, worse, hide their identities, they may feel additional stress and frustration from 'bottling it up' (Bell, 1990; Coser, 1979; Worden et al., 1985). As symbols of a marginalized cultural community, they may also worry about how their performance will affect others in their cultural group (Hooks, 1989; Kanter, 1977).

We do not want to end this section on such a pessimistic note. In addition to the pain of loneliness, guilt, self-doubt, and shaky self-esteem, some tempered radicals also report feeling authentic as a result of having a 'rather unorthodox, complex identity' (McIntosh, 1989), and feeling encouraged by others who can relate to the complexity of their commitments (Gilkes, 1982; Hooks, 1989). We turn now to a discussion of strategies that help tempered radicals effect change and simultaneously sustain their ambivalent identities despite the pressures described above.

Strategies of Change and Ambivalence

In general, tempered radicals create change in two ways: through incremental, semi-strategic reforms and through spontaneous, sometimes unremarkable, expressions of authenticity that implicitly drive or even constitute change. In this section, we discuss two change-oriented strategies – small wins and local, spontaneous, authentic action – and discuss how they relate to change, with the additional benefit of sustaining tempered radicals' identities and purposes.

The other two strategies we discuss – language styles and affiliations – work in the reverse fashion. They are directed at authentic identities, but also implicitly provoke and redefine change.

The process and politics of change in organizations has been addressed extensively in a variety of literatures, including work on radical change and community organizing (e.g., Alinsky, 1972), innovation (e.g., Frost and Egri, 1991; Kanter, 1983), 'championing' (e.g., Howell and Higgins, 1990; Kanter, 1983), upward influence (e.g., Kipnis et al., 1980; Mowday, 1978), 'issue selling' (Dutton and Ashford, 1993), and impression management (e.g., Goffman, 1959; Rafaeli and Sutton, 1991). These literatures issue prescriptions that might be useful to the tempered radical as change agent. However, none of these literatures focuses on how problematic and painful identity politics are for the change agent, in part because they do not assume a change agent who is dissident with the organization's fundamental premises. Steering a course between assimilation and separatism is a central and defining issue for the tempered radical.

The tempered radical bears some semblance to the boundary spanner role described in the organizational literature (Pfeffer and Salancik, 1978; Scott, 1984; Thompson, 1967), who must bridge two organizations that have different goals and resources. The tempered radical is different from this classic boundary spanner in the important sense that part of her core identity is threatened by or threatening to the dominant coalition of either or both of the organizations. Even so, tempered radicals may usefully employ some of the strategies of traditional boundary spanners, such as buffering the core aspects of their function in the organization from their change agent role (tempered radicals may be found in roles that are not explicitly chartered to deal with change) or creating bridging strategies with critical external groups.

The change agents in the organizational literature generally do not have broader visions of change in mind. Although terms like 'revolutionary' and 'deep' are sometimes used to describe change, those terms rarely refer to system change that challenges the embedded assumptions of the status quo (Alinsky (1972) and Frost and Egri (1991) are exceptions). In our review of strategies for tempered radicals, we refer occasionally to these literatures but also break with them.

Small Wins

A small wins approach (Weick, 1984, 1992) addresses several problematic aspects of tempered radicalism and seems to be a viable strategy for change and identity maintenance. First, small wins reduce large problems to a manageable size. Big, unwieldy problems produce anxiety, which limits people's capacities to think and act creatively (Weick, 1984). A colleague created a small win recently when she convinced the dean of a business school to delay the start of the tenure clock until new recruits' dissertations were complete. (For a variety of systemic reasons, women begin jobs before completing dissertations more frequently than men). While this policy change goes only a short way toward ending gender-based discrimination, it is a tangible first step with potentially large ramifications.

Second, small wins can be experiments. They may uncover resources, information, allies, sources of resistance, and additional opportunities for change (Weick, 1984). Small wins often snowball as they create opportunities and momentum for additional small wins. Weick argued that the real power of small wins as a strategy for social change comes in the capacity to gather and label retrospectively a series of relatively innocuous small wins into a bigger 'package' that would have been too threatening to be prospectively adopted. For example, a multipronged work and family policy could have been envisioned in the 1970s but might have been too sharp a departure and perhaps even too radical a label to propose then. However, a gradual accretion of different aspects of the program – from flex-time to on-site child care – has resulted by the 1990s in many companies (almost a quarter of a representative national sample) having or discussing what are now labelled 'work/family programs' (Osterman, 1994). A series of small wins is 'less likely to engage the organizational immune system against deep change' (Frost and Egri, 1991, p. 242).

As experiments, small wins act as a system diagnostic. With relatively minor visibility, risk, and disruption, small wins can test the boundaries of an organization's capacity for change. Even 'small losses' can be a source of discovery (Sitkin, 1992). Alinsky (1972) warned that reformers could miss change opportunities not only by 'shooting too high' but also by 'shooting too low'. The tempered radical never really knows what too high means until she steps over the line or what too low means until she learns of opportunities lost. Moreover, the line between too much and too little is constantly shifting.

Third, a small wins approach encourages picking battles carefully. Tempered radicals possess a limited amount of emotional energy, and they have access to limited legitimacy, resources, and power. The Chancellor's assistant described this problem:

> I have to choose very carefully when I's going to go against the party line. ... Like when there's a woman up for tenure and she's been turned down I'm the last person to comment before it goes to the Chancellor. I have to decide who to fight for. Because if every time a woman comes along who's been turned down I say, 'Oh my God, what a horrible injustice' then I won't have any credibility with the Chancellor. So I have to take my shots carefully when it's close, because the Chancellor is a very choosy constituent.

Of course, often the tempered radical does not have a neat menu of battles from which to select rationally. To quell rage even temporarily in a way that feels inauthentic can be neither desirable nor possible. The tempered radicals we most admire are those who have been able to draw courage from their anger and sometimes pick battles with fierce drive and reckless abandon.

Fourth, small wins are therefore often driven by unexpected opportunities. To be poised to take advantage of opportunities, the tempered radical's vision of the specific course of change must be somewhat blurry. Relatively blurry vision and an opportunistic approach enable an activist to take advantage of available resources, shifting power alliances, lapsed resistance, heightened media attention, or lofty corporate rhetoric to advance a specific change (Alinsky, 1972; Martin et al., 1990). We are reminded of a story told by one tempered radical of another. After receiving an invitation to a corporate Christmas party to which spouses and significant others were invited, a lesbian executive (who had not yet come out at work) informed her boss that she was going to bring her girlfriend. Her boss refused to accept this guest. Enraged, she took the issue (along with samples of corporate rhetoric about diversity) to the CEO, who welcomed her guest and 'talked to' her boss. Born out of range and frustration, this woman's courageous act turned out to be a significant intervention that produced real and symbolic change in the organization.

While a small wins approach can help a tempered radical push change while maintaining her identity, we should point to some risks associated with the small wins approach. First, tempered radicals in high positions may lose sight of the fact that, for lower level employees, some changes may be urgent, or the order of changes may matter a great deal. Although it may not matter in the long run which type of change comes first, employees may be desperate for child care solutions, but able to live quite easily without a policy about delayed partnership reviews.

Second, being driven solely by opportunity may mean that tempered radicals follow, rather than lead, change. They may achieve only those small wins that were there for the asking. Efforts that are too tentative or small may set a change process backwards by making people feel an issue is closed – 'OK, we have a day care facility and have solved the "work/family problem."' Small wins may distract people from a more fundamental issue, provide a premature sense of completion, or steer a change effort off course.

Even taking these cautions into account, the small wins approach is attractive. Immediate action means that commitments are not being deferred. The accumulation of small wins changes the organizational landscape for later battles, as 'outcomes of current political activity form the basis of the future deep structure of interaction' (Frost and Egri, 1991, p. 282). Further-more, as the organization gradually changes, the tempered radical's alignment struggles also shift. The only way for the tempered radical to locate the appropriate degree of resistance is to push continuously against the limits and keep the organization in flux. Smircich's notion of aligning as ongoing, local actions avoids reifying the organization and its limits:

> There isn't really 'an organization' out there that I am aligning myself to, rather my actions of aligning are doing organizing for myself and others.... [The organization is not] some independent hard separate reality, imposing itself on us, somehow disconnected from the very patterns of activity from which it is constituted. (Smircich, 1986, pp. 6–7)

Because it involves continuous pushing, a small wins approach sustains the tension between what it means to be an insider and what it means to dissent.

In our discussions with tempered radicals, we have heard of few instances in which tempered radicals who 'pushed too hard' were not given a 'second chance', even if they did push beyond what was organizationally appropriate. If small wins are used as an experiment, then successive tactics can become bolder and better attuned to the environment. An advantage for the tempered radical of being an insider is precisely to learn the dynamics of the local system and be able to act more confidently within it. As several tempered radicals have reminded us, enacting and celebrating small wins help sustain tempered radicals.

Local, Spontaneous, Authentic Action

A second way that change takes place – local, spontaneous, authentic action – is less strategic than small wins. It happens when tempered radicals directly express their beliefs, feelings, and identities. For example, a female surgeon explained how she changed her work environment by behaving more authentically. When she treated each member of her surgical team with respect and displayed compassion toward patients on her rounds, she demonstrated an alternative style of professional behavior. Her treatment of nurses in the operating room modeled new ways for the residents to behave toward nurses and may have helped alter the nurses' and residents' expectations of how teams share power and how surgeons should treat nurses. By acting in a way that was simply authentic, she created resistance to the authoritarian model that others on her team had taken for granted.

Acting authentically, as simple as it sounds, counteracts many of the disadvantages of sustaining ambivalence that we discussed earlier. The tempered radical who behaves authentically, even if this means inconsistently, may not feel dissonant. She and others may be able to accept her ambivalence as complexity (in the person and situation) rather than as insincerity or hypocrisy. The authenticity with which she behaves minimizes the possibility that she will experience feelings of fraudulence, self-doubt, or guilt.

Language Styles

Earlier we described how tempered radicals, forced to adopt the language of insiders to gain legitimacy, risk losing their outsider language and identity. In this section, we describe some strategies that can be used to counter the cooptive power of insider language. First, speaking in multiple languages and to multiple constituencies can help. While it is easy to imagine how one might speak different languages to different constituencies (e.g., academic to academic audiences, applied to applied audiences), it is harder to see how one might speak multiple languages to the same constituency. For example, some individuals choose to do 'diversity work' because of their commitment to social justice, their identification with a marginalized group, and their insights into the dynamics of disadvantage and privilege. Those who work in corporations learn to speak the language of insiders: in this case, to talk about diversity in 'bottom line' terms (e.g., recruitment and retention in a changing labor market, innovations born of diverse approaches, access to a broader customer base). However, tempered radicals may be most effective if they speak to each constituency in both languages. They do not channel their language so that business people hear only bottom line rationalizations, nor so that community organizers hear only the social justice reasons for proposed changes. Unexpected internal allies can be discovered in using the language of social justice inside the corporation.

The tempered radical might counter the cooptive power of insider language by using her insider knowledge and facility with the language to deconstruct it and then reconstruct alternative worlds. A few scholars in the management field have begun to deconstruct the traditional discourse in an attempt to expose assumptions, question what has been left unsaid, dislodge the hegemony of the traditional texts, and make room for alternative conceptions of organizing and management (e.g., Calás, 1987; Calás and Smircich, 1991; Gray, 1994; Kilduff, 1993; Martin, 1990; Meyerson, 1994). As a provocative illustration of this genre, Mumby and Putnam (1992) deconstructed the concept 'bounded rationality' and then used this deconstruction to reconstruct organizing in terms of 'bounded emotionality'.

A linguistic strategy that helps avoids cooptation by harnessing the dominant language is captured in the metaphor of jujitsu, a martial art in which the defender uses the energy of the attacker against itself. Tempered radicals can effect change by holding those in power to their own rhetoric and standards of fair play. In our study of corporate ethics officers, we observed this 'linguistic jujitsu'. Lower level employees appropriated the language of ethics to bolster their claims for more ethical treatment. This tactic worked particularly well in those companies that defined ethics broadly in terms of 'treating each other fairly, with dignity and respect'. Once such language was publicly espoused by management in ethics training sessions, employees could use it to push for more responsive and accessible grievance channels and other changes consistent with 'fairness, dignity, and respect'. Managers' fear of losing credibility persuaded them to be responsive to claims that invoked their own language (Scully and Meyerson, 1993).

Affiliations

Another approach tempered radicals may find helpful is to maintain affiliations with people who represent both sides of their identity. Almost all of the tempered radicals we interviewed emphasized the importance of maintaining strong ties with individuals, communities, or groups outside of their organization. These outside affiliations act as sources of information, resources, emotional support, and, perhaps most important, empathy. Affiliations with communities, organizations, and people help mitigate against the difficult emotions associated with ambivalence. Affiliations help keep the tempered radical from suppressing her passion and rage and from acting in a way that makes her feel fraudulent or guilty. They keep her fluent in multiple languages.

The tempered radical's understanding of oppression and injustice can only be preserved by continuing to identify with outsiders. Identifying as an outsider reminds her of her own privilege as an insider (Worden et al., 1985). Bell (1990, p. 463) argues that a Black woman professional can access her bicultural experience as a source of inner strength and empowerment', giving her a feeling of spiritual, emotional, and intellectual wholeness'. Affiliations help tempered radicals guard against losing their losing their ability to speak as outsiders. For example, Hooks (1989) cautions Black women against losing sight of how their minds have been 'colonized', and furthermore, warns against viewing identity politics as an end in itself rather than as a means to an end. Ties to the community are part of 'the struggle of memory against forgetting' (Hooks, 1989).

In our own experience as organizational scholars we have learned to treasure our outside affiliations. For example, our ties to women's studies programs and women's political organizations have served as sources of emotional and intellectual vitality. Our ties to friends and colleagues who are more radical in their approaches have sustained our ambivalent course by encouraging our commitments and nurturing our radical identities. We know two or three people who have taken more radical courses, and we try to imagine them reading our papers. Imagining as well as receiving their feedback helps us to sustain our commitments. Outside affiliations can also provide a sense of independence. One tempered radical claimed that his outside activities as an activist had become a crucial source of self-esteem when he felt alienated from his profession.

In addition to outside ties, connections to like-minded people inside the organization are a source of sustenance. Sometimes tempered radicals are hard to find precisely because their public personae are tempered. Reformers who think the system needs only minor changes and tempered radicals engaged in small wins en route to more massive changes may be difficult sometimes to distinguish. However, sometimes tempered radicals find each other and can build coalitions. Some tempered radicals report that they experience joy and connection because they have a strong sense of community inside as well as outside the organization (e.g., Gilkes, 1982; Worden et al., 1985). Even if membership and energy are in flux, there may be a collective momentum that outlives individuals' lulls. In a study of collective action inside organizations (Scully and Segal (in progress)), one member of a grassroots coalition reported its importance to her for maintaining organizational and personal attention to diversity issues:

> [The diversity issue] tends to peak and valley. It's not consistent energy, even from the grassroots. I think it goes up and down. I think because of the grassroots efforts, it hasn't been dropped … . The grassroots efforts have been instrumental even during the lower periods in bringing it back up to a peak, so I don't think you can do without the grassroots efforts.

We have seen each other through peaks and valleys and benefited from our long-standing collaboration on this project and on projects that grew out it. When one of us felt confused or pulled by the tension inherent in our ambivalent stance, the other could help redefine the tension in terms of excitement or challenge. We did 'cooptation check-ins' by phone. When we listened to each other talk about our joint project, we could hear the other's, and sometimes our own, language. We could hear in each other the changes in how we described and thought about our project. We should admit, however, that despite our efforts to keep each other on course, we sometimes failed and became complicit in each other's 'digression'. Yet, we can without hesitation recommend collaborating with another of like heart and mind.

Conclusion

This paper has focused on the tempered radical as an internal change agent quite different from those more commonly portrayed in the literature. Although tempered radicals face many of the same challenges, they also confront unique challenges associated with their ambivalent identities and their broader definition of ultimate change. This paper contributes to the literatures on change from within organizations by introducing a fundamentally different type of change agent than the protagonists of these other literatures. We hope that this paper also gives tempered radicals a kind of legitimacy, inspiration, and sense of community.

The labor of resistance may be divided among those who push for change from the inside, from the outside, and from the margin, each effort being essential to the others and to an overall movement of change. The importance of maintaining affiliations with colleagues and friends who are more and less radical than oneself may be crucial for tempered radicals, not only as a means to sustain their ambivalent course, but also as a way to make their struggles collective. Tempered radicals may be playing parts in movements bigger than themselves and their organizations. In the course of effecting change, they are helping prepare for bigger changes that more radical outsiders may be better positioned to advance. Tempered radicals can also support insiders who push for big changes from positions of power. Thinking in terms of a collaborative division of labor among activists helps resist the counterproductive tendency, particularly among liberals and radicals, to judge who is being the best and most true advocate for change.

Our effort to recognize tempered radicals comes at a crucial time. Those who do not neatly fit – mostly white women and people of color – have been fleeing mainstream organizations at a high and costly rate (Cox, 1993). Some leave because they can no longer tolerate the seemingly glacial pace of change, others leave because they are tired of being devalued and isolated, and still others leave simply because they no longer have the energy to 'play the game'. This exodus has serious repercussions for organizations.

Tempered radicals represent a unique source of vitality, learning, and transformation. Particularly as organizations attempt to become more global, multicultural, and flexible, they must learn to nurture those organizational members that will push them through a continuous transformation process. As the tempered radical's own survival depends on transforming the organization to achieve alignment, so too the contemporary organization may well depend on aligning with new voices and players in a diverse, global environment.

References

Alinsky, S. D. (1972) *Rules For Radicals,* New York, Vintage Books.

Bell, E. L. (1990) 'The bicultural life experience of career-oriented Black women', *Journal of Organizational Behavior,* vol. 11, pp. 459–77.

Bem, D. J. (1972) 'Self-perception theory' in Berkowitz, L. (ed.) *Advances in Experimental Social Psychology,* New York, Academic.

Calás, M. B. (1987) *Organizational Science/fiction: The Postmodern in the Management Disciplines,* Unpublished doctoral dissertation, Amherst, MA, University of Massachusetts.

Calás, M. B. and Smireich, L. (1991) 'Voicing seduction to silence leadership', *Organization Studies,* vol. 12, pp. 567–601.

Cohn, C. (1987) 'Sex and death in the rational world of defense intellectuals', *Signs: Journal of Women in Culture and Society,* vol. 12, no. 4, pp. 687–718.

Collins, P. H. (1986) 'Learning from the outsider within: The sociological significance of Black feminist thought', *Social Problems,* vol. 33, no. 6, pp. 514–32.

Coser, R. L. (1979) 'Structural ambivalence and patterned mechanisms of defense', *Training in Ambiguity: Learning Through Doing in a Mental Hospital,* New York, Free Press.

Cox, T. (1993) *Cultural Diversity in Organizations: Theory, Research Practice,* San Francisco, CA, Berrett-Koehler.

Culbert, S. A. and McDonough, J. (1980) 'The invisible war: Pursuing self-interest at work' in Frost, J., Mitchell, V. F. and Nord, W. R. (eds) *Organizational Reality: Reports from the Firing Line,* pp. 202–11.

Demo, D. H. (1992) 'The self-concept over time: Research issues and directions', *Annual Review of Sociology,* vol. 18, pp. 303–26.

DeYoung, K. (1988) 'Jackson is symbol to some U.K. Blacks and sellout to others', *London Herald Tribune,* p. 1.

Dutton, J. E. and Ashford, S. J. (1993) 'Selling issues to top management', *Academy of Management Review,* vol. 18, no. 3, pp. 397–428.

Ferguson, K. E. (1984) *The Feminist Case against Bureaucracy,* Philadelphia, PA, Temple University Press.

Festinger, L. (1964) *Conflict, Decision and Dissonance,* Stanford, CA, Stanford.

Foy, N. (1985), 'Ambivalence, hypocrisy, and cynicism: Aids to organization change', *New Management,* vol. 2, no. 4, pp. 49–53.

Frost, P. J. and Egri, C. P. (1991) 'The political process of innovation' in Staw, B. S. and Cummings, L. L. (eds) *Research in Organizational Behavior,* 13, Greenwich, CT, JAI, pp. 229–95.

Gecas. V. (1982) 'The self-concept', *Annual Review of Sociology,* vol. 8, pp. 1–33.

Gilkes, C. T. (1982) 'Successful rebellious professionals: The Black woman's professional identity and community commitment', *Psychology of Women Quarterly,* vol. 6, no. 3, pp. 289–311.

Goffman. E. (1959) *The Presentation of Self in Everyday Life,* New York, Doubleday.

Goffman. E. (1963) *Stigma,* Englewood Cliffs, NJ, Prentice-Hall.

Goffman. E. (1969) *Strategic Interaction,* Philadelphia, PA, University of Pennsylvania.

Gray, B. (1994) 'A feminist critique of collaborating', *Journal of Management Inquiry,* in press.

Harrigan, B. L. (1977) *Game Mother Never Taught You: Corporate Gamesmanship for Women,* New York, Warner Books.

Hasenfeld, Y. and Chesler, M. A. (1989) 'Client empowerment in the human services: Personal and professional agenda', *The Journal of Applied Behavioral Science,* vol. 25, no. 4, pp. 499–521.

Hochschild, A. R. (1983) *The Managed Heart,* Berkeley, CA, University of California.

Hollander, E. (1958) 'Conformity. Status, and idiosyncrasy credits', *Psychological Review,* vol. 65, pp. 117–27.

Hooks, B. (1984) *Feminist Theory from Margin to Center,* Boston, MA, South End Press.

Hooks, B. (1989) *Talking Back: Thinking Feminist, Thinking Black,* Boston, MA, South End Press.

Howell, J. M. and Higgins, C. A. (1990) 'Champions of technological innovation', *Administrative Science Quarterly,* vol. 35, no. 2, pp. 317–41.

Jackall, R. (1988) *Moral Mazes: The World of Corporate Managers,* New York, Oxford.

Kahn, R., Wolfe, D., Quinn, R., Snoek, D. and Rosenthal, R. (1964) *Organizational Stress: Studies in Role Conflict and Ambiguity,* New York, Wiley.

Kanter, R. M. (1977) *Men and Women of the Corporation,* New York, Basic Books.

Kanter, R. M. (1983) *The Change Masters,* New York, Simon and Schuster, Inc.

Kilduff, M. (1993) 'Deconstructing organizations', *Academy of Management Review,* vol. 18, no. 1, pp. 13–31.

Kipnis, D., Schmidt, S. M. and Wilkinson, I. (1980) 'Intraorganizational influence tactics: Explorations in getting one's way', *Journal of Applied Psychology,* vol. 65, pp. 440–52.

Kolb, D. and Williams, S. (1993) 'Professional women in conversation: Where have we been and where are we going?' *Journal of Management Inquiry,* vol. 2, March, pp. 14–26.

Krieger, S. (1991) *Social Science and the Self: Personal Essays on an Art Form,* New Brunswick, NJ, Rutgers.

Lenski, G. E. (1954) 'Status crystallization: A nonvertical dimension of social status', *American Sociological Review,* vol. 19, pp. 405–13.

McIntosh, P. (1989) 'Feeling like a fraud: Part Two', paper presented at the Stone Center, Wellesley, MA, Wellesley College.

Marris, P. (1975) *Loss and Change,* Garden City. NY, Anchor.

Martin, J. (1990) 'Deconstructing organizational taboos: The suppression of gender conflict in organizations', *Organization Science,* vol. 1, pp. 339–59.

Martin, J., Scully, M. and Levitt, B. (1990) 'Injustice and the legitimation of revolution: Damning the past. Excusing the present, and neglecting the future', *Journal of Personality and Social Psychology,* vol. 59, pp. 281–90.

Merton, R. K. (1976) *Social Ambivalence and Other Essays,* New York, Free Press.

Meyerson, D. E. (1994) 'From discovery to resistance: A feminist read and revision of the stress discourse', Working Paper, Ann Arbor, MI, University of Michigan.

Mowday, R. (1978) 'The exercise of upward influence in organizations', *Administrative Science Quarterly,* vol. 23, pp. 137–56.

Mumby, D. K. and Putnam, L. L. (1992) 'The politics of emotion: A feminist reading of bounded rationality', *The Academy of Management Review,* vol. 17, no. 3, pp. 465–86.

Osterman, P. (1994) 'Explaining the diffusion of employer-based benefits: The case of work/family programs', unpublished paper, Cambridge, MA, Sloan School of Management, MIT.

Park, R. E. (1928) 'Human migration and the marginal man', *American Journal of Sociology,* vol. 33, pp. 881–93.

Pfeffer, J. and Salancik, G. R. (1978) *The External Control of Organizations,* New York, Harper and Row.

Rafaeli, A. and Sutton, R. I. (1991) 'Emotional contrast strategies as means of social influence: Lessons from criminal interrogators and bill collectors', *Academy of Management Journal,* vol. 34, pp. 749–75.

Reinharz, S. (1992) *Feminist Methods in Social Research,* New York, Oxford University Press.

Scott, W. R. (1984) *Organizations: Rational. Natural, and Open Systems* (2nd edn), Englewood Cliffs, NJ, Prentice-Hall.

Scully, M. and Meyerson, D. (1993) 'The separation of law and justice: The implementation of ethics programs at two companies in the defense industry', *Employee Responsibility and Rights Journal,* vol. 6, p. 4.

Scully, M. and Segal, A. (1994) 'Passion with an umbrella: The mobilization of grassroots activists in organizations', unpublished paper, Cambridge, MA, Sloan School of Management, MIT.

Shklar, J. N. (1984) *Ordinary Vices,* Cambridge, MA, Belknap.

Sitkin, S. (1992) 'Learning through failure: The strategy of small losses' in Staw, B. and Cummings, L. L. (eds) *Research in Organizational Behavior,* 14, Greenwich, CT, JAI, pp. 231–66.

Smircich, L. (1986) 'Can a radical humanist find happiness working in a business school?' Paper presented in the symposium. *Alignment in the Development of Social Science—Towards a New Role for Organizational Development,* Annual Meetings of the Academy of Management, Chicago.

Stonequist, E. (1937) *The Marginal Man,* New York, Russell and Russell.

Sutton, S. E. (1991) 'Finding our voice in a dominant key'. unpublished paper, University of Michigan.

Thompson, J. D. (1967) *Organizations in Action,* New York, McGraw-Hill.

Warner, J. (1993) 'Mixed Messages', *Ms* 4, 3, November/December, pp. 20–25.

Webster's New World Dictionary (1975).

Weick, K. E. (1979) *The Social Psychology of Organizing,* Reading, MA, Addison-Wesley.

Weick, K. E. (1984) 'Small wins: Redefining the scale of social problems', *American Psychologist,* pp. 40–49.

Weick, K. E. (1992) 'Wisdom in the 90s: Adaptation through small wins', Hale Lecture #4, Ann Arbor, MI, University of Michigan.

Weigert, A. and Franks, D. D. (1989) 'Ambivalence: A touchstone of the modern temper' in Franks, D. D. and McCarthy, E. (eds) *The Sociology of Emotions,* Greenwich, CT, JAI.

Worden, O., Chesler, M. and Levin, G. (1985) 'Racism, sexism, and class elitism: Change agents' dilemmas in combatting oppression' in Sargent, A. (ed.) *Beyond Sex Roles* (2nd edn), St. Paul, MN, West Publishing Co., pp. 451–69.

Part VI
Tools and Techniques

Introduction

Part VI adopts a different format to the rest of the book. Previously we have walked through the generic issues relating to the management and or leadership of change, in this part we are presenting you with an inventory of tools and techniques that you may wish to use at various stages throughout the processes of planning, implementing and evaluating change.

The tools and techniques section is presented in alphabetical order rather than by trying to categorise the tools and techniques. The objective here is that this gives you greater freedom to decide how and where you use each of the techniques. To illustrate, you may wish to use de Bono's six thinking hats as a tool for describing the change necessary, you may wish to use the same tool for generating potential objectives for change and you may wish to use the tool to evaluate those objectives.

Each element is presented in a specific way which outlines the history of the model, shows you the model itself, describes the uses, tells you how you can use the model and then considers the strengths and limitations of each model.

The consideration of each is necessarily limited and is presented to give you a flavour for some of the tools and techniques available to people leading or managing change. We have therefore provided an additional reference at the end of each element where you can find information should you wish to.

We have tried to include within this part some newer or less well known tools and techniques and we would encourage people to try using these instead of the traditionally used methods, to see if they offer any new insights which can help inspire practice.

6–3–5 Method

History

The 6–3–5 method was first described by Warfield et al. in 1975. The model is a group technique for generating ideas in a systematic way. The technique involves 6 people, each of whom generates three ideas. The ideas are circulated around the group at five minute intervals (hence 6–3–5).

Model

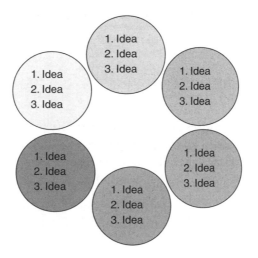

Uses

The 6–3–5 Model can be used to:

    Identify the causes of problems
    Identify opportunities
    Generate options for change
    Evaluate options for change
    Consider support for or resistance to change
    Consider how to deal with resistance to change.

How to use

1. The group decide on the key theme for the session (e.g. The causes of falling quality standards).
2. The group sit in a circle and each person is given a sheet of paper. They are given five minutes on which to write the three issues/causes that they feel are most important.
3. After five minutes each piece of paper is passed around to the person sitting on the left. This person then has five minutes to add to, to elaborate on the list which has just been passed to them.
4. After five minutes each piece of paper is passed again to the person sitting on the left and they too elaborate on the comments made by the first and second person.
5. The process continues until everyone receives their own piece of paper back.
6. The facilitator gathers all the pieces of paper together for the group to evaluate.

Strengths

The model is useful as it gives people the opportunity to surface their own ideas and perspectives and then allows other people to build on these. As such the data gathered is far richer than it would be from a traditional brainstorming session or from using nominal group technique.

Limitations

The model only allows for the generation of ideas. It is still reliant on an effective means of evaluting the suggestions/ideas generated.

_____ *Reference* _____

Warfield, J.N., Geschka, H. and Hamilton, R. (1975) *Methods of Idea Management*, Columbus, Ohio, The Academy fro Contemporary Problems. Van Gundy, A.B. (1988) *Techniques of Structured Problem Solving* (2nd edn), New York, Van Nostrand Reinhold.

Awakishi Diagram (a reversed Ishikawa diagram)
(Adapted from Newman, 1995)

History

The Awakishi diagram is a development from the Ishikawa cause and effect diagram. Unlike the Isikawa diagram, this is fundamentally concerned with trying to work out what one needs to do, what action one needs to take in order to achieve the desire effects, in other words, in order to achieve the solution.

Model

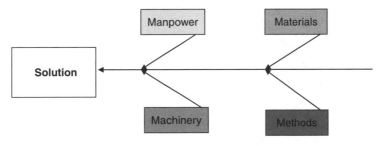

Uses

The Awakishi diagram is useful as a mechanism for working out what actions or activities need to take place in order to bring about a desired solution. It is based on the principle that those managing the change have clear objectives as to what it is they need to achieve. As such it may be that people have used problem solving tools and techniques to arrive at their solution or that the desired output of the change has simply been dictated to people.

How to use

1. The solution, once identified should be mapped in the solution box.
2. The group then need to identify the range of factors which need to happen, or the range of things that need to be changed, in order to bring about that solution.

3. The group then need to prioritise these factors to find the headings of the 'fish-bones' (labelled as Manpower, Materials, Machinery and Methods in our diagram). It is possible to use more than four here depending on how complex the change is.
4. Once the main fish-bone headings are in place people can start to add the contributory spines, i.e. what exactly needs to happen with 'Materials' in order to achieve the objective set? See worked example below.

Worked example

In the example below a company that paints kitchen cupboard doors has been told to increase the number of doors they paint per day.

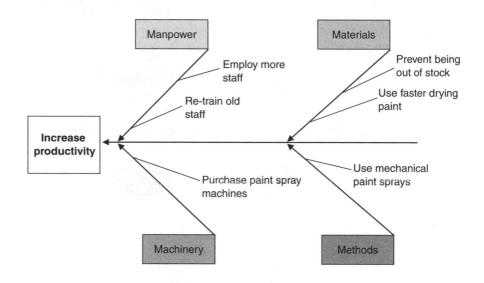

If we expand on one of the spines we can illustrate the level of detail that can be included in an Awakishi diagram.

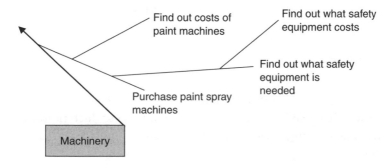

Strengths

The strengths of an Awakishi diagram lie in the fact that they allow you to map clearly the key areas which need be acted upon to bring about the desired change. The process can also help you to map out your thinking in terms of the sequence of event that precedes each of the activities.

Limitations

The diagram tends to present an image of each of the key areas as being distinctive from the other areas, as though activity in each of these areas could take place in isolation. In reality all are interconnected and thinking about successful change implies that people need to be aware of the connections between the factors.

Reference

Newman, V. (1995) *Made-to-Measure Problem Solving*, England, Hampshire, Gower.

Breadth versus Depth Matrix

History

In planning organisational change it has traditionally been important to scope the boundaries of that change. By doing so, those leading the change are able to work within clearly defined perimeters within which they can set the objectives for change. Likewise it has traditionally been seen as important to consider the impact that the change will have on those affected, that is, to see where and why you can expect to meet resistance. This matrix pulls those two factors together so that those planning the change can clearly see the relationship between the extent to which the change may disrupt the procedural aspects of the organisation and the extent to which the change may disrupt the human aspects of the organisation.

Model

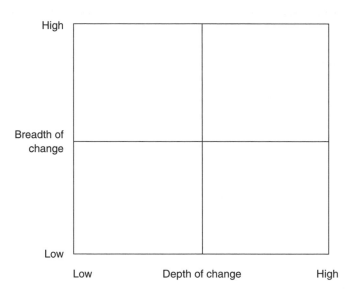

Key

Breadth of change = the extent to which the changes planned spread across all the different parts of the organisation. Breadth is deemed to be high when the change involves lots of different areas, different process and systems, different disciplines and different people. The breadth of change is deemed to be low when it is focussed on one particular area, department, process or group of people.

Depth of change = the extent to which the changes planned challenge the accepted ways of doing things within the organisation. The depth of change is deemed high when the change planned moves people outside their 'range of stability' (Arnold et al., 1994: 432). This means that the people involved in the change feel that the change challenges their psychological, emotional or physical confidence, making them feel uncomfortable. The depth of change is deemed low when people can easily cope with minor adaptations in the ways in which they work.

Uses

The model is used for helping those planning the change to see the scope of the change alongside the ways in which this will affect the people involved.

Implications

1. Where the breadth of the change is high and the depth of the change is high, this would imply the need for high profile support for the change, consistent and organisation wide communication and a staged socio-technical approach which balances the acquisition of new skills and competences with support for the individuals involved.
2. Where the breadth of the change is low and the depth of the change is high, this would imply the need for local level coaching and mentoring to support people through the process of change.
3. Where the breadth of change is high and the depth of change is low, this would imply the use of multi-disciplinary teams or quality circles to come up with newer and more effective ways of working.
4. Where the breadth of change is low and the depth of change is low, then local level procedural adaptations may be negotiated or imposed.

How to use

Based on your description of the change, consider the number of departments affected by the change you plan. You can do this by considering these as a percentage of the overall number (i.e. the change will affect 7 of the 14 departments thus 50% of the organisation will be, in one way or another, involved) or by the number of employees in each department, in which case, although 7 of the 14 departments are affected, these only constitute 30% of the overall workforce.

Next consider the extent to which you are challenging the ways in which people do things. Are the changes that you are planning likely to make people feel uncomfortable? Are they likely to doubt their ability to cope?

Once you have a generic mapping you can then take this to the next level of abstraction by selecting those groups that you feel will be most affected by the change. At this level you should think of breadth in terms of the number of routines or processes being changed, and depth as the level to which these routines and processes will be disrupted.

Strengths

The strengths of the model lie in its surfacing the need to consider the extent to which the planned changes will affect the wider organisation, and the idea of aligning this with a consideration of the significance of that disruption.

Limitations

This is only a starting place for thinking. It is for the person planning the change to then consider whether or not it is feasible to meet the demands of all of these stakeholders, whether or not some are simply told what they have to do, whilst others have a more contributory part of the process of change.

Reference

Arnold, J., Cooper, C.L. and Robertson, I.T. (1998) *Work Psychology: Understanding Human Behaviour in the Workplace*, London, Financial Times.

Demands, Constraints and Choices Model
(Adapted from Rosemary Stewart, 1982)

History

The demands, constraints and choices model was devised by Rosemary Stewart. In her original paper the model characterised the context within which managers worked. The notion of demands and constraints was seen to frame what actions managers could and should take. Testament to the usefulness of this framework is that since its inception it has been used in many guises from problem-solving to strategic planning.

Model

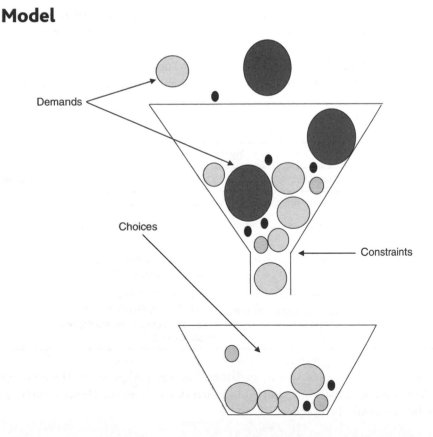

Uses

The adapted demands, constraints and choices model can be used to recognise the context within which decisions are made. As such it allows for those planning the change (or those involved in strategic planning or problem-solving) to devise courses of action which are aimed at achieving their objectives whilst being appreciative of the limitations placed on them by the environment.

How to use

Note your responses in a framework similar to the one provided in Table 1 (an example is provided *in italics* in this table)

1. Determine what the objectives of the change are.
2. Write down a list of the relevant stakeholders.
3. Write down a list of the relevant organisational issues.
4. Systematically write down what each of the groups/contexts in answers to 2 and 3 want to see as the outcome of the change that you are planning.
5. Systematically write down the ways in which each of the groups/contexts in answers to 2 and 3 can limit what it is you want to achieve.
6. Do this group by group and item by item until columns 1, 2 and 3 are completed.

Table 1

Group/Issue	Demands	Constraints	Choices
My line Manager	Greater efficiency	No additional resource	
My staff	Less pressure of work	Reluctant to change patterns of work	
Organisational strategy	High level of customer service	Cannot stop delivering service to make improvements	
Other departments	Greater efficiency To keep pace with their changes	They need us to keep delivering whilst making any changes They don't communicate these in sufficient time	

7. Once each of the stakeholders/issues has been aligned to the relevant demands and constraints, you should then think about the choices you have. Choices should be noted in column 4.

Strengths

The strengths of the model relate to its ability to encourage people to think about the wider stakeholder, environmental and organisational issues which may have an impact on the change that they are planning. It is useful for highlighting areas of competing interest or conflicting demands.

Limitations

The model offers no solutions, it simply indicates those issues that complicate the process of trying to plan effective change. The model also requires people to make a value judgement regarding the level of abstraction they take the assessment to, that is do they consider absolutely everyone and everything, or do they consider only those people and groups that they consider to be relevant.

Reference

Stewart, R. (1982) 'A model for understanding managerial jobs and behaviour', *Academy of Management Review*, vol. 7, no. 1, pp. 7–13.

Force Field Analysis

History

The force field analysis was devised by Kurt Lewin in the 1940s. Although often thought of as a unitary model, his force field analysis was just one element of his wider thinking which included action based research, group dynamics and the three step approach to change. The logic underpinning the force field model was that in order to successfully bring about change within an organisation, one must first understand the pressure and the tensions which are maintaining the status quo. (Burnes, 2004) That it is only by understanding what encourages people to remain as they are, that one can work out how best to persuade them towards change.

Model

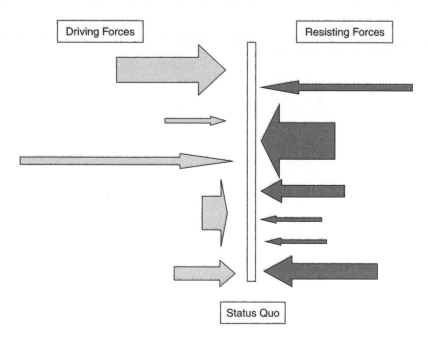

Uses

Lewin's force field model can be used as a tool to determine where people and/ or conditions are supportive of change and where people and/or conditions are resistant to change. Once the drivers and the resisters for change are mapped out, then those leading the change can decide what action they need to take. Lewin advocated that it was not sufficient to simply try and increase the drivers for change. Any attempt to do so would result in a similar increase in the forces of resistance. Therefore what will emerge is a position of stalemate. Rather, that those who are resisting change need to be persuaded towards the value of the change. The emphasis is on decreasing the forces resisting the change whilst at the same time increasing the forces driving the change.

How to use

Within this framework each of the arrows represents an issue which is driving the change forward or an issue which is resisting (or likely to resist) the change. In identifying what these are, it is worth considering both environmental conditions and specific individuals or groups of people. As such, you may identify that a particular group of workers are likely to resist change but it is more useful to consider why they might resist that change, for example perhaps they feel they lack the necessary skills or fear for their job security.

A useful way of representing this idea of drivers for and resisters to change is by the breadth and the length of the arrows. The wider the arrow the more intense the resistance will be, the longer the arrow the more prolonged that resistance is likely to be. By doing this it helps to prioritise which aspect of resistance you need to deal with first.

1. Brainstorm a list of the stakeholders affected or likely to be affected by the change being proposed. Alternatively, brainstorm a list of environmental circumstances in which the proposed change will take place. (It may be useful to use a PESTLE {Political, Economic, Socio-cultural, Technological, Legal and Environmental} framework to do this.)
2. Divide the list(s) that you have into forces driving for the change and forces driving against the change. Should any groups or issues arise that appear neutral, i.e. they are neither driving for nor pushing against the change, these can be kept to one side. However, don't discard this list as, the change processes and dynamics themselves change and people previously not interested may suddenly become interested.
3. Consider what factors you need to establish about people's resistance to change. Is it important to know how powerful these people are? Is it important to know how long their resistance or support will last? Is it important to know how opposed to the change they are? You should select two of these and represent one by the length of the arrow and the other by the breadth of the arrow.

4. Using the framework pictured above you should now map the most significant drivers for change and the most significant resisters against the change.
5. The mapping can be used as the basis for gathering further information or to feed into the process of planning the change.

Strengths

The model gives you a useful visual impression of the relationship between those pushing for and those pushing against the change. This allows you to see where more information is required or why you need to focus your attention.

The generic framework is very adaptable. It allows you to useful specifically relevant titles to the arrows to increase the depth of analysis. As such you could use the width and the length of the arrows to indicate a range of features, for example the 'strength of resistance' (are people vehemently opposed to what you plan or marginally unhappy), 'the power of resisters' (how able are groups/people to undermine your plan), 'the likely duration of resistance' (will this be a long fought battle or will people soon come around to your ways of thinking) or any other factors pertinent to your specific change.

Limitations

The model gives you a picture at one moment in time. As change is a dynamic it might be dangerous to plan the whole change programme around a single analysis.

The model doesn't offer any insights into why they are resistant. It is for the people managing the change to find that out if necessary. The model tells you where you might need to take action, but not what action you need to take.

―――――――――――――――――― *Reference* ――――――――――――――――――

Burnes, B. (2004) 'Kurt Lewin and complexity theories: back to the future', *Journal of Change Management*, vol. 4, no. 4, pp. 309–25.

Ishikawa: Cause and Effect Diagram

History

The cause and effect diagram was devised in the 1960s by Kaoru Ishikawa, one of the founding fathers of Quality Management. The diagram is also known as the fish bone diagram because of its resemblance to the skeleton of a fish.

Model

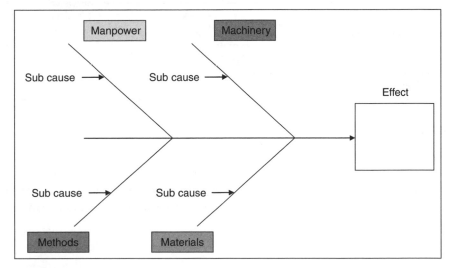

Uses

The cause and effect diagram is a useful tool for making sure that change efforts are focused on the areas most likely to produce the desired outcomes. The model encourages people to breakdown the issues that are causing the problem into specific areas. Most commonly the headings of manpower, machinery, materials and methods are used although these can be changed to more appropriate headings in different circumstances. An example might be that in a marketing context the headings of product, price place and promotion might be deemed more appropriate.

How to use

Having identified the problem (the effect), groups then brainstorm a list of areas which might contain the potential causes of the problem. Once this list has been generated the group then prioritise those causes which they feel are most significant. These become the headings for the spines. The group then consider each spine in turn and identifies the sub causes under each. (See worked example)

Worked Example

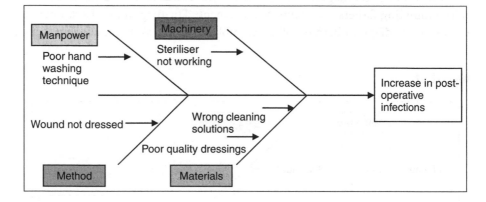

Strengths

The cause and effect model encourages people to think about the issues which provoke the problem, rather than focussing attention simply on the effects of that problem. As such it allows people to tackle the root causes rather than just the symptoms.

Limitations

The effectiveness of the model is dependent on people being able to accurately identify the causes of the problems. Where the causes are inappropriately identified, the focus of any subsequent changes will be inappropriate.

Reference

Slack, N., Chambers, S., Harland, C., Harrison, A. And Johnston, R. (1998) *Operations Management*, London, Prentice Hall.

McKinsey's Seven 'S' Model

History

McKinsey's Seven 'S' Model was devised by Peters, Waterman, Athos and Pascale in the 1970s. The premise of the model is that successful change is based on an understanding of the interdependence between seven variables. These variables consider what Peters and Waterman refer to as 'the hardware-strategy and structure' (1982: 11) of the organisation, as well as 'the software of the organization-style, systems, staff (people), skills, and shared values' (ibid).

Model

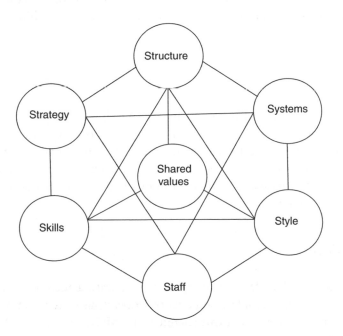

Key

Structure – Structure is deemed to be the positional relationships within the organisation which have an impact on work flow and on social relationships. Issues such as the extent of any hierarchy, levels of responsibility and authority, span of control and the magnitude of centralisation or decentralisation all warrant consideration.

Systems – Systems are described as the routines, processes and procedures necessary for the organisation to fulfil its purpose and achieve its goals and objectives.

Style – Style relates to the attitudes and behaviours of the organisation's managers and how they control and influence people towards the achievement of the organisations goals.

Staff – Staff refers to the nature and types of personnel groups which work within the organisation.

Skills – Skills are the technical, behavioural, cognitive and interpersonal attributes which exist within and across the various groups within the organisation.

Strategy – Strategy is the long-term plan of the organisation which moves the organisation forward from where it is today to where it wants to be tomorrow.

Shared Values – Shared values relate to the culture of the organisation, the implicit and explicit understandings about the way people do things.

Uses

The model provides a useful framework for thinking about the wider implications of a single episode of organisational change. If one visualises each area of the model as being connected to the others, then changes to one of the aspects (for example 'systems') of the model will create a tension on the other aspects of the model. Alternatively the model can be used to look for opportunities to improve the status quo.

Illustration

Clearoni Hospital has decided to use a new operating technique for routine eye surgery. This is a simple change to one operating system, however, when we look at the implications of this change using McKinsey Seven S Model, the following issues are raised:

Staff – The medical, nursing and ancillary staff need to be aware of how this new process changes their roles and responsibilities.

Skills – Likewise, each group needs an opportunity to acquire and refine the new skills needed to successfully implement the new procedure.

Style – Line managers may have to adopt a more supervisory role until such time that their staff are competent in the new techniques.

Systems – If the new technique takes more time or less time than the previous technique then the whole system for planning operating time will need to be re-visited.

Shared values – the motives for the change will need to be consistent with the values of the organisation. If the new procedure is seen to be efficient but less effective, then people may resist the change.

Structure – Those involved in the change need to be clear where the authority and the responsibility for implementing the change lies.

Strategy – If the new procedure presents a more efficient way of working then the organisation might need to re-evaluate its plans for the future.

How to use

Framing your answers within the context of the change you are planning:

1. Brainstorm the list of staff likely to be affected by the change.
   For each group of staff identified, make a note of what the impact is likely to be.
2. Next think about the skills that these people have and will need if the change is to be successful.
   You might wish to prioritise those skills which are most important.
3. Next think about the style of management that you, or the supervisors/line managers involved need to use to deal with the staff.
   Here you are thinking about whether you should consult with them, inform them or just impose the change on them.
4. Next consider what systems you need to introduce or improve in order to successfully introduce the change.
   These can be new operational systems, adapting old systems or getting rid of ineffective systems.
5. Next consider how the change will influence workflow patterns and the hierarchy.
   Is the current organisational structure sufficiently adaptable to deal with new processes?
6. Next consider how the changes planned fit in with the wider elements of the organisation's corporate, tactical and operational strategies.
   Here you are looking at the inter-connectedness of a wide range of organisational change processes and programmes.
7. Lastly, what are the cultural implications of the change processes you are implementing and of the ways in which you manage the change?
   Do the changes mean that the organisation now values different attributes, skills or competencies?

Strengths

The Seven S Model is good for generating a wider and more organisationally aware views of the impact of the change that you are planning. It generates a wide range of insights and allows those managing the change to see not only each of the factors in isolation, but also to consider the relationship between the factors.

Limitations

The model is basically focussed on an inward view of the change. There is a need also to consider the external stakeholders and the environmental context within which the change takes place. The model can also generate vast swathes of information which may be more or less relevant.

—————————————— *Reference* ——————————————

Peters, T. and Waterman, R. (1982) *In Search of Excellence: Lessons from America's Best-Run Companies*, London, Harper-Collins.

Mind Maps

History

Mind maps were first devised by Tony Buzan in the 1960s. They provide a means by which people can explore the ideas and the issues related to a central theme. Mind maps can be used by individuals to note the connections between key themes or can be used by groups, as an idea generating tool similar to brain storming.

Model

The example below relates to a student mapping out their ideas on leadership.

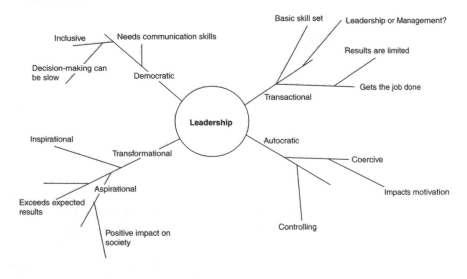

Uses

Mind maps can be used for a range of things. They can be used to identify the causes of problems, to generate solutions to problems or objectives when planning processes of change. They can also be used to clarify the implications or the consequences of specific objectives. In each of these situations, mind maps are used to generate a range of ideas, options or alternatives which can then advise action. However, mind maps can also be used to help you to revise or remember specific facts.

Where they are used to help you remember the connections between specific themes, rather than simply map these out as part of a problem solving process, then the use of colour may help with re-call. If we re-work the above example to illustrate.

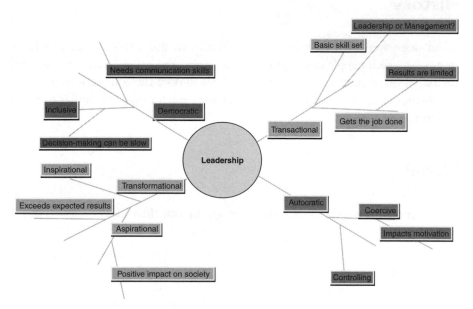

By highlighting each of the leadership types in a different colour it becomes easier to make the association between the colour, the type of leadership and the ideas and connections that you made when thinking about each of the issues.

How to use

Mind maps can be used by just one person to clarify their own ideas, or by a group. When using mind maps the important issue is the central focus (the hub). Because the generation of ideas will widen the ways in which you are thinking, it is useful to be relatively focussed in deciding on the central focus (the hub). If using mind maps as a problem solving technique then you should articulate the problem as succinctly as possible. If using them as a means of generating options, then you should be clear in the central hub about what it is you want to achieve. From that point you simply generate ideas and their associations.

If using mind maps as a group, there are a number of approaches. You can put one large map in the centre of a table and allow everyone free rein to draw their own ideas on the map. Alternatively you can allocate a specific spine to a person or a group of people and then share the ideas at the end of the session. It is also useful to consider a rotation system, by which each person goes around the spines (or indeed adds spines) in turn, adding their ideas as they go around.

Strengths

Mind maps are an excellent tool for generating a wide range of ideas and options. They can be used in the short term for problem-solving or decision-making. They can be used as an evaluative tool to look at the implications of decisions or they can be used in the longer term as tools for revising and remembering.

Limitations

There are no major weaknesses with mind maps as long as the central hub is sufficiently clear. Failure to be clear can lead to the generation of masses of unconnected ideas. Some people use mind maps regularly and find them extremely useful, for others, the visual format doesn't sit well with their preferred style of learning.

Reference

Buzan, Tony (2006) *Mind Mapping: Kickstart Your Creativity and Transform Your Life*, London, BBC Active.

Nominal Group Technique

History

Nominal Group technique was comprehensively described by Delbecq et al in 1975. It is traditionally seen as a team based approach to problem-solving. One or more teams of between 5 and 10 members go through a structured approach to diagnosing problems and/or generating potential solutions.

Model

There is no formal structuring model with Nominal Group Technique, rather this is dependent on a free flowing interactive process to generate results.

How to use

Participants are gathered together in a room and each is given a pen and some paper. The issue to be discussed is then introduced by the facilitator. In introducing the issue it is important that the facilitator be as 'neutral' as possible. No opinions should be given, no anticipated results, nothing that may influence or skew the thinking of the group members. Once the introduction to the topic has been made the people within the group generate a list of their own ideas. The facilitator will advise the team of the time they have to do this, (usually about 10 minutes) and within that time frame each individual works on his or her own to generate a list of potential ideas/options/solutions.

Once the ideas have been generated the facilitator goes around the table and asks each participant in turn to put one idea forward to the group. People within the group are allowed to ask questions or seek clarification from the person proposing the idea, but are not allowed to be openly critical of the idea. The facilitator writes up all the ideas on a master sheet. The process continues until all the ideas from all the participants have been transferred to a master sheet. The last stage involves anonymous voting. Each of the participants votes for what he or she feel are the ten most important/relevant/potentially viable options. They vote for these in rank order and the facilitator is responsible for coordinating the voting process and advising people of the result.

Strengths

Nominal Group Technique allows for the gathering of a wide range of ideas/options/solutions. It allows everyone to contribute by having a structured approach to feedback and the voting system can be re-visited following discussions if the results of this are unclear.

Limitations

Nominal Group Technique produces results based on consensus rather than on well reasoned facts and figures. As such, the potential solutions generated here may in practice be unworkable.

———————————— *Reference* ————————————

Delbecq, A. L. and Van de Ven, A. H. (1971) 'A group process model for problem identification and program planning', *Journal of Applied and Behavioural Science*, vol. 7, no. 4.

Power versus Interest Map

History

Power versus interest maps have traditionally been used to consider the potential impact that stakeholders can have on decisions made by the managers of an organisation. These decisions may be strategic in terms of accessing new markets or developing new products, or internal changes such as re-structuring. There are a number of manifestations of the matrix, what we have presented here is our perspective.

Model

Power versus interest map

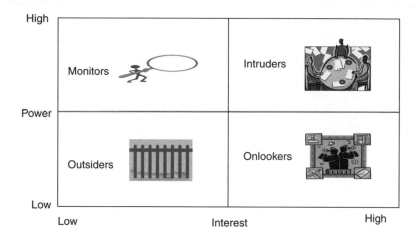

Uses

Here we are mapping the relationship between power (the ability to intervene) and interest (the extent to which people are concerned) of stakeholders. The idea of mapping that relationship is so the people can anticipate the responses of the various groups to the changes that they are planning. This allows those directing the change to then make proactive decisions regarding the extent to which people are consulted about the change, the extent to which the change is communicated to them or the extent to which people are simply subject to the change being imposed.

Categories

Monitors

These are groups or individuals who are powerful enough to be able to support or undermine the change. They may be shareholders, commissioning bodies, funders, or internal management structures. What is important to recognise is that they can work against you, i.e. they can force you to alter your plans. Contrarily they can work with you, i.e. they can influence people around to your ways of thinking.

However, because they are mapped on the matrix in the 'low interest' category, in this particular context they are really not concerned about the nature or the consequences of the change that you are considering. For them neither the costs of the change or the benefits that may be brought about by the changes are important. Because of this, rather than intervene in the change, they simply observe.

Intruders

These are groups or individuals who are powerful enough to support or mine the change, and who are interested enough in the changes taki to take action. As with the Monitors, they may be internal to the org for example trade unions or a senior manager, or they may be exte organisation, e.g. shareholders or local pressure groups. The important thing for you and the change that you are involved with is that, if these people are supportive, then they can be a great positive influence for change, however, if they disagree with that changes or the consequences of that change, they may well intervene to force you to alter the changes you have planned or even to prevent you taking action altogether.

Onlookers

Onlookers are groups or individuals who are very interested in the changes planned. The changes may have an impact on them personally or may have consequences for people or for things that they care about. Despite being interested in what is happening, these people have very little power to do anything. They cannot influence the change in any way.

Outsiders

...ups or individuals who rate low on both interest and power. ...hen, why do we bother considering these groups when ...ssues of change. The answer to that is that these are ...ir position as 'outsiders' may change if we alter or ... This idea of movement between the categories ... consider later that change may not always ...d out. Likewise it is important to consider ...ular, there is seldom just one change taking ...e who find themselves in the 'outsider' category for one change, may find themselves in the intruder category for another change.

How to use

The first stage of the process is to brainstorm a list of stakeholders. This can either be done in a free format or could be related to the far, the near and the internal environment in which they exist. This can be done from an individual perspective or as a group (also consider using nominal group technique). It is important also to consider potential stakeholders, namely groups of people who may not be particularly interested in your organisation now, however, they will be if you bring about the planned changes.

Next think about the extent to which each of the stakeholder groups will be interested in the changes that you have planned. Think about this from their perspective, what will the impact of the changes be and is that important to them? Next you should think about what the stakeholders can legitimately do to stop or at least force you to change your plans for change. Once you have mapped the stakeholders you can then think through logically how you will deal with each of the groups.

Strengths

The model encourages those planning a change process to think in advance of the ways in which the stakeholders and the potential stakeholders may respond to their plans. This allows them time to consider whether or not they need to deal with the stakeholders, how they will deal with the stakeholders and how they will respond to their concerns.

Limitations

The model still requires those planning the change to make a value judgement as to which stakeholders they should respond to and how.

Process Flow Charts

History

Process flow charts were first created by Frank Gilbreth in 1921. Since then they have traditionally been associated with assessing the effectiveness of operational systems. The focus on each of the stages of a process allows people to walk through the series of activities which lead to a specific output. Process flow charts are basically a road map which allows us to see where the systems are working well, where they are working less well and where they are not working at all.

Model

The process flow chart uses a series of symbols to represent specific activities, these are:

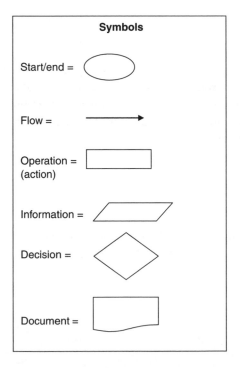

Uses

The process flow chart model is traditionally used as a means of finding out where problems exist within established processes or for seeking opportunities to improve processes usually as part of a wider programme of Quality Improvement. However, in wider applications it can be used to map the process of planning or implementing change. To illustrate, a process mapping system has been used below to guide people through the description stage of organisational change.

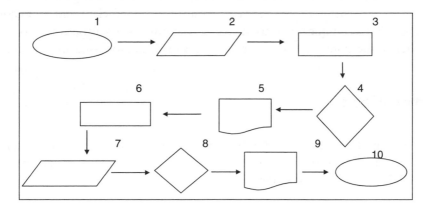

Note:
1 = Start
2 = Gather information on what seems to be the problem
3 = Evaluate the information
4 = Decide which problems/issues are clear and which you need more information about
5 = Record that decision
6 = Devise a list of potential objectives
7 = Gather information on the feasibility of these
8 = Decide on objectives for change
9 = Record decision
10= Stop

How to use

To construct a process flow chart people 'walk through' the entire process from beginning to end, recording each activity using the symbols above. There is no need to record every single sub activity and a local decision needs to be made as to what factors are worthy of recording and what factors are not. The purpose in mapping out each of the stages in the process is so that you get a clearer idea of what is adding value and what is not, that is, which activities are useful and which are redundant. It is also useful to note a time along the process arrows as this allows you to see where the process slows for whatever reason.

Strengths

Process flow charting is an excellent tool to use when reviewing long established organisational processes. Often, emergent change within the organisation adds new elements which accrue over years, resulting in inefficient and ineffective systems. The technique is also useful for determining where problem are occurring across the system, such that any changes made are focussed and specific.

Limitations

Process flow charting is limited to the mapping of one process at a time and it is important to look at the wider implications of making changes to one process. (See McKinsey's Seven S Model)

Reference

Slack, N., Chambers, S., Harland, C., Harrison, A. and Johnston, R. (1998) *Operations Management*, London, Prentice Hall.

Six Thinking Hats

History

Six thinking hats is one of many thinking tools devised by Edward de Bono. (1999). De Bono argued that the problem with much of our thinking is that we try to look at things from six different perspectives simultaneously. As such we confuse what might be considered our emotional and intuitive responses with those based on well-reason arguments and data. In order to help clarify our thinking, de Bono suggests that we disaggregate this mass of intermingled thought and try to consider each of our perspectives in isolation. The eventual pulling together of all the trains of thought then gives us a richer sense of what we want or need to do next.

Model

White hat The white hat represents the logical, objective and neutral ways of thinking. When wearing the white hat we should be thinking about the facts and the figures, what we know for sure, what are we certain about.

Red hat The red hat represents the emotional side of our thinking. When wearing the red hat we are encouraged to think intuitively, what was our first reaction to the situation? What do our instincts tells us we should do?

Black hat The black hat represents caution and negativity. What are the problems with what we want to do? What can stop us from achieving our goals? What are the limitations of what we are trying to achieve?

Yellow Hat The yellow hat represents the opposite to the black hat. Here we are trying to think optimistically about the situation. What can we do? What can we achieve? What factors are supporting and enabling us to achieve our goals?

Green Hat The green hat encourages to think outside the box. Rather than manage change in the same ways as before or seek the same solutions to problems (even if these have been successful), the green hat encourages us to do new things, to do things differently, to come up with creative and innovative ways forward.

Blue Hat The blue hat encourages us to think about systems and processes. To look at the functional and operational changes we need to make in order to progress our ideas about change.

Uses

De Bono's six thinking hats allows people to think about change from a range of different perspectives. By doing this it allows people to generate wider insights into the problems which create the need for change, the ways in which we describe that change and the plans we make to instigate and manage that change.

How to use

The six thinking hats model can be used by individuals or by teams, and for diagnosing the need for change or planning change.

In diagnosing the need for change people are encouraged to describe the situation/problem from the perspective of wearing each of the hats. From a team perspective this can be done either by allowing each person to wear every hat (i.e. to write down their own views from every perspective). The team then exchange ideas at the end. Alternatively individual team members can be allocated a particular colour hat to wear. That is each person is charged with thinking about the change from just one perspective. The output of either should be a brief outline of the key points that the group need to take forward. For example it may be that whilst thinking with the black hat on, a serious consequence of inaction has surfaced. As such the team then need to make sure that action is taken quickly to stop the situation from deteriorating.

In planning change the same process is adopted but with the process being prospective rather than retrospective. Here people are looking at each of their planned actions from the view point of each of the hats, to see how these views reinforce what they are planning to do, or offer alternative solutions.

Strengths

The strength of the model is that it allows for individuals and teams to generate a wealth of information about the situation. It also provides interesting insights from which people can reflect on the ways in which they view things, the opinions that they hold and how these relate to others and to practice.

Limitations

The limitations relate to the time it takes to implement, especially where change is needed rapidly. It also needs to be consolidated by some of the wider and more practically oriented analyses.

Reference

De Bono, E. (2000) *Six Thinking Hats* (Revised 2nd edn), London, Penguin.

The Lotus Blossom Technique

History

The Lotus Blossom technique was devised by Yasuo Matsumura, Director of Clover Management Research in Chiba City, Japan. The model is thought to be based on a Darwinian way of thinking, in that, rather than trying to randomly generate a range of disconnected ideas, thinking starts with a central focus around which connected thoughts and ideas form themes. Each one of these themes is then disaggregated from the original model and used to form the central focus of the next level of thinking.

Model

Based on the image of a lotus flower the model consists of a circular centre point surrounded by a number of circles (petals). In the central circle you write the core theme, and in each of the surrounding circles you write a related theme. When all the circles are complete, then each petal is used as the central circle for the next flower.

Example

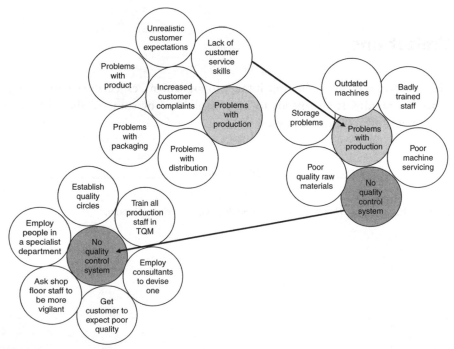

Uses

The lotus flower model can be used to:

Identify the causes of problems
Break down problems into constituent parts
Generate potential solutions
Generate options for change
Identify the consequences of those options.

How to use

The diagram can be used by individuals as a means of surfacing the issues mentioned above. The key here is that the central circle needs to be specific and focussed. The relevance of the ideas generated will depend on the appropriateness of the centre circle which provokes those ideas. It is useful to have some understanding beforehand about the level of abstraction you need or want to take the analysis to. Whilst you can continue to develop more and more themes, generally speaking you should set a limit to your ideas, be this related to control, responsibility, feasibility or level of detail.

The diagram can also be used as a group technique wherein you can either allow everyone to contribute to each idea (petal) or you can allocate specific ideas (petals) to individuals and then feedback to the main group at the end of the session. To do either of these, people should gather as a group, and the main focus of the session is communicated to them. The facilitator (who can be a group member also) explains the process to the group. As such, the main diagram of a lotus blossom is put before the whole group (on paper on a table, as a flip chart or white board or projected onto a screen). If every member is contributing to each petal then the facilitator coordinates putting the ideas generated on to the diagram. There may be a need to prioritise or vote for the items considered by the group to be salient. Where particular areas are being allocated to particular people, this can only be done after the first round of idea generation, when each of the petals in the first lotus blossom diagram has been completed. At that point the facilitator either allocates roles or people volunteer to take a particular petal and work on creating the next flower from this.

Strengths

The lotus blossom technique allows for individuals and groups to surface not only the main issues, but also to consider the consequences of these issues.

Limitations

If not carefully controlled people can become so subsumed with ideas and the implications of these that they are no better off in determining a way forward. The technique also requires a closure process from which the actual course of action to be taken by the group of the individual is planned.

_____ *Reference* _____

http://www.personneltoday.com/articles/2001/05/01/8607/thought-processes.html last accessed 11.09.08

TROPICS Model

History

The TROPICS model was devised by Paton and McCalman (2000) to provide a framework which could distinguish between the need for hard systems change and soft systems change. Hard systems change is change focussed on a clearly defined issue or problem. Because the focus is so clear, the change process here can be meticulously planned and enacted. Soft systems change is change in circumstances characterised by vagueness and or complexity. As such change needs to be an on-going developmental process rather than a one off management project.

Model

Factors

Time Scales	Clearly defined-short to medium term = A	Poorly defined-medium to long term = B	A = Hard systems B = Soft systems
Resources	Clearly defined and stable = A	Poorly defined and variable = B	A = Hard systems B = Soft systems
Objectives	Clear and quantifiable = A	Subjective and value oriented = B	A = Hard systems B = Soft systems
Perceptions	Shared by all involved = A	Different or disparate = B	A = Hard systems B = Soft systems
Interest	Clearly defined stakeholder groups = A	Poorly defined or complex stakeholder groups = B	A = Hard systems B = Soft systems
Control	Single source of power = A	Multiple sources of power = B	A = Hard systems B = Soft systems
Source	Drivers for change are internal = A	Drivers for change are external = B	A = Hard systems B = Soft systems

Uses

The TROPICS model provides a useful framework for considering the level of complexity involved in planning change. It helps people to recognise the degree of clarity with which they are able to define the changes necessary and to consider the nature of the relationship between each of the factors. The results of the analysis are an indication as to whether the change being considered could be managed as a distinct programme of change or whether it is more appropriately undertaken as an on-going process of organisational development. Such issues are significant because they have implications for the resourcing of the change and for the timescales within which the organisation can expect to achieve the desired results.

How to use

You should begin by writing down a description of the change that you are planning or that you have been asked to consider. Describe the change in as much detail as you can at this stage as this will help to frame your thinking as you move through the listed criteria.

Then you can work down the list of topics listed on the left hand side of the table, and think about the extent to which the change that you are planning, more closely matches one or other of the two statements given. You should rate your response as A or B accordingly.

Where the answers you have given are all A's or all B's, then the approach to change is relatively clear. All B's would imply that a hard systems approach is favoured. One in which process and procedural issues drive the change forwards. All A's would imply a more humanistic approach to change, one in which people participate in or are at least a communicated with as part of the change process. However, as McCalman and Paton note, it would be highly unusual for change to be so clearly defined. Instead they advocate that the distribution of responses is a good starting place for thinking about what factors you need to respond to and how.

Strengths

The strengths of the model are that it provides a convenient framework which encourages those managing change to think logically through both practical and perceptual issues related to the change. Although, in some circumstances it offers a convenient classification of the type of change needed, it does this in a contingent way, noting that the framework should be used to provoke thought rather than prescribe action.

Limitations

The limitations of the model relate to the notion that once the change has been classified, it is for the person managing the change to decide how significant each of the factors are. They also need to consider any tensions that arise between these issues and how they plan to deal with those tensions alongside the change itself.

Reference

McCalman, James and Paton Robert. A. (1992) 'Change Management', *A Guide to Effective Implementation*, London, Paul Chapman Publishing.

The SFA Balance Sheet

History

The SFA Balance sheet is a hybrid model formed by combining Johnson and Scholes (1999) Suitable, Feasible, Acceptable (SFA) model of strategy evaluation, and the decision-balance sheet structure as described by Van Gundy. (1988) The objective here was to consolidate the SFA model by creating a framework through which positive and negative considerations could be mapped.

Model

	Positive	Negative	Yes if
Suitable			
Feasible			
Acceptable			

Uses

The SFA balance sheet can be used as a means of assessing potential plans for change. The model encourages people to consider whether:

1. The change planned actually meets the objectives for the change (suitable) or not
2. The costs of meeting those objectives (human and non-human resources) are reasonable (feasible) or not
3. The processes and the outcome of change will be agreeable to the stakeholders (acceptable) or not.

How to use

First write down a description of the change in as much detail as is possible. You will use this to frame the ways in which you think about your responses to the questions of suitability, feasibility and acceptability. Write down as much as you can about what you propose to do; you need to consider the process from planning, through implementation to evaluation of the outcomes.

Using this as the basis for thinking you should consider the issue of suitability. Based on your plan for change what are the positive features that relate to it being able to achieve its intended outcomes? List these in the positive column. Next think of the negative features, what factors in your plan either don't achieve the objectives or detract from achieving them? Write these down in the 'negative' column. Lastly try to think about how you could achieve more or how you could convert the negatives in to positives. Make notes on these in the 'yes if' column.

You should now repeat the process for the feasible and acceptable columns.

Once you have completed the balance sheet you need to consider, on balance, whether your plan for change is a good one which can be implemented largely along the lines that you had previously decided. Whether the plan needs minor alterations, perhaps converting some of the 'yes-ifs' to positives, or whether the plan is destined to fail and you need to rethink your approach.

Strengths

The SFA balance sheet presents a useful mechanism for surfacing the range of issues which arise under the suitable, feasible and acceptable headings. It allows people to judge the values of these factors such that they can use this understanding to further plan or to implement the change. It is of particular use with groups, where a broader range of issues are surfaced.

Limitations

The model is simply a tool for assessing the value of the plan of change you propose. It is fundamentally subjective and although it is possible to introduce numerics particularly in the feasibility section, it is dependent of the willingness of the participants to be honest and open about the change they have planned.

_____ *References* _____

Johnson, G. and Scholes, K. (1999) *Exploring Corporate Strategy*, Essex, England, Prentice-Hall.
Van Gundy, A.B. (1988) *Techniques of Structured Problem Solving*, 2nd edn, New York, Van Nostrand-Reinhold.

Index